D1156348

SILVER BURDETT & GINN
SOCIAL STUDIES

Our Country's Communities

Richard H. Loftin
Former Director of Curriculum and Staff Development
Aldine Independent School District, Houston, Texas

W. Frank Ainsley, Jr.
Associate Professor of Geography
University of North Carolina at Wilmington,
Wilmington, North Carolina

SILVER BURDETT & GINN
MORRISTOWN, NJ • NEEDHAM, MA
Atlanta, GA • Cincinnati, OH • Dallas, TX • Menlo Park, CA • Deerfield, IL

W. Frank Ainsley, Jr., Associate Professor of Geography, University of North Carolina at Wilmington

Val E. Arnsdorf, Former Professor, College of Education, University of Delaware, Newark, Delaware

Herbert J. Bass, Professor of History, Temple University, Philadelphia, Pennsylvania

Richard C. Brown, Former Professor of History, State University of New York College at Buffalo

Patricia T. Caro, Assistant Professor of Geography, University of Oregon, Eugene, Oregon

Kenneth S. Cooper, Professor of History Emeritus, George Peabody College for Teachers, Vanderbilt University, Nashville, Tennessee

Gary S. Elbow, Professor of Geography, Texas Tech University, Lubbock, Texas

Elaine Fay, Former Director of Education, New Jersey Historical Society, Newark, New Jersey

John W. Florin, Associate Professor and Chairman, Department of Geography, University of North Carolina at Chapel Hill

Alvis T. Harthern, Professor of Early Childhood Education, West Georgia College, Carrollton, Georgia

Timothy M. Helmus, Social Studies Instructor, City Middle and High School, Grand Rapids, Michigan

Bobbie P. Hyder, Elementary Education Coordinator, Madison County School System, Huntsville, Alabama

Theodore Kaltsounis, Professor and Associate Dean, College of Education, University of Washington, Seattle, Washington

Richard H. Loftin, Former Director of Curriculum and Staff Development, Aldine Indpendent School District, Houston, Texas

Mary Garcia Metzger, Dean of Instruction, Dowling Middle School, Houston, Texas

Clyde P. Patton, Professor of Geography, University of Oregon, Eugene, Oregon

Norman J.G. Pounds, Former University Professor of Geography, Indiana University, Bloomington, Indiana

Arlene C. Rengert, Associate Professor of Geography, West Chester University, West Chester, Pennsylvania

Robert N. Saveland, Former Professor of Social Science Education, University of Georgia, Athens, Georgia

Charles A. Stansfield, Jr., Professor of Geography, Glassboro State College, Glassboro, New Jersey

Edgar A. Toppin, Professor of History and Dean of the Graduate School, Virginia State University, Petersburg, Virginia

Billye Joyce Barron, Teacher, Alamo Elementary School, Galveston, Texas

Elois Carey, Teacher, Lincoln School, Toledo, Ohio

Adele Kehoe, Teacher, Tess Corners School, Muskego, Wisconsin

Loraine Reddrick, Teacher, Forest Hills School, Wilmington, North Carolina

Margaret E. Robinson, Teacher, Blessed Sacrament – St. Mary's School, Bridgeport, Connecticut

Alfred Velasquez, Teacher, Missouri Avenue Elementary School, Roswell, New Mexico

Beverly Wong Woo, Teacher, Kimball Elementary School, Seattle, Washington

© 1990 Silver, Burdett & Ginn Inc. All rights reserved. Printed in the United States of America. This publication, or parts thereof, may not be reproduced in any form by photographic, electrostatic, mechanical, or any other method, for any use, including information storage and retrieval, without written permission from the publisher.
ISBN 0-382-12862-1

CONTENTS

3 Our Country's Farms and Resources

MAPS

ATLAS

GRAPHS

Graph Appendix

Tools for Studying Our World

This year you will be learning about some cities and towns in your country. You will find out where people live. You will read about where they work and how they use their land and water. You will enjoy learning about what they do to have fun.

In Unit 1 you will learn about some tools that will help you understand your world. One of the most useful tools you can use is a map. Reading a map can help you find places where you want to go. Maps can show you where things are and how far away they are. If you learn how to use a map, you probably will never get lost.

(*Left*) Betty and her mother and friends are hiking in a big park. Their map helps them find interesting places to visit. (*Right*) A map of the zoo helped Matt and his aunt find the elephants. Now their map will help them find the monkey cages. It will also tell them how far they have to walk to get there.
■ What might Betty have in her backpack?

Bus drivers need maps, too. They also need another tool that helps them to get to the right places on time. They need a timetable. A timetable is a list that tells them what time they are supposed to arrive at certain places. This kind of timetable is also called a schedule.

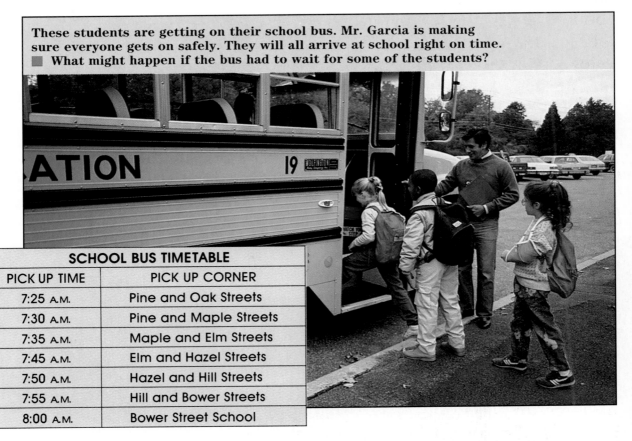

These students are getting on their school bus. Mr. Garcia is making sure everyone gets on safely. They will all arrive at school right on time.
■ What might happen if the bus had to wait for some of the students?

SCHOOL BUS TIMETABLE	
PICK UP TIME	PICK UP CORNER
7:25 A.M.	Pine and Oak Streets
7:30 A.M.	Pine and Maple Streets
7:35 A.M.	Maple and Elm Streets
7:45 A.M.	Elm and Hazel Streets
7:50 A.M.	Hazel and Hill Streets
7:55 A.M.	Hill and Bower Streets
8:00 A.M.	Bower Street School

People who ride on buses use timetables too. They need to know what time their bus will stop for them and what time they will get where they are going.

Without any timetables, people would be too early or too late for their jobs. Students would miss their school bus. Or they might have to wait a long time for the bus.

Tables, like maps, give you important information. In Unit 1, you will learn about tables and maps and many other ways to get helpful facts.

1 Using Maps

The Earth

In what ways is the globe like the earth?

VOCABULARY

model	North Pole	South Pole	east
globe	north	south	west

Models   Have you ever played with miniature trains or toy trucks? Do you have any dolls? Each of these is a **model** of a real thing. (Words in heavy type are in the Glossary, which starts on page 282. Glossary words are pronounced.) A model is made to

One of the automobiles in the photographs above is a model of the real automobile.
■ How can you tell which is the real automobile?

look like a real thing. The main difference between a real thing and a model is that a model is smaller. In the picture on page 4, the model car on the right is made to look just like the real car on the left.

A **globe** is a special kind of model. It is a model of the earth. The picture at the left below shows what the earth looks like from space. The picture of the globe at the right shows the same part of the earth. The globe, like the earth, is shaped like a ball.

One of the photographs above shows the real earth. The other photograph shows a globe.
■ Which picture tells you about the names of places on the earth?

Sally Ride (1951–)

When Sally Ride was a little girl, she spent most of her time after school playing baseball and football with the boys in her neighborhood. She was almost always the only girl chosen for a team. And she was always the first player chosen. When Sally was 10 years old, she began to play tennis. Soon she was one of the best young players in the country.

All through her school years, Sally continued to love tennis and other sports. But she became very interested in studying science, especially outer space. In 1978 she was one of 35 people who were picked from among 8,000 young scientists to train as astronauts.

The training program got Sally Ride ready for the shock of blast-off in a spaceship. It prepared her for having no weight in space. She learned to parachute. And she learned how to make repairs on a spaceship.

Sally Ride did so well in training that she was the first one chosen from her group to fly in space. And on a June day in 1983, Sally Ride was once again first. She became the first American woman to go into space.

The flight of the spaceship *Challenger* lasted 6 days. Sally Ride and the rest of the crew kept very busy carrying out scientific tests. When the *Challenger* finally landed, Sally Ride returned to her home in Texas.

"The thing that I'll remember most about the flight I took," said Sally Ride, "is that it was fun!"

Direction   One of the many things we can learn from a globe is direction. Look at the picture of the globe on this page. Find the **North Pole**. The North Pole is a very special place. It is the most northern place on the earth. **North** is the direction toward the North Pole. Find the **South Pole**. It too is a very special place. It is the most southern place on the earth. **South** is the direction toward the South Pole. North and south are opposite each other.

North and south are two directions. Two other directions are **east** and **west**. If you face north, east will be to your right. West will be to your left. If you face south, where will east be? East and west are opposite each other. North, south, east, and west are the four main directions. Knowing these directions helps us understand where places are.

Look again at the picture of the globe on this page. Suppose you wanted to locate a place somewhere between the north arrow and the east arrow. You could say that the place is between the directions north and east. An easier way would be to say that the place is in the northeast. What direction is between east and south? Between south and west? Between west and north? The four in-between directions—northeast, southeast, southwest, and northwest—also help us to understand where places are.

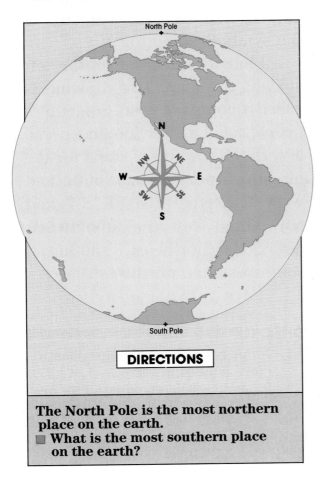

DIRECTIONS

The North Pole is the most northern place on the earth.
■ What is the most southern place on the earth?

CHECKUP

1. What is a model of the earth called?
2. What are the four main directions?
3. **Thinking Critically** What can you find on a globe that is not shown on the real earth?

Maps

How do symbols help us to read maps?

VOCABULARY

map	symbol
key	compass rose

Maps with Symbols   The globe is one tool that helps us learn more about the earth. But it is not the only tool we can use to learn about the earth. Another tool is a **map**. Maps, like globes, show us what the earth looks like. There are many different kinds of maps.

Most maps show what the earth looks like from directly overhead. The photograph on the next page was taken from an airplane. Now look at the map on page 9. The map shows the same place as the photograph. Find some unusual shapes in the photograph. Find those same shapes on the map.

Notice that the map has a special part called the **key**. Most maps have keys. A key shows the **symbols** used on a map. The symbols stand for real places and things. Always look at the key to find out what real places and things the symbols stand for.

Find the drawing on the left side of the map. The drawing is called a **compass rose**. Sometimes people call it a direction finder. The letters N, E, S, and W stand for the directions north, east, south, and west. The letters NE, SE, SW, and NW stand for the in-between directions northeast, southeast, southwest, and northwest.

This picture shows a wall map.
■ Where are the teacher and the student pointing?

CHECKUP

1. Name two tools that help us learn more about the earth.
2. What do the symbols stand for on the map on page 9?
3. **Thinking Critically**   Make a list of the kinds of maps you have seen.

The map below shows the same area as the photograph above.
The map uses symbols for the real things you see in the photograph.
How many tennis courts does the map show?

DRAWING A MAP

KEY

Apartment Buildings	Golf Course
Parking Lots	Pond
Tennis Courts	Roads
Swimming Pool	Other Land

Scale

Why do maps have to be drawn to scale?

VOCABULARY
scale

Scale on Drawings   In order to show the correct size of places, maps are drawn to **scale**. Before we talk about scale on a map, let us see how scale is used in drawings. Look at the two drawings of an airplane on the next page. Both drawings show the same airplane. But each drawing is drawn to a different scale. The first one is drawn to a scale of 1 inch to 20 feet. This means that 1 inch on the drawing stands for 20 feet on the

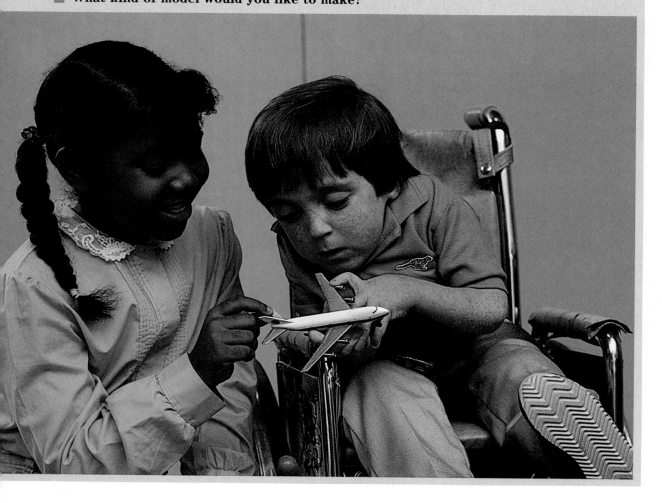

These two friends are playing with a model airplane that they made. Many people enjoy making models of trains, cars, and airplanes.
■   What kind of model would you like to make?

real airplane. The drawing is about 5 inches long. Since each inch stands for 20 feet, you have to add five groups of 20 to find out how long the real airplane is. It is about 100 feet long (20 + 20 + 20 + 20 + 20 = 100).

The second drawing is smaller, so the scale is different. On this drawing, 1 inch stands for 25 feet.

The drawing is about 4 inches long. To find the length of the real airplane this time, you must add four groups of 25 (25 + 25 + 25 + 25 = 100). The answer is still 100 feet. Although the scale has changed, the size of the real airplane stays the same. No matter what size the drawing is, the size of the object is the same.

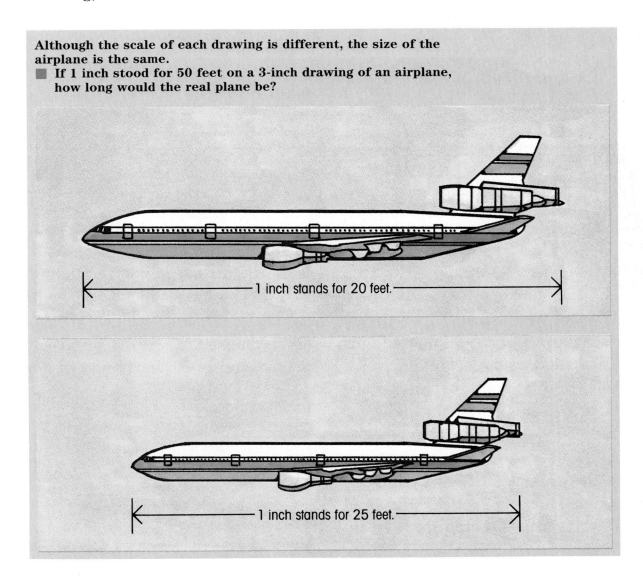

Although the scale of each drawing is different, the size of the airplane is the same.
◼ If 1 inch stood for 50 feet on a 3-inch drawing of an airplane, how long would the real plane be?

1 inch stands for 20 feet.

1 inch stands for 25 feet.

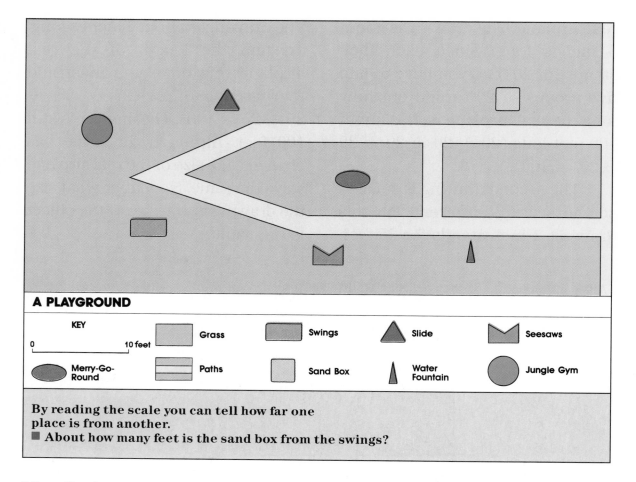

A PLAYGROUND

KEY

0   10 feet

Grass

Swings

Slide

Seesaws

Merry-Go-Round

Paths

Sand Box

Water Fountain

Jungle Gym

By reading the scale you can tell how far one place is from another.
■ **About how many feet is the sand box from the swings?**

Map Scale

Now let us see how scale is used on a map. At the top of this page is a map of a playground. Look at the key on the map. Now find the numbered line. It is called a map scale. The scale helps you find out how big a place is. It also helps you find how far one place is from another.

The scale on the map above tells you that each inch on the map stands for 10 feet in the real playground. The map has a scale of 1 inch to 10 feet. Use your ruler to find out how long the playground is on the map. You will see that it is 6 inches long. Since each inch stands for 10 feet, you have to add six groups of 10. The real playground is 60 feet long ($10 + 10 + 10 + 10 + 10 + 10 = 60$).

CHECKUP

1. What does a map scale tell you?
2. Why can't a map be drawn to the full size of the place it shows?

3. **Thinking Critically** How would you use scale to draw a map of your classroom?

Communities and States

Which is larger, a community or a state?

VOCABULARY

| community | law |
| state | capital |

Communities In the last lesson, you used a map of a playground. A playground is often part of a **community**. A community is a place where people live, work, and play.

Communities have homes, stores, places of worship, and many

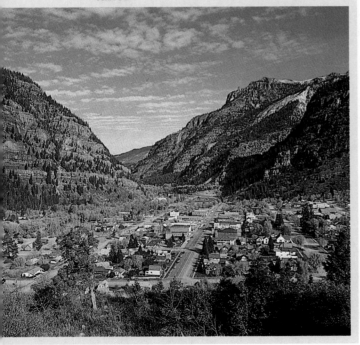

This is a community in the state of Colorado.
■ From where is the photograph taken?

other buildings. Cities and towns are communities. Cities are larger than towns. What is the name of your community? Is it a city? Is it a town? Can you name some cities and towns near you?

States The map on page 14 shows some communities in the **state** of California. As you can see from the map, a state is much larger than a city or a town. A state is made up of many different communities.

Every state has a special city in which the state leaders make **laws** and plans for the whole state. A law is a rule that people must obey. This special city where state laws and plans are made is called the state **capital**. Look at the key on the map on page 14. Find the symbol for a state capital in the key. Now find the capital of California on the map.

CHECKUP
1. How is a state different from a community?
2. What is a state capital?
3. **Thinking Critically** List the places in your community where people can play and have fun.

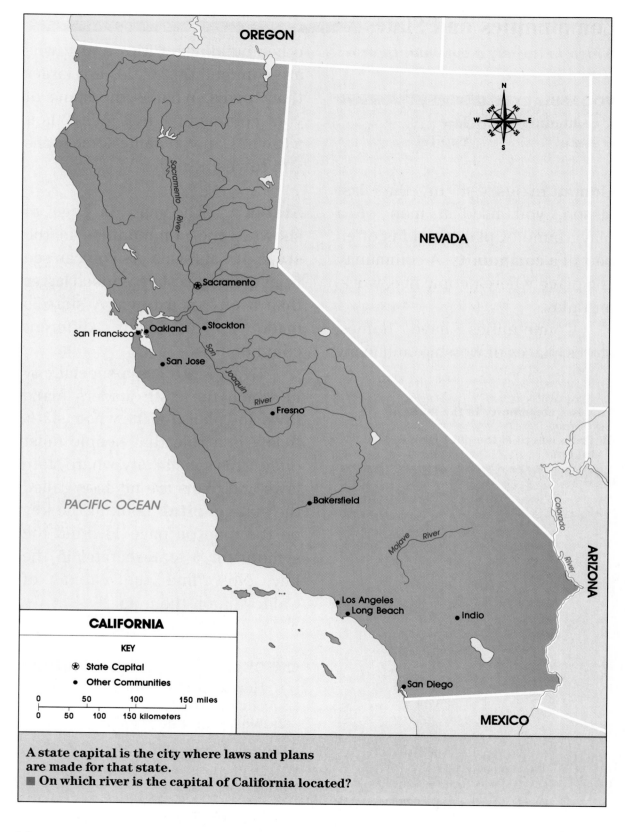

CALIFORNIA

KEY

⊛ State Capital
● Other Communities

A state capital is the city where laws and plans
are made for that state.
■ On which river is the capital of California located?

Our Country

What are some physical features found in our country?

VOCABULARY

physical feature	ocean
peninsula	border
island	gulf
mountain	river
plain	lake

Small States and Large States

Our country, the United States of America, is made up of 50 states.

Some states are large. Alaska, Texas, and California are our three largest states. Some states are small. Our three smallest states are Rhode Island, Delaware, and Connecticut. Find these six states on the map of our country below.

People Some states are home to many people. More people live in California than in any other state. New York and Texas are two other

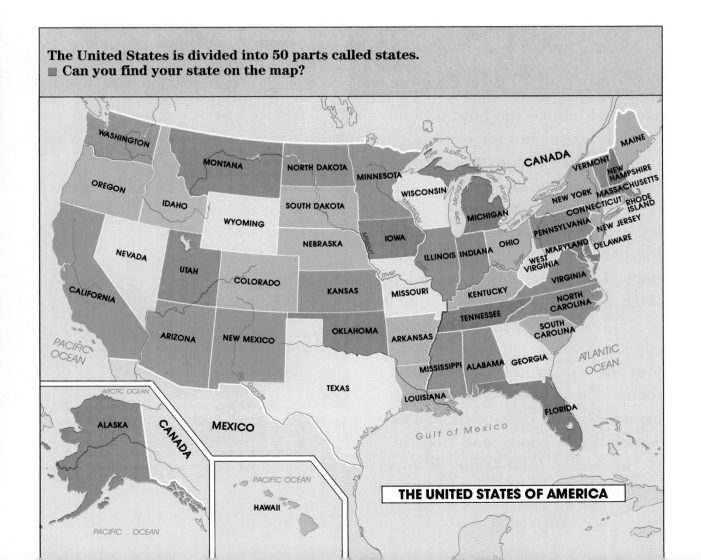

The United States is divided into 50 parts called states.
■ **Can you find your state on the map?**

THE UNITED STATES OF AMERICA

states that have many people. Some states have few people. Wyoming has the fewest.

States and Physical Features

A **physical** (fiz′ ə kəl) **feature** is a part of the earth. Our country is so large that we have examples of all physical features. Most of Florida is a **peninsula**. That is, it has water almost all the way around it.

One of our states, Hawaii, is made up entirely of **islands**. An island is a body of land with water all around it.

Some states, such as Alaska, California, and Colorado, have high **mountains**. A mountain is land that rises high above the land around it. Find the symbol for mountains in the key on the map of the United States on pages 254–255.

One large part of our country is very flat. All you can see is flat grasslands stretching for miles and miles. Land like this is called a **plain**. Nebraska is a plains state.

There are four large bodies of salt water on the earth. Each large body of salt water is called an **ocean**. The names of the oceans are the Atlantic Ocean, the Pacific Ocean, the Indian Ocean, and the Arctic Ocean. Find these oceans on page 18.

These pictures show three different kinds of physical features in our country.
■ Can you name the three shown above and one that is not shown?

16

The community of Juneau in the state of Alaska is located near a body of water called a channel.
■ What physical features can you see behind the community?

Three of these oceans **border** on, or touch, our country. One state that borders on the Atlantic Ocean is North Carolina. Name the other states that touch the Atlantic Ocean. Five of our states border on the Pacific Ocean, but only one state borders on the Arctic Ocean. Can you name these six states?

Some of our states border on a **gulf**. A gulf is part of an ocean or sea that pushes into the land. Look at the map on pages 254–255. Name the states that border on the Gulf of Mexico.

The United States also has many **rivers** and **lakes**. A river is a long, narrow body of water that flows through the land toward a larger body of water. A lake is a body of water that has land all around it. Is the community you live in located near a river or a lake?

CHECKUP
1. How many states are there in the United States?
2. Which state is one of the largest in size and has the largest number of people?
3. Which state is a group of islands in the Pacific Ocean?
4. **Thinking Critically** What physical features are found in your community or state?

17

Continents and Hemispheres

What is the difference between a continent and a hemisphere?

VOCABULARY

| continent | Equator |
| hemisphere | |

Continents   Mexico is the name of the country to the south of the United States. Canada is the name of the country to the north of the United States. Look at the map on the opposite page. Find Canada and Mexico. The United States, Canada, and Mexico are part of the **continent** of North America.

A continent is a very large body of land. You can see that the West Indies and the countries of Central America are also part of North America. Can you find all seven countries of Central America on the map on page 19? Which Central American country is the farthest away from the United States?

There are six other continents on the earth. They are South America, Europe, Africa, Asia, Australia, and Antarctica. On the map below, find the earth's seven continents.

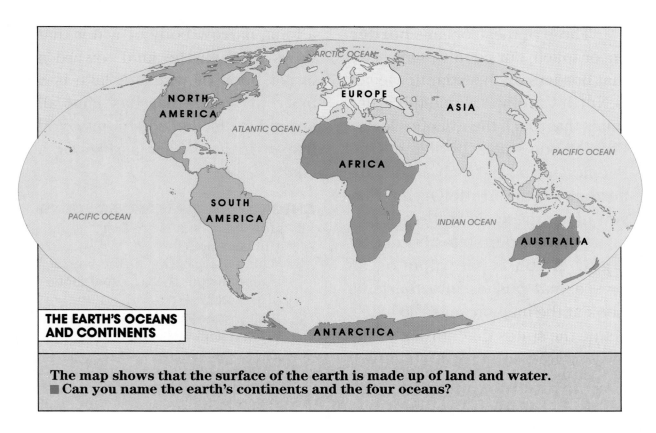

THE EARTH'S OCEANS AND CONTINENTS

The map shows that the surface of the earth is made up of land and water.
■ Can you name the earth's continents and the four oceans?

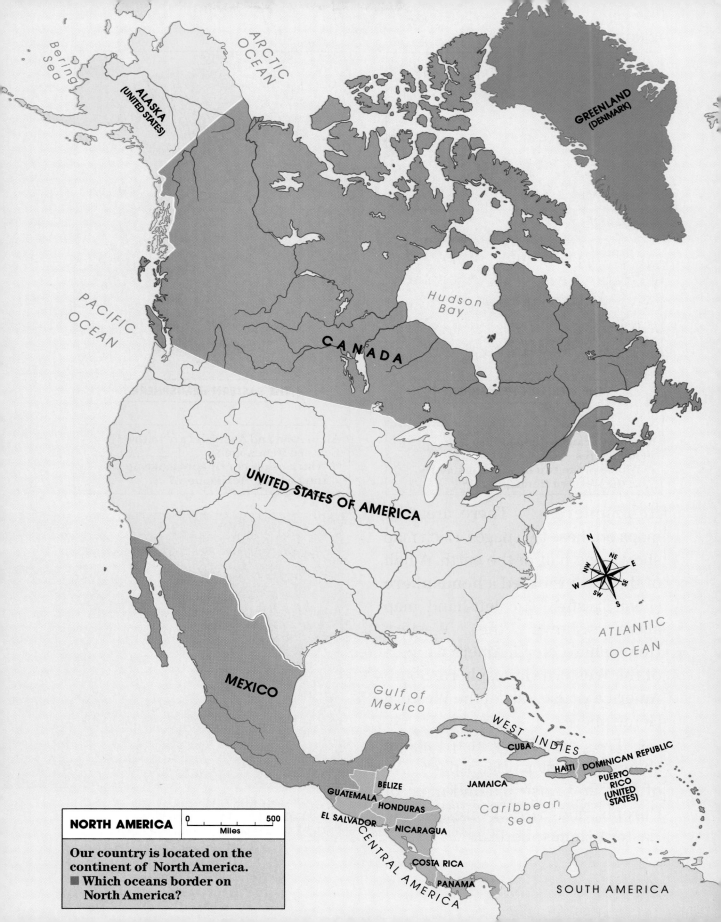

ARCTIC OCEAN

Bering Sea

ALASKA
(UNITED STATES)

GREENLAND
(DENMARK)

Hudson Bay

CANADA

PACIFIC OCEAN

UNITED STATES OF AMERICA

N
NW NE
W E
SW SE
S

ATLANTIC OCEAN

MEXICO

Gulf of Mexico

WEST INDIES

CUBA

DOMINICAN REPUBLIC

HAITI

JAMAICA

PUERTO RICO
(UNITED STATES)

GUATEMALA

BELIZE

HONDURAS

EL SALVADOR

NICARAGUA

Caribbean Sea

COSTA RICA

CENTRAL AMERICA

PANAMA

SOUTH AMERICA

NORTH AMERICA

0 Miles 500

Our country is located on the continent of North America.
■ **Which oceans border on North America?**

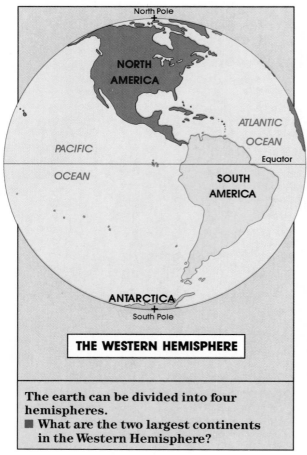

THE WESTERN HEMISPHERE

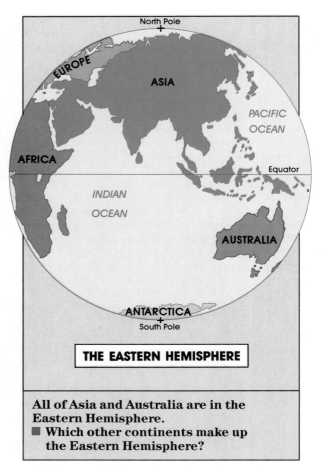

THE EASTERN HEMISPHERE

The earth can be divided into four hemispheres.
■ What are the two largest continents in the Western Hemisphere?

All of Asia and Australia are in the Eastern Hemisphere.
■ Which other continents make up the Eastern Hemisphere?

Hemispheres There are four maps on these two pages. Each map shows one half of the earth. A half of the earth is called a **hemisphere** (hem′ ə sfir). The left-hand map above shows the Western Hemisphere. North America is part of the Western Hemisphere. South America is also part of the Western Hemisphere.

The right-hand map above shows the Eastern Hemisphere. All of Asia and Australia and most of Europe and Africa are in the Eastern Hemisphere.

The Amazon River, shown above, is the largest river in the world. Part of the Amazon is located close

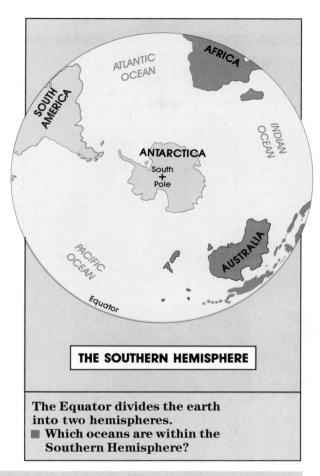

THE SOUTHERN HEMISPHERE

The Equator divides the earth into two hemispheres.
■ Which oceans are within the Southern Hemisphere?

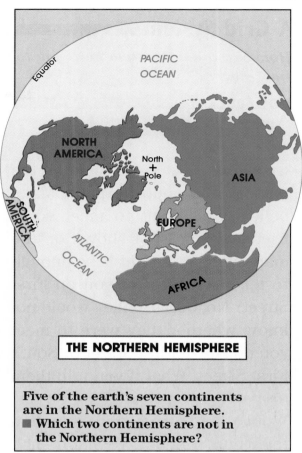

THE NORTHERN HEMISPHERE

Five of the earth's seven continents are in the Northern Hemisphere.
■ Which two continents are not in the Northern Hemisphere?

to the Equator.
■ Can you find the Amazon River on the map on page 257?

The **Equator** (i kwā′ tər) is a line that is used on maps. It divides the earth into two other halves. They are the Southern Hemisphere and the Northern Hemisphere. All of Antarctica and Australia are in the Southern Hemisphere. So are parts of Africa and South America and just a small part of Asia.

CHECKUP

1. How many continents are there?
2. What is a hemisphere?
3. **Thinking Critically** Which two continents, do you think, might be thought of as one continent? Why?

A Grid System

How can a grid system help you to find places?

VOCABULARY

grid system

Crossing Lines   Look at the map on the opposite page. Make believe you want to meet some friends at the spot shown on the map by an X. Would it be enough to tell them to meet you on First Street? No, because they would not know whether they were to meet you on North First Street or South First Street. What if you told them to meet you on North First Street? Would that be enough information for your friends? Probably not, because North First Street is a long street.

So how could you best tell your friends where to meet you? What if you told them to meet you at the corner of North First Street and West Third Avenue? Put a finger at the top, or northern end, of West Third Avenue. Put a finger of your other hand on the far right of North First Street. Now move both fingers, one down and the other across, until they meet. They should meet at the place marked by an X on the map. This crossing of lines is called a

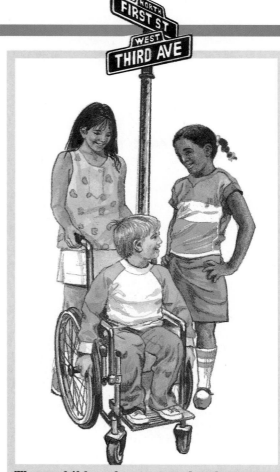

These children know exactly where to meet.
■ What helps them find the place?

grid system. By using the grid system, you can find and describe the location of places on the map.

CHECKUP

1. What is a grid system?

2. **Thinking Critically** Suppose you were on the corner of South Third Street and East Second Avenue. In which directions would you go to meet your friend on the corner of North First Street and West Third Avenue?

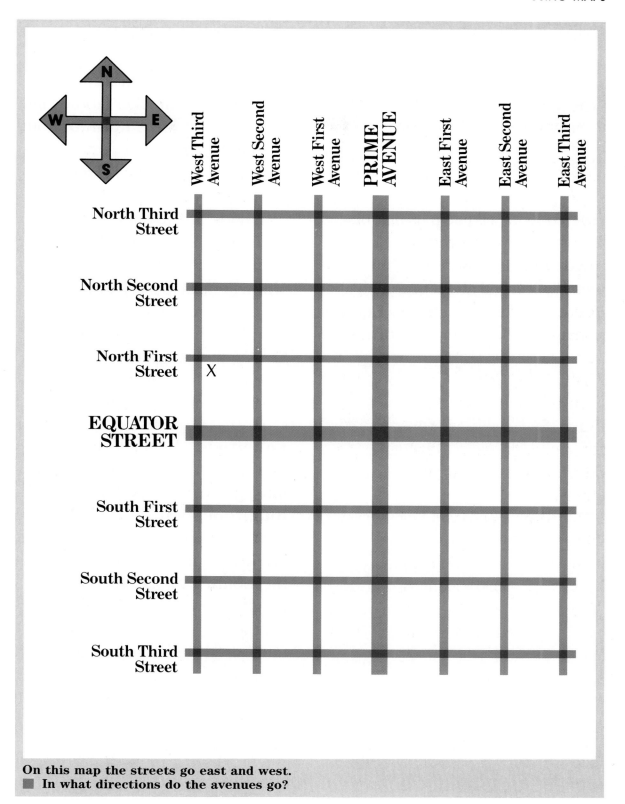

On this map the streets go east and west.
In what directions do the avenues go?

Latitude and Longitude

What are lines of latitude and longitude?

VOCABULARY

latitude	Prime Meridian
degree	Greenwich
longitude	

Latitude To help us find places on maps, mapmakers use lines of **latitude** (lat′ ə tüd). You have already learned about one such line. It is called the Equator. The Equator is halfway between the North Pole

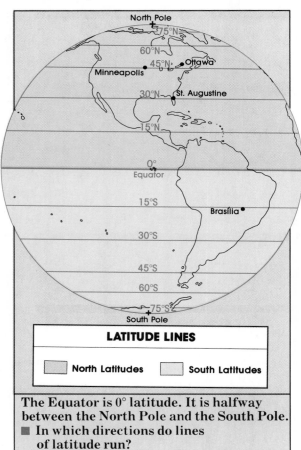

LATITUDE LINES

☐ North Latitudes ☐ South Latitudes

The Equator is 0° latitude. It is halfway between the North Pole and the South Pole.
■ In which directions do lines of latitude run?

and the South Pole. It is a very special line of latitude. It is numbered 0°. All other latitude lines measure distances north or south of the Equator. This distance is measured in **degrees**. The symbol for degrees is °.

Look at the map on this page. You will see that the city of Minneapolis (min ē ap′ ə ləs), Minnesota, is located at 45 degrees north latitude. A short way to show 45 degrees north latitude is 45°N. St. Augustine (sānt ô′ gə stēn), Florida, is located near 30 degrees north latitude, or 30°N.

Longitude Lines of another kind are drawn on maps to help us find places. These are lines of **longitude** (lon′ jə tüd). Look at the map on page 25. Longitude lines are drawn from the North Pole to the South Pole. A special line of longitude is called the **Prime Meridian** (mə rid′ ē ən). It is numbered 0°. All other longitude lines measure distances east or west of the Prime Meridian. The Prime Meridian passes through a place in England called **Greenwich** (gren′ ich). Half of all longitude lines are west of Greenwich. The

This community is located in Antarctica, not far from the South Pole.
■ **Can you find Antarctica on the map on pages 252–253?**

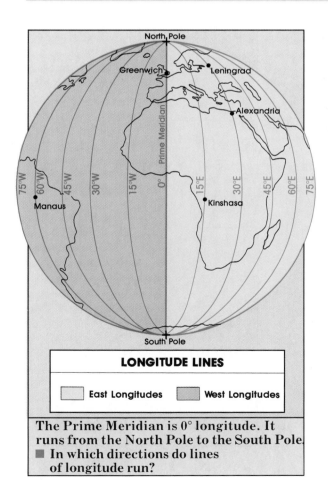

LONGITUDE LINES

☐ East Longitudes   ■ West Longitudes

The Prime Meridian is 0° longitude. It runs from the North Pole to the South Pole.
■ In which directions do lines of longitude run?

other half of these lines are east of Greenwich.

Let us find the city of Manaus (mə naůs′), Brazil, on the map. Manaus is in the Western Hemisphere. To make the city easier to find, you could tell someone that Manaus is at 60° west longitude on the map.

Now find Leningrad, in the Soviet (sō′ vē et) Union. Leningrad is east of the Prime Meridian. It is at 30° east longitude.

CHECKUP

1. What do lines of latitude measure?
2. What do lines of longitude measure?
3. **Thinking Critically** How are the Equator and the Prime Meridian alike?

25

Using Latitude and Longitude

How can latitude and longitude help us find places on the earth?

VOCABULARY

coordinates

Putting It All Together   The map on these two pages shows a few cities. The map also has lines of latitude and longitude. These lines help us to find places, just as streets and avenues do. The lines of latitude and longitude are like the streets and avenues in that they too form a grid system.

If you wanted to tell someone where to find Leningrad, you could just say that it is in the Soviet Union. However, the Soviet Union is the largest country in the world, so you would have to give some more information.

You could say that Leningrad is at 60° north latitude and 30° east longitude. Another way to show this would be to write 60°N/30°E. These would be the grid **coordinates** (kō ôr′ də nits) for Leningrad. Coordinates are a set of numbers used to find a place on a map or globe. If you know the latitude and longitude of a place, you can easily find it on a map. You do this by finding the place where the line of

latitude and the line of longitude cross. To find Leningrad, put one finger on the line marked 60° north latitude. Put a finger of your other hand on the line marked 30° east longitude. Now move your fingers

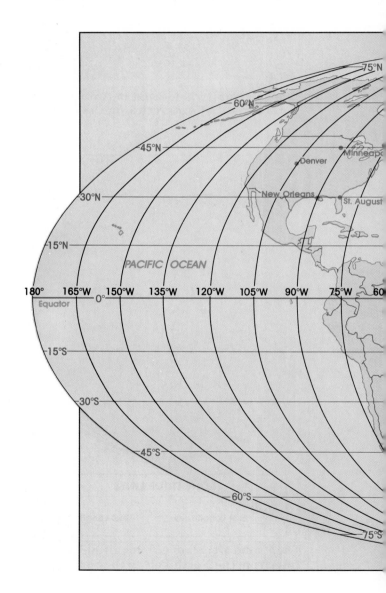

toward each other on these lines. The place where these two lines meet is the location of Leningrad.

Now can you find New Orleans, Louisiana? The grid coordinates are 30° north latitude and 90° west longitude. Give the grid coordinates of the other cities on the map.

CHECKUP

1. How are lines of latitude and longitude like streets and avenues on a map?
2. What are Alexandria's coordinates?
3. **Thinking Critically** Use its coordinates to find which hemispheres the city of Brasília is located in.

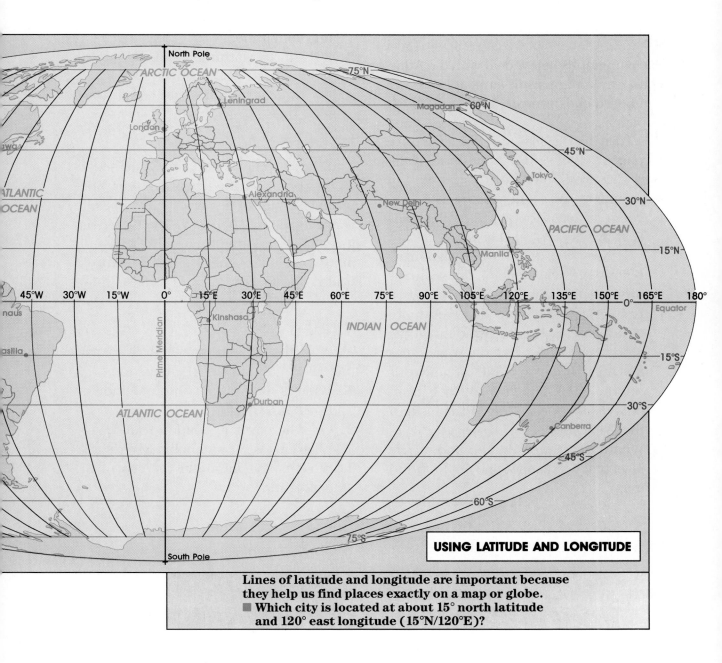

USING LATITUDE AND LONGITUDE

Lines of latitude and longitude are important because they help us find places exactly on a map or globe.
■ Which city is located at about 15° north latitude and 120° east longitude (15°N/120°E)?

Using the Atlas and the Gazetteer

THE ATLAS

Your book has a special section called the Atlas. The Atlas is made up of different maps. These maps tell many interesting things about the world in which we live.

SKILLS PRACTICE

The paragraphs below deal with the Atlas. Read each paragraph and answer the numbered questions on a separate sheet of paper.

Turn to the first map in the Atlas, on pages 252–253. It is a flat map of the world. It shows the seven continents and the countries on each continent.

1. Name at least four physical features that are shown on the map.

Now look at the two smaller maps below the world map. Those maps are called *insets*. An inset shows a part of the big map. It gives more detail. Locate the West Indies on the world map. Notice that the West Indies has lines drawn around it. The words on the map tell you to "see inset below." Look carefully at the inset of the West Indies.

2. What information do you find on the inset that you cannot find on the world map?

Turn now to the second map in the Atlas. It is titled "The United States of America." The map shows lines of latitude and longitude for every five degrees. Name the city found at or near the following lines of latitude and longitude.

3. 35° north latitude and 90° west longitude (35°N/90°W)
4. 40° north latitude and 105° west longitude (40°N/105°W)

THE GAZETTEER

Another special section in your social studies book is called the Gazetteer. This is a dictionary of geographical names. It is arranged alphabetically. The Gazetteer gives information about cities, rivers, mountains, and other physical features. It also shows latitude and longitude for cities.

SKILLS PRACTICE

Turn to the Gazetteer, which starts on page 263, and answer the questions.

1. What is the latitude and longitude of Portland, Oregon?
2. On what river is London found?
3. Where does the Columbia River start?
4. What is special about the city of St. Augustine?

CHAPTER 1 REVIEW

MAIN IDEAS

1. A globe is a model of the earth.
2. Maps show what the earth or parts of the earth look like.
3. The key and its symbols help to explain what the map shows.
4. The scale on a map shows how far one place is from another.
5. Directions and lines of latitude and longitude help to locate places on a map.

VOCABULARY REVIEW

Copy the sentences below and fill in the blanks with the right vocabulary term. Write on a sheet of paper.

a. model	**f.** physical features
b. latitude	
c. symbols	**g.** border
d. community	**h.** scale
e. compass rose	**i.** Equator
	j. globe

1. A _____ is a model of the earth.
2. A _____ is a small copy made to look like a real thing.
3. Map _____ stand for real things and places.
4. A small drawing that shows direction on a map is called a _____ .
5. The map _____ tells how far one place is from another.
6. The states of Montana and Vermont _____ on the country of Canada.

7. Rivers, lakes, and mountains are all parts of the earth; they are called _____ .
8. A place where people live, work, and play is called a _____ .
9. The _____ is a line shown on maps halfway between the North Pole and the South Pole.
10. Lines that run east and west on maps are called lines of _____ .

CHAPTER CHECKUP

1. What do we call a body of land with water all around it?
2. Why is a state capital a special kind of city?
3. List the continents of the world.
4. **Thinking Critically** How are lines of latitude and longitude alike and how are they different?

APPLYING KNOWLEDGE

Locate all the states that border on the Atlantic Ocean, the Gulf of Mexico, or the Pacific Ocean. Use this information to make a chart like the one shown below. The map of the United States on pages 254–255 will help you fill in your chart.

STATES BORDERING ON OCEANS OR GULF		
Atlantic Ocean	Gulf of Mexico	Pacific Ocean

2 Using Social Studies Tools

Tables, Graphs, and Diagrams

How can tables, graphs, and diagrams help us?

VOCABULARY

table	population	pie graph
pictograph	line graph	diagram
bar graph		

Tables   In the last chapter you learned something about maps and globes. You saw what helpful tools maps and globes can be. You learned that maps and globes can help you find places on the earth. In this chapter

you will learn about other tools that can help you find out about the world in which you live.

One of these tools is a **table**. A table lists facts and information. Tables can show you all kinds of information. You could make a table showing how many students in your class have a birthday in each month of the year. You could make a table showing how many students in your class own a dog, a cat, a bird, a rabbit, or other animal.

Tables are helpful also because they are very accurate. They give you exact information. The table that appears on page

Rachel is making a table telling how many students in each grade of her school have a dog. The other two students are working on another way to show the same facts.
■ Do you know what they are making?

31

32 shows the amount of cotton produced in the five leading cotton-growing states of our country. The table gives the name of each state in one column. The amount of cotton in *bales* is given in the other column. A bale of cotton is a large bundle of cotton pressed into one package.

To find out which state grows the most cotton, in a year, place your finger on the table under the largest number of bales. Then move your finger straight across to the left. Which state is under your finger? Which state grows the next largest amount of cotton? Which state grows less than 1 million bales of cotton?

This cotton mill is located in west central Texas.
■ Can you tell what is in the truck on the left?

UNITED STATES: LEADING GROWERS OF COTTON	
State	*Number of Bales of Cotton*
Texas	4,000,000
California	3,000,000
Mississippi	1,600,000
Arizona	1,000,000
Louisiana	700,000

Texas grows the most cotton.
■ Which state grows the least?

Graphs Graphs are another important tool. They also can show information or facts. A graph can show you *how much, how many,* or *how fast.* It can also show *how much more, how many more,* or *how much faster.*

Reading a graph is an important social studies skill. It is a skill everyone should have. Sometimes graphs can tell you something more easily than words can.

Pictographs On this page you saw a table showing the leading growers of cotton in the United States. The information in that table can also be shown on a graph. One kind of graph is called a **pictograph**. A pictograph uses symbols instead of numbers. Look at the graph below. Notice that each symbol stands for 1 million bales of cotton. Four symbols are shown for Texas. That means that Texas produced 4 million bales of cotton.

In a way, a graph is like a picture. By looking at the graph, you can quickly see which states grew the most cotton. You can also get an idea about how much cotton each state grew. To get that kind of information from the table on page 32, you would have to look more closely.

If you wanted exact numbers, a table would be more helpful than a graph. The best thing about a graph is the way it shows relationships. That is, it shows how big one thing is compared with another. Look at the graph below. You can see that *compared* to the amount of cotton produced by Louisiana, the amount of cotton produced by Texas is much greater. You can easily see the *relationship* between the amount of cotton produced by Louisiana and the amount produced by Texas. Compare the table on page 32 to this graph.

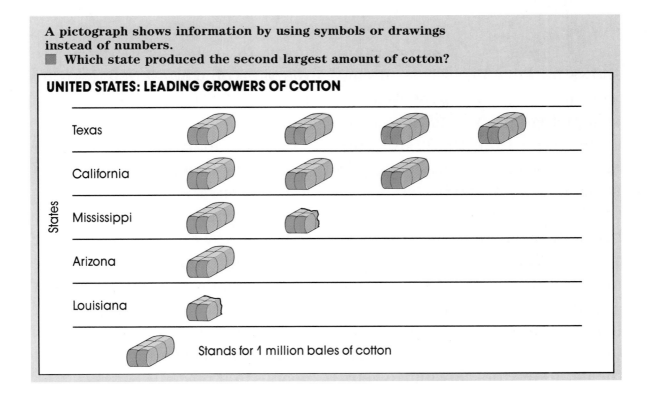

A pictograph shows information by using symbols or drawings instead of numbers.
■ Which state produced the second largest amount of cotton?

UNITED STATES: LEADING GROWERS OF COTTON

Stands for 1 million bales of cotton

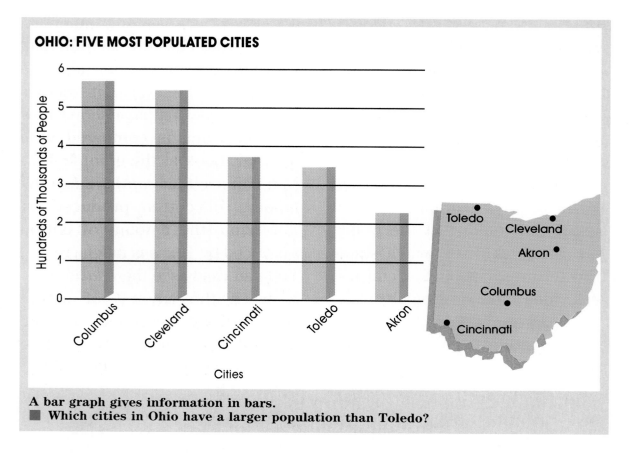

OHIO: FIVE MOST POPULATED CITIES

Hundreds of Thousands of People (y-axis: 0, 1, 2, 3, 4, 5, 6)

Cities (x-axis): Columbus, Cleveland, Cincinnati, Toledo, Akron

A bar graph gives information in bars.
■ Which cities in Ohio have a larger population than Toledo?

Bar Graphs A **bar graph** shows information in bars. It can show the same kinds of information as a pictograph. You have to read a bar graph from the bottom up and then across to the side. Look at the bottom of the bar graph on this page. It is marked *Cities*. Each bar shows a different city. Now look at the left side of the graph. It is marked *Hundreds of Thousands of People*. The numbers show how many people there are. Find the bar for Akron. Run your finger up the bar to the top. Now move your finger from the top of the bar to the left. You will see that there are about 227,000 people living in Akron.

Now look at the bar for Columbus. Run your finger up the bar and then across to the side. Your finger should be a little more than halfway between the line for 5 hundred thousand and the line for 6 hundred thousand. That means that the **population** of Columbus is about 566,000. Population means the number of people in a place.

Line Graphs Everything changes over time. You change. You are taller now than you used to be. You probably weigh more, too. Your family changes. Maybe there are more people in your family than there were a few years ago. Your community and your state also change over the years.

Line graphs help you see change that takes place over time. They also help you to compare information so you can see quickly and clearly the ways in which things change. Look at the line graph at the bottom of this page. It shows how many people lived in North Carolina in 6 different years. It also shows you how the population of the state of North Carolina has grown over a 50-year period.

Reading a line graph is not very different from reading a bar graph. In the line graph on this page, the dates are shown at the bottom, and the numbers of people are shown at the left side. Find the dot for 1970. You will see that there were about 5 million people in North Carolina that year.

Graphs often help you to see relationships or connections between two or more things. The two related things on the line graph on this page are years and numbers of people.

A line graph can also give information about population.
■ About how many people lived in North Carolina in 1980?

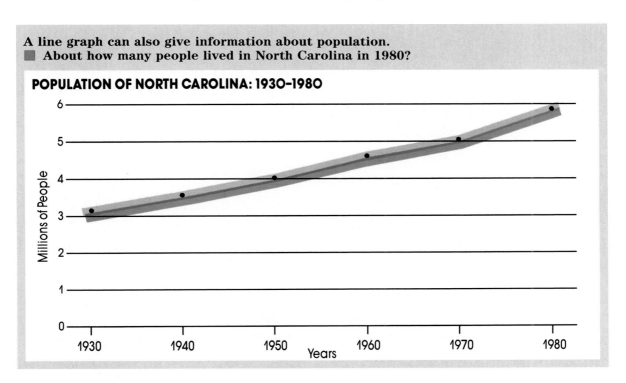

POPULATION OF NORTH CAROLINA: 1930–1980

Millions of People

Years

Pie Graphs   **Pie graphs** show you how much of one thing there is in a whole. Look at the pie graph on this page. You can easily see why it has its name. Notice that in this graph, the whole pie stands for all the land in the United States.

The pie is not cut into equal parts. That is because it shows the amount of land in each of the five largest states. It also shows—in the sixth and largest piece of the pie— the amount of land in the rest of the country. Which state has the most land? Which is our fourth largest state? If you wanted exact information about the amount of land in these five states, which would be more helpful—this pie graph or a table that tells how much land is in each of the five states?

Graph Appendix   On pages 273–281, there is a special graph

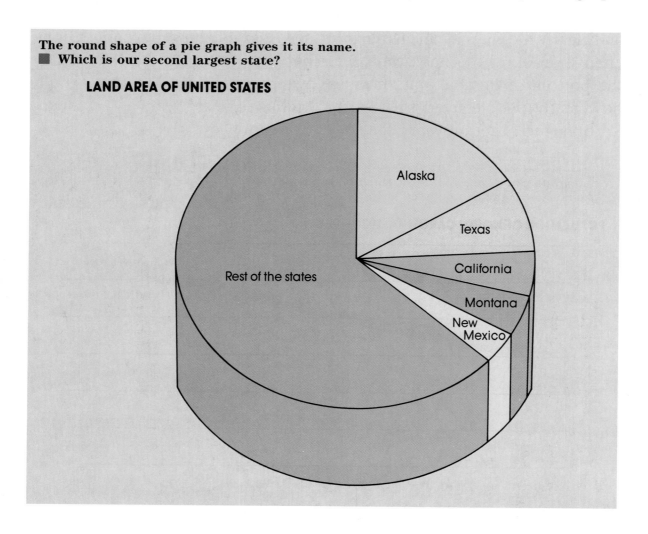

The round shape of a pie graph gives it its name.
■ **Which is our second largest state?**

LAND AREA OF UNITED STATES

Alaska
Texas
California
Montana
New Mexico
Rest of the states

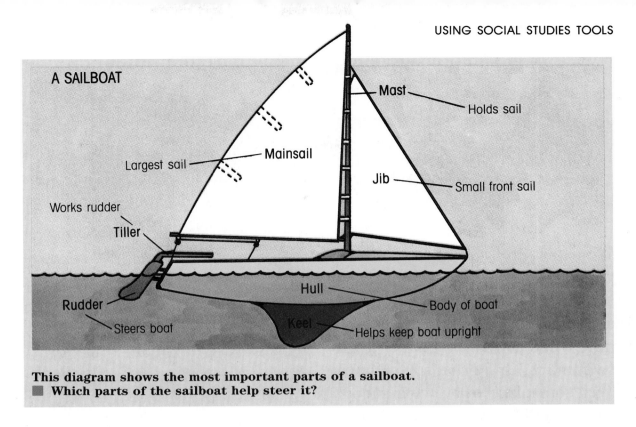

A SAILBOAT

Mast — Holds sail

Largest sail — Mainsail

Jib — Small front sail

Works rudder
Tiller

Rudder — Steers boat

Hull — Body of boat

Keel — Helps keep boat upright

This diagram shows the most important parts of a sailboat.
■ Which parts of the sailboat help steer it?

section called a Graph Appendix. Look at these graphs that show information about the United States and other countries.

Diagrams   **Diagrams** (dī′ ə grāmz) are another important tool to help you find out more about your world. A diagram is a drawing with labels. A diagram can show what a thing is and can explain how it works. It can tell you what the important parts of the thing are.

The diagram on this page shows you the important parts of a sailboat. The labels tell you what each part is and how it helps the boat sail through the water.

A diagram can also explain how something works or the order in which something happens. You can use a diagram to explain some things that cannot be easily explained by words. Many of the toys and bicycles that you buy have diagrams with them. These diagrams help you see how the toy or bike should be put together.

CHECKUP

1. In what way is a table more helpful than a graph?
2. Why would a diagram be helpful to show someone how to use a can opener?
3. **Thinking Critically** Give two relationships, or comparisons, between a teacher and a student.

Using a Thermometer

How do you read a thermometer?

VOCABULARY

weather	thermometer
climate	temperature
natural resource	precipitation

Weather and Climate Have you ever had to change your plans because it was colder than you had expected? Or maybe there was a time when it was too cloudy to go swimming. Or perhaps you have lived someplace where your school was closed because of a storm.

Rain, snow, wind, heat, and cold are all part of **weather**. Weather is the way the air is at a certain time. The weather may change from day to day or even from hour to hour. It might be sunny this morning and cloudy this afternoon. Or it might be dry today and wet tomorrow.

The kind of weather a place has over a long period of time is called its **climate**. A good climate is a great **natural resource**. A natural resource is something found in nature that is useful to people. The United States of America has many important and valuable natural resources.

Tom is looking at a thermometer. Why might the outdoor temperature be important to him?

Thermometer A useful tool that tells us something about the weather and the climate is called a **thermometer**. Thermometers are used to measure the **temperature** of the air. Another way of saying this is that a thermometer tells us how hot or how cold the air is. If you had a thermometer hanging outside your window, you would be able to tell if it was cold enough to need a coat outdoors or if the weather was warm enough for you to wear shorts.

In order to find out what the temperature is, you have to be able to read a thermometer. There is a diagram of a thermometer on this page. Notice the black numbers and lines along the sides of the thermometer. The numbers and lines help you to know the temperature of the air. The numbers show the temperature in *degrees*. In Chapter 1 you learned that latitude and longitude are measured in degrees. Degrees are also the units in which temperature is measured. The lines on the thermometer diagram mark each five degrees.

The red line in the middle of the diagram shows the liquid inside the glass tube of the thermometer. When the air becomes colder, the liquid falls in the glass tube. When the air gets warmer, the liquid rises in the glass tube.

Find the top of the red line and put one of your fingers on it. Then move your finger to the left. What number does your finger touch? The temperature shown by this diagram of a thermometer is 70 degrees Fahrenheit. A shorter way to write this is 70°F. At about what temperature does water freeze?

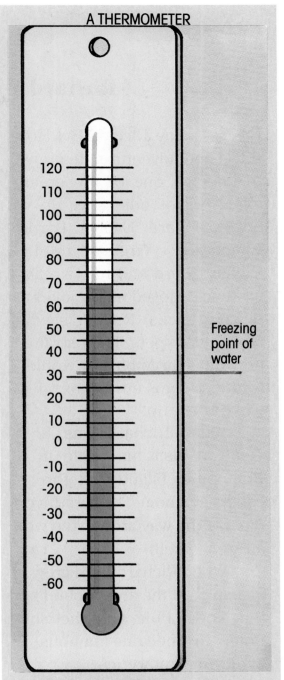

A THERMOMETER

Freezing point of water

This is a Fahrenheit (far′ ən hīt) thermometer. It was developed by Gabriel Fahrenheit, a scientist who was born over 300 years ago.
■ Why must the temperature be at least as low as 32°F before people might ice-skate outdoors?

Richard E. Byrd (1888–1957)

Even as a boy, Richard Byrd loved travel and adventure. He grew up to become one of the greatest explorers of our time. He was born Richard Evelyn Byrd in Winchester, Virginia, in 1888. Richard Byrd and his two lively brothers enjoyed telling jokes and playing tricks. Richard's whole family liked pets. Their strangest pet was a large bird. It would fly to their rooms every morning to wake them up.

When Richard was 12, he went to visit his uncle in the Philippine Islands. Before he came back home, he had traveled most of the way around the world all by himself.

When Richard Byrd grew up, he explored the area around both the North Pole and the South Pole. He became famous for exploring Antarctica.

Byrd took many scientific instruments, including some thermometers, wherever he went. In Antarctica he found that the

average temperature in September was 29 degrees below zero (−29°F). The warmest weather was in December when the temperature went up to 24°F.

Byrd spent almost the whole winter of 1934 in a little hut by himself. For weeks the temperature was between −64°F and −71°F. Ice covered even the inside of the hut. When Byrd finally left his lonely camp, he brought back to American scientists not only facts about temperature but facts about many other branches of science. Byrd brought back one other thing from Antarctica—a whole flock of penguins!

The Temperatures of a City Different places in the world have different temperatures. Also, not many places have exactly the same temperature all year round.

Look at the temperature graph on this page. The letters along the bottom of the graph stand for the months of the year. The numbers along the left side stand for degrees of temperature. In the Michigan city of Grand Rapids, the temperature of the air in September is 63°F. What is the temperature of the air in January?

Precipitation   You can see that to understand the weather and climate of a place, you must know about the temperatures of its air. You must also know about its **precipitation** (pri sip ə tā′ shən). Rain, snow, and all the other forms of water that fall to the earth are called precipitation.

Precipitation is measured in the inches of water that fall into a special tool called a *rain gauge* (gāj). A diagram of a rain gauge is shown on this page. Notice the numbers on the ruler inside the gauge. They show how much rain or other precipitation has fallen into the gauge.

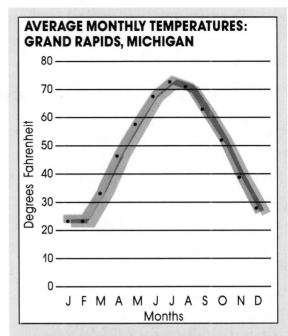

AVERAGE MONTHLY TEMPERATURES: GRAND RAPIDS, MICHIGAN

Degrees Fahrenheit

J F M A M J J A S O N D
Months

The dots on the line graph stand for each month's temperature.
■ What is the temperature of Grand Rapids's air in July?

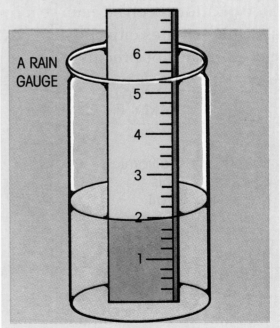

A RAIN GAUGE

Using a rain gauge is an easy way to measure precipitation.
■ How much rain has fallen into this rain gauge?

The amount of precipitation that a place receives over time is very important. It is a very valuable natural resource. People and animals must have water to live. Plants need water to grow. But all places do not have the same amount of precipitation. Some places have plenty of rainfall each year while others receive very little.

Places that have little rain often have a problem getting enough water for people and plants. Sometimes water must be brought in from other areas.

Look at the table on this page. It shows the amount of precipitation received each year by six United States cities. Which city has 23 inches of precipitation?

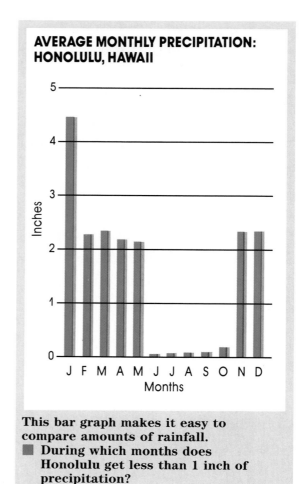

AVERAGE MONTHLY PRECIPITATION: HONOLULU, HAWAII

This bar graph makes it easy to compare amounts of rainfall.
■ During which months does Honolulu get less than 1 inch of precipitation?

SIX UNITED STATES CITIES: AVERAGE YEARLY PRECIPITATION

City	Inches
Bakersfield, California	6
Chicago, Illinois	34
Honolulu, Hawaii	23
Nashville, Tennessee	47
St. Louis, Missouri	37
Washington, D.C.	40

Bakersfield receives the least precipitation.
■ Which city receives the most?

No city has exactly the same amount of precipitation each month of the year. Look at the precipitation graph on this page. It shows how much rain the city of Honolulu gets each month. In which month does Honolulu get the most rain?

CHECKUP

1. What is the difference between weather and climate?
2. What name is given to the unit used to measure temperature?
3. **Thinking Critically** You have read that a good climate is a great natural resource. What does a good climate mean to you?

Reading a Time Line

What can we learn from a time line?

VOCABULARY

time line

When it Happened You have learned that maps and globes, and tables, graphs, and diagrams are tools that help you learn more about the world in which you live. A **time line** is another kind of tool. Time lines show you when certain things happened. They also help you see the order in which these things happened.

A time line, like a map, is a scale drawing. The time line on this page is 6 inches long. It shows 12 years in the life of a girl named Maria. It begins in 1980 and ends in 1992. Each inch on the time line stands for 2 years in Maria's life.

Find the word *Born* on the left side of the line. Notice that this word is written above the year 1980. That means that Maria was born in 1980. During what year did Maria begin school?

Think of some things you might put on your own time line.

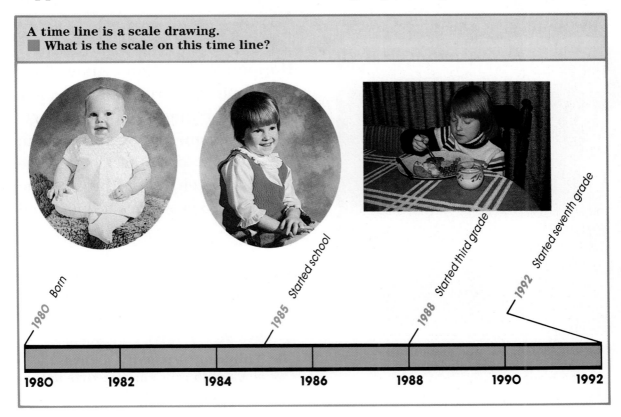

A time line is a scale drawing.
What is the scale on this time line?

1980 Born
1985 Started school
1988 Started third grade
1992 Started seventh grade

| 1980 | 1982 | 1984 | 1986 | 1988 | 1990 | 1992 |

43

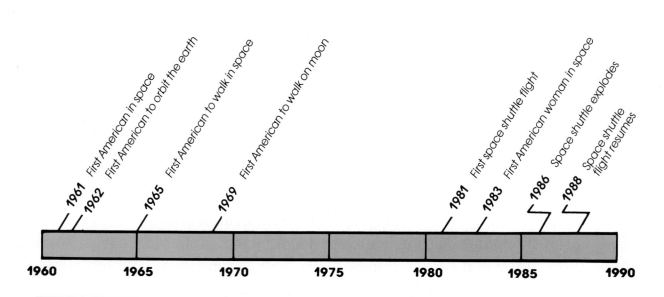

First American in space 1961
First American to orbit the earth 1962
First American to walk in space 1965
First American to walk on moon 1969
First space shuttle flight 1981
First American woman in space 1983
Space shuttle explodes 1986
Space shuttle flight resumes 1988

1960 1965 1970 1975 1980 1985 1990

A time line tells when things happened.
■ When did the first American woman make a flight in space?

Edwin Aldrin, Jr., was one of two
Americans who were the first to walk
on the moon.
■ When did this event occur?

The Order in Which Things Happened Many time lines show much more than 12 years. Look at the time line on this page. It shows some important dates in the history of America's space program. Each inch of the time line stands for 5 years. What happened in 1962?

CHECKUP

1. What do time lines show you?
2. What is the scale used on the time line on page 43?

3. **Thinking Critically** Why is the scale different on the two time lines in this lesson?

Reading a Graph

SOCIAL STUDIES TOOLS

In this chapter you learned about several tools that can help you learn about the world in which you live. One of these tools is the bar graph. The first bar graph below shows the number of farms in the United States in four different years. The second graph shows the average size of farms in the same four years.

SKILLS PRACTICE

Use the bar graphs on this page to answer the questions in the next column. Sometimes you might have to use both graphs to answer a question.

1. About how many farms were there in the United States in (**a**) 1954? (**b**) 1963? (**c**) 1973? (**d**) 1983?
2. Were there more farms in 1983 or in 1954?
3. About how many acres did the average farm have in (**a**) 1954? (**b**) 1963? (**c**) 1973? (**d**) 1983?
4. As the number of farms in the United States became fewer, what happened to the size of the remaining farms?
5. What are you able to learn by reading both graphs that you would not be able to find out by reading only one of the graphs?

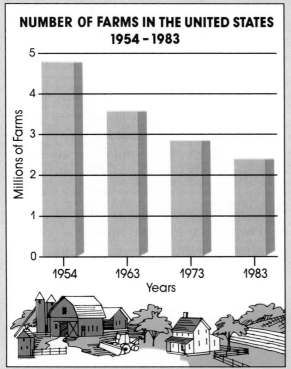

NUMBER OF FARMS IN THE UNITED STATES
1954–1983

Millions of Farms — Years

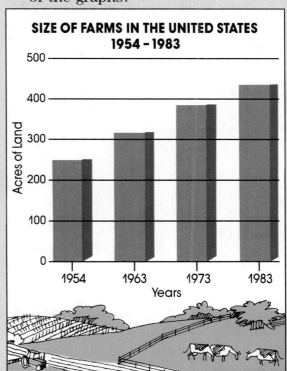

SIZE OF FARMS IN THE UNITED STATES
1954–1983

Acres of Land — Years

45

CHAPTER 2 REVIEW

MAIN IDEAS

1. Tables list facts and information in a very accurate way.
2. Graphs give us facts in forms that make the information quickly understandable. But the information may not be as complete and correct as the information in tables.
3. Graphs can show us relationships and change and can help us compare one piece of information with another.
4. Diagrams can show us how something works and its important parts.
5. The kind of weather a place has over a long period of time is its climate.
6. A thermometer can tell us the temperature of the air.
7. Time lines help us see when particular events took place and the order in which they took place.

VOCABULARY REVIEW

Copy the sentences below and fill in the blanks with the right vocabulary term.

a.	pictograph	**f.**	weather
b.	bar graph	**g.**	climate
c.	line graph	**h.**	time line
d.	pie graph	**i.**	diagram
e.	table	**j.**	natural resource

1. A _____ is a very accurate listing of information.
2. _____ is made up of rainfall, snowfall, wind, and temperature.
3. A graph that uses symbols instead of numbers to stand for things is called a _____ .
4. A _____ uses dots connected by lines to show information.
5. A _____ uses bars of different sizes to give information.
6. The rainfall, snowfall, wind, and temperature in a place over a long period of time is its _____ .
7. A _____ is used to show when events took place.
8. A _____ is drawn in the shape of a circle.
9. A drawing that can show you how something works and what its important parts are is called a _____ .
10. Something that is found in nature and that is useful to people is called a _____ .

CHAPTER CHECKUP

1. How might a diagram help you put together a model car?
2. Name the forms of precipitation.
3. **Thinking Critically** If you were studying the history of your community, how might a time line help you?

APPLYING KNOWLEDGE

1. Prepare a 12-inch time line of the birthdays in your classroom. Each inch can stand for a month. Place each student's birthday on the time line in the correct place and in the correct order.
2. Prepare a pictograph using the birthday information to show how many birthdays are in each month.

SUMMARIZING UNIT 1

REVIEWING VOCABULARY

1. globe   A globe is a model of the earth. A globe helps us learn about directions. What are the four main directions and the four in between directions?

2. continent   Continents are very large bodies of land. How many are there, and what is the name of each one?

3. Equator   The Equator is a line used on globes and maps. The Equator divides the earth into two equal parts. What are the names of these parts? In which hemisphere is the United States located?

4. climate   Climate is the kind of weather that a place has over a long period of time. Describe the kind of climate that would be good for growing things? Explain your answer.

5. time line   Time lines show the order in which events took place. They also help you see when certain things happened. How is scale used on a time line?

EXPRESSING YOURSELF

1. Making your own symbols   Maps and map symbols help us understand places. If you drew a map of your classroom, what map symbols would you use?

2. Using directions   If you wanted to tell people how to go from your classroom to other places in your school, you could use map directions. If they wanted to go to the library, you might say "Go north to the first hallway and then turn east." What directions would you give them if they wanted to find the cafeteria?

3. Using a grid system   Grid systems help us find places. Make a grid system of your classroom. Number each row of desks in the front of your class from left to right. Then give each row from the front to the back a letter. Who is sitting at 1-A? Who is at the desk at 2-C?

4. How would life be different?   Our country has many different physical features. How might your life be different if you moved from the mountains to the seashore?

5. Which would you use?   Tables and graphs help us understand information. Which of them would you use if you wanted to find exact information?

47

Learning About Different Communities

People like to be near other people. So they live in villages, towns, and cities. Almost all the people in the world live in some kind of community.

People need food and clothes and places to live. They need schools and jobs and many other things. Communities, large and small, provide these things for the people who live in them. In Unit 2 you will learn something about what it is like to live in large communities and in smaller communities.

This family is returning to their home high above the city streets.
■ **What do you think they have been shopping for?**

Many people, like Debbie and her mother, live in small communities. Debbie's mother travels to work in a nearby city. Other people, like the Alaskan children below, live in small towns far away from any city.

Debbie is happy to see her mother when she gets home from her job in the city.
■ How might Debbie's mother get to and from her job?

There is only one store in the tiny town where these friends live.
■ How do you think they get their food and other things they need?

There are many things that are fun to do in a big city. There are many ways to have fun in a small town too. People enjoy living in big communities, small communities, and communities that are in between.

Does your community have special places where people go to have fun? What else do you know about your community? In Unit 2 you will learn how to find out many things about your own community as well as about other towns and cities.

When the weather is pleasant and no rain is expected, it's a good time for a picnic. A park in a city or in a town is a good place for a picnic.
■ What do you suppose is in the picnic basket?

Watching a parade is fun. So is a picnic under a shady tree. Some people like to fish in a clear, clean stream. Do you have a favorite thing you enjoy doing? Can you do it in your own community?

(*Left*) Children and grownups alike are enjoying this parade.
(*Right*) These children are hoping to catch some fish for dinner.
■ Which picture shows a big city? How can you tell?

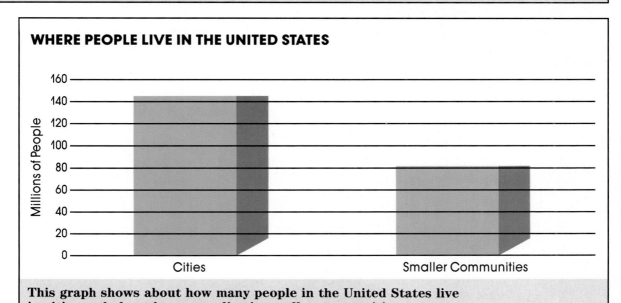

WHERE PEOPLE LIVE IN THE UNITED STATES

Millions of People

160
140
120
100
80
60
40
20
0

Cities   Smaller Communities

This graph shows about how many people in the United States live
in cities and about how many live in smaller communities.
■ Where do more people live in the United States, in cities or in
smaller communities?

51

3 Studying One Community

Learning Through Maps

How do maps help you learn about your community?

VOCABULARY

port   county

Let's Learn About Our Community   We all live in communities. Each of us may think that our community is the most important one. The truth is that every community is important. Every community has its own special people and places.

The city of Wilmington, North Carolina, is located on the Cape Fear River. Wilmington was settled in 1732.
■ Why, do you think, was this location for a city a good one?

We cannot learn about all of our communities. Instead we will visit a class in one community. The students in this class will tell us how they learned about their community. We can use many of these same ways to study our own community.

We will visit a class of girls and boys who go to Forest Hills Elementary School. The school is in Wilmington, North Carolina. Look up Wilmington in the Gazetteer on pages 263–267. Then find Wilmington on the map on page 56. You can see that Wilmington is in southeastern North Carolina.

A Good Way to Begin The students told their teacher, Mrs. Reddrick, that they wanted to learn more about their community. Mrs. Reddrick asked them what they already knew about Wilmington. The students discovered that they really knew a lot. They knew that Wilmington is a **port** city. A port is a place where ships can be safe from the big waves and strong winds of stormy seas. The boys and girls knew that many ships come to their city's port every year.

Mrs. Reddrick then asked the students to tell her what they wanted to study. This helped her to group the class so that students with the same interests could work together.

Now we will look at each group to see how they studied their community and what they learned.

Learning from Maps Antonio, Tonya, Ben, and Kelsey had moved to Wilmington during the summer. They wanted to make maps. These maps would help them find places in their new community. They decided to make four maps. Mrs. Reddrick gave them some maps to

(Left) Mrs. Reddrick helps her class learn about their city and state. (Right) Kelsey, a student in Mrs. Reddrick's class, points to the location of Wilmington.
■ What tells you that this class is studying about North Carolina?

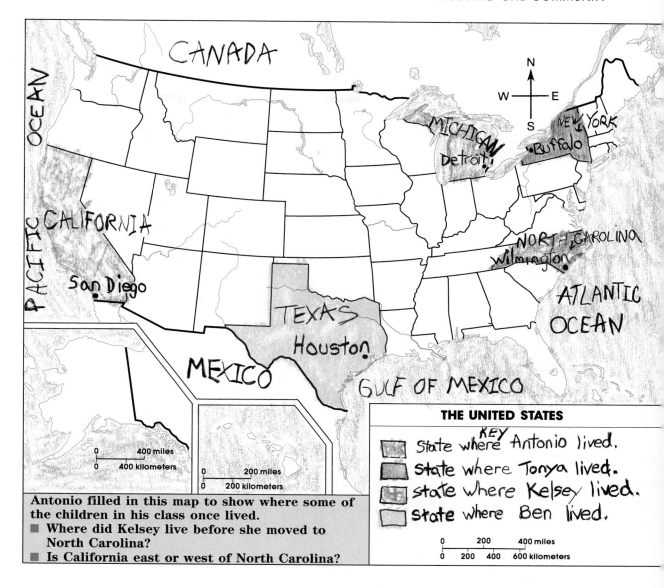

THE UNITED STATES

KEY

State where Antonio lived.
State where Tonya lived.
State where Kelsey lived.
State where Ben lived.

Antonio filled in this map to show where some of the children in his class once lived.
■ Where did Kelsey live before she moved to North Carolina?
■ Is California east or west of North Carolina?

use. These maps showed the outlines of certain places. The maps also showed a compass rose and a scale of miles. The girls and boys filled in the maps and made map keys.

Antonio filled in a map of the United States. He colored North Carolina red and put a black dot where Wilmington is located. Antonio also colored the states where he, Tonya, Ben, and Kelsey used to live. He put black dots where their old communities are located. Then he filled in the names of all these places. Look at Antonio's map above. Where did he live before moving to Wilmington?

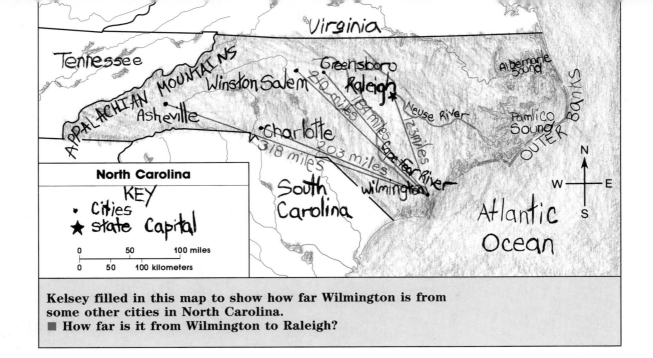

North Carolina

KEY
- • Cities
- ★ state Capital

| 0 | 50 | 100 miles |
| 0 | 50 | 100 kilometers |

Kelsey filled in this map to show how far Wilmington is from some other cities in North Carolina.
■ How far is it from Wilmington to Raleigh?

Tonya colored in Wilmington, its neighbors, and other communities in her county.
■Name the communities in New Hanover County that border Wilmington.

New Hanover County

Key
- Wilmington
- Wilmington's Neighbors
- Other Parts of the County

| 0 | 5 | 10 miles |
| 0 | 5 | 10 kilometers |

Kelsey wanted to make a map of North Carolina. She located Wilmington on her map. She also showed other cities in the state and how far they are from Wilmington. Kelsey drew in the Appalachian Mountains, the Cape Fear River, the Neuse River, Albemarle Sound, Pamlico Sound, and the Outer Banks.

Tonya's map shows the **county** named New Hanover County. A county is a political division. Most of our states are divided into counties. Besides showing the shape of New Hanover County, Tonya's map shows some of the communities in the county.

Ben colored in a map of Wilmington. He colored the bodies

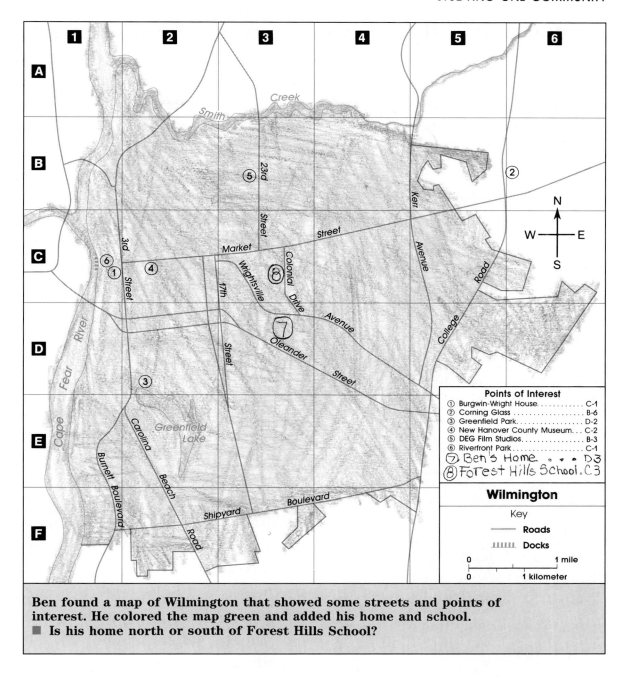

Points of Interest
① Burgwin-Wright House C-1
② Corning Glass B-6
③ Greenfield Park D-2
④ New Hanover County Museum . . . C-2
⑤ DEG Film Studios B-3
⑥ Riverfront Park C-1
⑦ Ben's Home . . . D3
⑧ Forest Hills School . C3

Wilmington

Key
—— Roads
⊥⊥⊥⊥⊥ Docks

0   1 mile
0   1 kilometer

Ben found a map of Wilmington that showed some streets and points of interest. He colored the map green and added his home and school.
■ **Is his home north or south of Forest Hills School?**

of water blue. He showed where some important places are located. He also placed his home and school on the map and in the map key. Ben's map is shown above. On which street is Ben's school?

CHECKUP

1. Which states border North Carolina?

2. **Thinking Critically** How was Kelsey's map different from Tonya's map?

A Community's History

How can you learn about your community's history?

VOCABULARY

card catalog   encyclopedia

Finding Some Important Places

Amanda, Jason, Gelene, and Jamie wanted to learn what their community was like a long time ago. Mrs. Reddrick told the students that there are special places in Wilmington that were important in the community's past. She said that in these places, people can learn a great deal about Wilmington's history.

The Governor Dudley Mansion, built about 1832, is one of many well-cared-for homes in Wilmington.
■ What can you learn from old homes?

"We can do that, too!" said Amanda. "We can visit the places we want to study."

"Yes," said Jamie. "But first we ought to use books to find out a little about the places we might want to visit."

"We will need a map of Wilmington, too," said Amanda. "We can look at the map to see where the special places are."

Gelene was happy. "I have a new camera. I can take some pictures of the places we visit. Maybe we can find some old pictures of Wilmington, too."

Learning in a Library

First the students decided to go to the school library to learn more about Wilmington. They went to talk to Mrs. Mowery, the librarian. She showed them how to look for the names of books in the **card catalog**. This is an alphabetical list of the books in the library. The cards are in drawers marked with the letters of the alphabet. Each card tells three things about a book. It tells the title of the book, the author's name, and what the book is about. Then Mrs. Mowery showed the students how to find the books

Mrs. Mowery helps the students find out about Wilmington in the library.
■ **What would you like to find out about in your community?**

on the shelves. They found four books about Wilmington. Mrs. Mowery also told the boys and girls to look in the **encyclopedias** (in sī kla pē′ dē əs).

She said, "These are sets of books that have a lot of information about many different things. Subjects are listed alphabetically in these books. You will find them on special shelves in the library."

The students found the encyclopedias. They looked up *Wilmington* in the encyclopedia marked *W*. The girls and boys found information that they could use. They also looked up information under the heading *North Carolina*.

Taking Field Trips The boys and girls gathered all the information they could find in books. Then they visited the places that they planned to write about in their report. They were given booklets at some of the places they visited. Each booklet described the place and told some things about what had happened there long ago.

At each place, Gelene took pictures. The other students made notes about what they had learned.

Then the boys and girls wrote a report about the places they visited. They used pictures to make the report more interesting. This is their report.

INTERESTING PLACES
IN AND AROUND WILMINGTON

THE U.S.S. NORTH CAROLINA

This giant battleship was built to help make our navy strong. The ship took part in almost every naval battle in the Pacific Ocean during World War II (1939–1945).

When the navy no longer needed the ship, it was to be sold as scrap metal. But people in North Carolina wanted to save the ship, so they raised money. School children helped by giving a dime each.

The U.S.S. North Carolina is anchored on the Cape Fear River across from downtown Wilmington. The ship is a memorial to the people who died in World War II.

THE BURGWIN-WRIGHT HOUSE

This house is named for its first two owners—John Burgwin and Joshua Wright. The house was built by John Burgwin in 1771. It is one of the oldest houses in Wilmington. It is also known as the Cornwallis Headquarters because the British General Cornwallis used the house in April 1781. When we visited the house, we saw that it had been made to look as it did during the War for Independence.

NEW HANOVER COUNTY MUSEUM

This museum has many pictures, models, and artifacts that show what life was like long ago. Artifacts are things that were made and used by people long ago.

One of the most interesting things we saw in the museum was a model of Wilmington. The model shows the waterfront during the Civil War period, from 1861 to 1865.

OLD BRUNSWICK TOWN

Brunswick Town, a few miles south of Wilmington, was an early port town on the Cape Fear River. The town is almost 275 years old. After

Wilmington became the main port on the river, most people moved away from Brunswick Town. The forest grew over and covered the old town.

In recent years, scientists have dug up many artifacts that show how the people at Brunswick Town lived long ago.

Today, visitors can walk along the original streets of the town and see where the buildings were. The old church walls still stand in the woods, and nearby is an old cemetery.

CHECKUP

1. In what ways did the students learn about historic places in their community?

2. Whom does the battleship U.S.S. *North Carolina* honor?

3. **Thinking Critically** Why do communities like Wilmington provide places for people to learn about the past?

Working in the Wilmington Area

*How can we gather information
about the businesses in a
community?*

VOCABULARY

area	import
chamber of commerce	export
product	dock
	container

Facts by Mail   Michael, Meg, Rebecca, Tony, and Lisha decided to learn about places where people work in the Wilmington **area**. Area is the land for several miles around a community. Michael and Meg wanted to learn about some of the largest companies in Wilmington. They were mainly interested in finding out which companies hired the most workers.

Meg and Michael asked Mrs. Reddrick, "Where do we start? There are so many different places where people work."

Mrs. Reddrick answered, "You might begin by writing a letter to the **chamber of commerce**. It is a group of business people. They have much information about the companies in the Wilmington area. Send your letter to Mr. Joseph Augustine. He will be glad to help you."

Information in a Chart   A week later, Meg and Michael received a package in the mail. The package was from Mr. Augustine. It was full of facts about businesses in and near Wilmington.

Meg and Michael learned that there are some places where a large number of people work. There are also some places where few people work. There were so many different places that Meg and Michael decided to make a chart. The chart

Mrs. Reddrick helps Meg write to the chamber of commerce.
■ What do you think Meg needs to put on the envelope?

602 Colonial Drive
Wilmington, North Carolina
28403

September 28, 1987

Mr. Joseph Augustine
Executive Vice President
Greater Wilmington Chamber of Commerce
P. O. Box 330
Wilmington, North Carolina 28402

Dear Mr. Augustine:

Our third grade class at Forest Hills School is studying about our community. We want to learn about the places where people work in the Wilmington area.

Please send us information about the different businesses and industries. We want to know their names and what they do or make. We also would like to know the number of people who work at these places.

Thank you for your help.

Sincerely,
Meg Marshall
and
Michael Borneman

Meg and Michael planned their letter carefully. They told Mr. Augustine who they were and why they were writing to him. When Meg wrote the letter, she showed her best handwriting.

■ How did Mr. Augustine know where to send the information?

PLACES WHERE PEOPLE WORK IN AND AROUND WILMINGTON

Business	Number of Workers
General Electric	2,450
Corning Glass	960
North Carolina State Ports Authority	700
DEG Film Studios	700
Snyder General	570
Cape Industries	540
Block Industries	325
Century Mills	300

There are many places where people work in Wilmington. Meg and Michael's chart lists only some of those places.
■ How many people work for North Carolina State Ports Authority?

showed some of the companies in the Wilmington area that hire the most people. Look at Meg and Michael's chart, above.

Observing and Listening
Lisha, Rebecca, and Tony told Mrs. Reddrick that they wanted to study one place where people in Wilmington work. The place they chose was the North Carolina State Ports Authority.

Mrs. Reddrick called the North Carolina State Ports Authority. She talked with Mr. Salisbury. He helps people learn about the port. He said that he would be happy to have the students visit him and see the port.

Mr. Salisbury was waiting for Lisha, Rebecca, and Tony when they arrived. "I want to tell you about the North Carolina State Ports Authority at Wilmington," he said. "Each year, hundreds of ships from all over the world come to Wilmington. Here they unload their **products**. Then they load other products onto their ships. Products are the things made or grown by companies or people and needed by other people or companies. Products bought from other countries are called **imports**. Products sold to other countries are called **exports**."

Lisha asked, "Mr. Salisbury, what are the main exports and imports of our port?"

Mr. Salisbury answered, "That's a very good question, Lisha. The most important exports shipped out of Wilmington are tobacco, paper products, lumber products, and cotton goods. Many of these products go to countries in Europe. These products also go to places as far away as China. The main imports that come here are oil products, sugar, molasses, burlap, farm equipment, and steel products.

"Let's go out to the **docks** and see what is happening today. A dock is a kind of platform where ships load and unload their goods.

"Look at the big ropes coming from each ship. They are tied to the dock and hold the ship in place. To get to the docks, the large ships are guided by tugboats up the channel in the middle of the river. The small tugboats gently guide the larger ships safely over to the docks. The tugboats also help the ships turn around in the river and head back out toward the ocean.

"When the ships reach the docks, they are unloaded and loaded by groups of people who are called dockworkers," explained Mr. Salisbury. "The dockworkers use cranes, bulldozers, and other machines to move the goods. Look at those stacks of large metal **containers**. They look like the trailer sections of large tractor-trailer trucks. Containers are full of smaller boxes of goods. The containers make it easier to load

The port of Wilmington is visited by many oceangoing ships.
■ **What tells you that ships from other countries visit the port?**

and unload ships. The containers are stored in stacks until they are taken either by truck or by train to other parts of the country. Notice the train tracks along the docks. Trains can pull up close to the ships. That helps to move the products quickly from the ships to the trains and then to market.

"This ship is named *Tadeusz Kosciuszko* (ta de′ üsh kôsh chüsh′ kô)," said Mr. Salisbury. "It is from Poland."

"Oh yes," exclaimed Tony. "All the containers have *Polish Ocean Lines* written on them. I've seen trucks carrying containers like those through Wilmington."

"Very good," said Mr. Salisbury. "I bet that children in other cities and states have seen them, too. Now let me show you one more thing. You can always tell if a ship is loaded or unloaded by how it sits in the water at the dock. See that large ship over there named the *Ming Sun*? It is from Taiwan. Look down at the side of the ship. The

(Left) The giant-sized metal boxes, called containers, are packed with different products. (Right) A huge crane on shore lifts a container from the dock and loads it onto a ship.
■ How does a container travel to the crane?

Not all products travel in containers. Here a chemical used in the textile industry is about to be loaded aboard a ship.
■ What safety clothing are the dockhands wearing?

bottom part is painted red. There are also numbers spaced one foot apart to show how much of the ship is below the water. Whenever you see a lot of red on the side of the ship above the waterline, you know that it is not loaded. The red painted section on a heavier, loaded ship would be below the water.

"Well, that is the tour of our port," said Mr. Salisbury. "I hope that you enjoyed it."

All of the children thanked Mr. Salisbury for the nice tour. The next day, Lisha, Rebecca, and Tony wrote a report about their tour of the port. They wrote about the many things they had learned by listening to Mr. Salisbury and by observing the interesting sights at the port.

CHECKUP

1. How did Meg and Michael gather information about businesses in Wilmington?
2. How did Lisha, Rebecca, and Tony find out about one special place where people in Wilmington work?
3. **Thinking Critically** Why is the North Carolina State Ports Authority important for people both inside and outside Wilmington?

A Special Place in Wilmington

Why is the movie-making company, DEG Film Studios, important to Wilmington?

VOCABULARY
architect

The Movie Industry Bryant, Melissa, Vaughn, Susan, and Mark wanted to learn more about DEG Film Studios. This is a large movie-making company that came to Wilmington in 1984.

"We have all heard about the movie studio," said Bryant. "Some of us have even seen the filming of scenes, or parts of movies."

"Yes," said Melissa, "but we would like to learn more about the movie industry. Why did this company choose Wilmington? What goes on at the studio when a movie is filmed?"

Mrs. Reddrick said, "I'll call someone at DEG Film Studios." She talked to Miss Bednarczyk (bə när′ sik), who agreed to give the class a tour of the studio and sets.

Visiting the Studio Miss Bednarczyk met Mrs. Reddrick and the class at the main gate. Miss Bednarczyk started by telling why Wilmington was chosen to be the

This is an aerial view of DEG Film Studios in Wilmington.
■ What does *DEG* stand for?

site of this movie studio. "About 3 years ago, Dino De Laurentiis decided to film the movie *Firestarter* here. He chose the Wilmington area because he saw a picture of Orton Plantation on the cover of a magazine. He wanted to use Orton Plantation in his film. De Laurentiis, who is from Italy, also liked Wilmington's fair weather and warm climate. He built his first United States studio here."

Henry Bacon (1866–1924)

Have you ever looked closely at the back side of a penny? If you have then you might have noticed a drawing that looks like a building. That building is the Lincoln Memorial. It is in Washington, D.C. The Lincoln Memorial honors Abraham Lincoln, the sixteenth President of the United States. A statue of President Lincoln is inside the memorial. Henry Bacon, who once lived in Wilmington, North Carolina, drew the plans for the Lincoln Memorial.

Henry Bacon moved with his family to Wilmington in 1880. He was 14 years old at the time. His family moved to Wilmington because his father was put in charge of building a dam on the Cape Fear River.

In 1884 Henry Bacon graduated from Tileston High School. After high school, he went to college and studied to be an **architect**. An architect is a person who draws the plans for buildings and then guides the builders. Bacon best liked to draw plans for monuments and memorials.

In 1923 Bacon received an award from President Warren G. Harding for his work on the Lincoln Memorial. If you visit Oakdale Cemetery in Wilmington today, you will be able to find the gravestone that marks where Henry Bacon is buried.

Author Steven King directs a movie on the set at DEG Film Studios.
■ **What jobs might be available at a movie-making company?**

Melissa asked, "What are those big buildings?"

"Five of those are what we call sound stages," explained Miss Bednarczyk. "A sound stage is where different scenes for movies are filmed. And that building over there is the special effects unit. That is where special kinds of lights, actions, or sounds are prepared. Our main building has offices and a cafeteria."

"What is that?" asked Vaughn, pointing his finger.

Miss Bednarczyk laughed. "What you are looking at is a street set. This set was built for the movie *Year of the Dragon*. It is like a city street in the Chinatown area of New York City."

Miss Bednarczyk said, "We also film scenes here in Wilmington. We get permission from the police department and from the property owners to use certain streets, houses, or businesses for outdoor filming."

Miss Bednarczyk went on to say that DEG Film Studios provided jobs for many people from the area. "We hire carpenters, electricians, painters, chefs, set makers, and other people to work on our films."

Mrs. Reddrick and the students thanked Miss Bednarczyk for showing them the movie studio. They all felt that it was truly a special place in Wilmington.

CHECKUP

1. Why did De Laurentiis choose Wilmington as a good place for his studio?
2. What is an architect?
3. **Thinking Critically** How, do you think, might the movie industry affect Wilmington?

Having Fun in Wilmington

How can people enjoy themselves in Wilmington?

VOCABULARY

| recreation | interview |

Conducting an Interview   Joe, Trisha, Todd, and Frances decided to find out about places where people have fun in the Wilmington area.

"Trisha and I want to learn about community parks and playgrounds," said Todd. "Let's ask Mrs. Reddrick how we can find out about these places."

Mrs. Reddrick told them about her friend Miss Trask. "Miss Trask is in charge of the Parks and **Recreation** Department of the city of Wilmington. Recreation is the activities that people do for fun. Maybe you can visit Miss Trask. I'll call her tonight."

Todd and Trisha made a list of questions to ask Miss Trask in the **interview**. An interview is meeting someone face-to-face to talk over a special subject.

A few days later, Trisha and Todd visited Miss Trask at her office. After their talk, the students wrote out the answers to some of their questions. Here is part of the interview.

Trisha and Todd prepared their questions for the interview with Miss Trask. They listen attentively as she answers the questions.
■ **Why is it important to be a good listener?**

An Interview with Miss Trask

Trisha: In our social studies class, we have been studying our community. We know there are many parks and playgrounds in Wilmington. Are there any plans for new ones?

Miss Trask: We have several large parks within our city. But there are several new areas that have been added to Wilmington. Local parks and recreation areas will be needed there.

Todd: What are some things that people do when they go to the parks?

Miss Trask: At Greenfield Park, people go boating. They also ride bicycles on the 7-mile (11-km) bicycle path around the lake. People use the swings and the two swimming pools.

Empie Park has a small castle in which children like to play. There are also large shelters with fireplaces for cookouts.

Riverfront Park is our newest park. Here people like to walk along the new walkways and look at the boats in the river.

Todd: Will there still be parks when we grow up?

Miss Trask: Almost all of our parks are owned by the community, the county, or the state. This means they belong to all of us. We are always trying to buy more land for parks. Sometimes, people give land for a park. Our community also has many miles of ocean beaches that all of us can use. We may never have as many parks as we would like to have. But there will be parks when you grow up.

At Greenfield Park in Wilmington, a family enjoys a walk together. Other people have fun boating.
■ What do you like to do when you visit a park?

Around Wilmington there are places for people to see ocean animals, build sand castles, and ride bicycles.
■ **Which of these things would you most like to do?**

Fun for Everyone Frances and Joe wanted to find out about some of the best places they could go to have fun. They asked their parents and neighbors about different things to do and places to visit in and around Wilmington.

Then Frances and Joe asked their friends for pictures of fun places to visit. They made a bulletin-board display with all the pictures they received.

CHECKUP
1. In what ways did Frances, Trisha, Todd, and Joe gather information about their community?
2. How did the students prepare for the interview?
3. **Thinking Critically** What questions would you have liked to ask Miss Trask about the parks and playgrounds in Wilmington?

Being a Good Citizen

How can we be good citizens of our community?

VOCABULARY

citizen   citizenship

Citizenship   Charlie, Theresa, and Ginny had heard about the **Citizen** of the Year Award. They told Mrs. Reddrick that they wanted to find out what made a person a good citizen.

Mrs. Reddrick said, "Well, a citizen is someone who is a member of a community, state, or country. **Citizenship** is how we live up to the responsibilities of being a citizen, or member, of our community, state, or country.

Theresa said, "We will ask a number of people what they think makes a person a good citizen."

"Yes," added Charlie. "We could then list what they say on a poster. That should give us an idea of how we can be good young citizens."

"That sounds like a great idea," said Mrs. Reddrick. "Do you know who you are going to ask?"

"Yes," answered Ginny. "We want to ask some teachers, the principal, and maybe even a police officer. We also will ask our parents for their ideas."

The students talked with many people. The poster lists the answers given most often.

Students can be good citizens at home, at school, and in their community.
■ Why are these students good citizens?

A GOOD CITIZEN IS SOMEONE WHO

- respects other people
- respects the property of other people
- obeys rules and laws
- helps others
- works to make the community, state, and country a better place to live

Learning About Your Own Community   In this chapter you have read how one class studied its community. Now it is your turn to learn some things about your own community.

As you study your community, you should try to answer some of the questions below. When you think of other questions, write them in a list.

IMPORTANT FACTS

What is the name of my community?
How did my community get its name?
What are the names of some nearby communities?
What is the name of my state?
Where is my state located in the United States?

MAKING A LIVING

About how many people live in my community?
What kinds of jobs do people have?
How do people travel to work?
What are some of the stores and businesses in my community?

THE PAST

Who were the first people to live in my community?
What did my community look like long ago?
Who were some famous people from my community?
What important things have happened in my community?

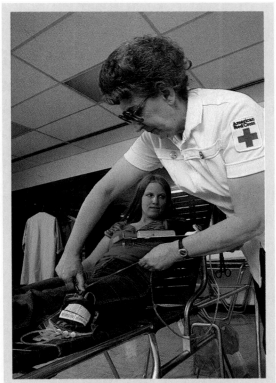

A *volunteer* offers to work without pay, usually to help others. The volunteers above are part of their community's blood donation program.
■ How are these volunteers helping?

INTERESTING PLACES

What are some interesting places that people visit when they are in my community?
Why do people visit these places?

CHECKUP

1. What are some ways in which students can be good citizens?
2. How can you gather information about your community?
3. **Thinking Critically** Why is it important for us to be good citizens?

Reading a Map

SKILLS PRACTICE

Every community is made up of neighborhoods. Look at the map of a neighborhood below. Answer the questions on a separate sheet of paper.

1. The jail is in box D-2. In what box is the school?

2. On what streets are the stores?

3. If you live on the corner of Elm Street and Washington Street, in which direction would you walk to go to school?

4. Using the scale, figure how far it is from the gas station to the police station?

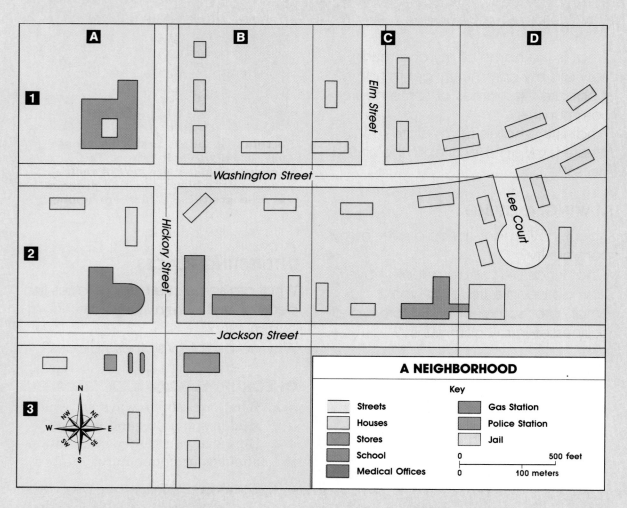

A NEIGHBORHOOD

Key

	Streets		Gas Station
	Houses		Police Station
	Stores		Jail
	School
	Medical Offices

0   500 feet

0   100 meters

CHAPTER 3 REVIEW

MAIN IDEAS

1. We all live in communities.
2. Maps can help us learn about our community by showing us where important places are and how to find our way around.
3. Many communities have well-known places that help people learn a great deal about their community's history.
4. There are often many different places to work in and around a community.
5. We can gather information about our community by writing to, listening to, and interviewing appropriate people; by reading; and by observing.
6. The movie-making company, DEG Film Studios, supplies jobs for some people in Wilmington and the area.
7. Wilmington, like most other communities, provides opportunities for fun and enjoyment.
8. We can be good citizens by doing everything possible to make our community, state, or country a better place in which to live.

VOCABULARY REVIEW

Write the numbers 1 to 10 on a sheet of paper. Match the words in the first part with their meanings in the second part.

a. chamber of commerce
b. port
c. card catalog
d. interview
e. product
f. citizen
g. architect
h. citizenship
i. area
j. encyclopedia

1. A safe place for ships

2. Someone who is a member of a community
3. Something that people make or grow
4. A group made up of business people who help the community
5. The land for several miles around a community
6. How people live up to the responsibilities of being a citizen
7. A list of the books in a library
8. Meeting someone face-to-face to talk over a special subject
9. A person who draws the plans for buildings and then guides the builders
10. A set of books that have information about a great many things

CHAPTER CHECKUP

1. What did the students learn about Wilmington from Ben's map?
2. How did the students use the library to find information?
3. Why did Meg and Michael write a letter to the chamber of commerce?
4. **Thinking Critically** List the ways you would study your community.

APPLYING KNOWLEDGE

1. List the places in your community that you think a visitor would like to see.
2. If your community has a chamber of commerce, write a class letter to it, asking for information.
3. Plan a museum for your town or city. List the things that you would put in the museum to help visitors learn about your community.

4 Learning About Cities

Cities Have a History

Why do cities begin and grow?

VOCABULARY

specialize	transportation
trade	crop
division of labor	religious freedom
valley	harbor
causeway	government

The Growth of Cities You learned in Chapter 1 that a city is a large community. Many people live, work, and play in cities all over the world.

This is New York City, the largest city in the United States. The tallest building in the picture is the Empire State Building. It has 102 stories, and is 1,250 feet (381 m) high.

■ Why, do you think, is this building called a *skyscraper*?

People have not always lived in cities. Long ago people moved from place to place in search of food. They hunted animals and gathered plants to eat. In time, some people learned to grow plants. Others learned to raise animals for food. People became farmers. They began to stay in one place to take care of their plants and animals.

Once they started farming, people found they could often grow more food than they could eat. When this happened, some people were able to stop farming. They started doing other kinds of work, such as making bowls

and dishes or weaving cloth. They could give some of what they made to the farmers in exchange for the farmers' extra food. They no longer had to grow all their own food.

Little by little, people came to live together in communities. No one person could make everything he or she needed in order to live. People found that their lives were better if they worked together. People could **specialize** (spesh′ ə līz). That means they could make just a few kinds of things. Then they could **trade,** or exchange, their extra products for other products that they might need. People could divide up the work. We call that **division of labor.** In time, some of these little communities of people who needed one another grew into cities.

Tenochtitlán   One community that grew in size was named Tenochtitlán (tā näch tē tlän′). It was built hundreds of years ago by the Aztec (az′ tek) Indians. The Aztecs lived in what is now the country of Mexico. Mexico City, its capital, now stands on the spot where Tenochtitlán was built long ago. Find Mexico and Mexico City on the map on page 256.

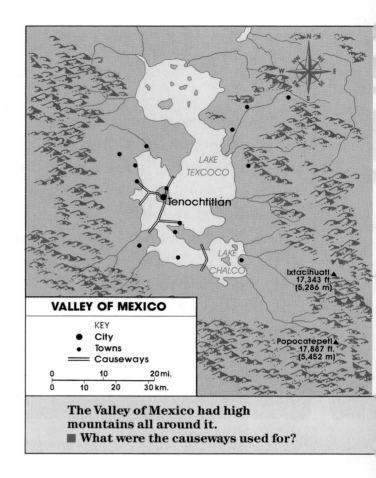

VALLEY OF MEXICO

KEY
- City
• Towns
═══ Causeways

0   10   20 mi.
0   10   20   30 km.

The Valley of Mexico had high mountains all around it.
■ What were the causeways used for?

Tenochtitlán was built on an island in the middle of a lake. This lake was in a **valley.** A valley is a lowland between hills or mountains. The Valley of Mexico had high mountains all around it. Many Aztecs had settled in the area because of the lake water and because it had rich farmland.

The map on this page shows the Valley of Mexico and the island on which Tenochtitlán was built. The Aztecs built **causeways** to connect their island to the land around it. The causeways were like bridges, but they were made of land.

Over many years Tenochtitlán grew larger as more people came to live and work there. By the time the first people from Europe came to Mexico, there was a big city at Tenochtitlán. It had beautiful buildings, wide streets, and room for many people.

All the communities in our country today were built long after Tenochtitlán began. Let us look at some of the reasons why different cities began and grew.

Cities and Natural Resources
Some cities began because they were located near important natural resources. You have already learned that the people of Tenochtitlán first settled there because of two great natural resources—water and good land for farming.

Water is useful for another reason. It gives people a way to travel and to move products from place to place. This is called **transportation.** Many cities have grown up along lakes, rivers, and oceans because of easy transportation. One such city is London in England. Find London in the Gazetteer that starts on page 263. The latitude and longitude are given for the city. Use that information to find London on the map on page 260.

On the left is a painting showing how Tenochtitlán probably looked long ago. On the right is a photograph of modern Mexico City.
■ **How are these cities alike? How are they different?**

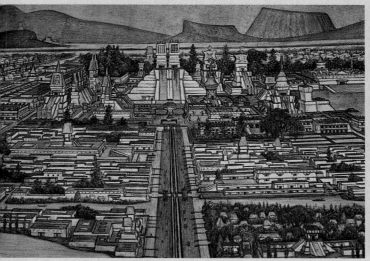

London More than 2,000 years ago, London was a small community on the banks of the Thames (temz) River. It started as a settlement of soldiers from an enemy country. The enemy had taken over this part of the land that is now England.

The soldiers in the small community needed food and other products. They bought some things they needed from people living nearby. Some people even moved to the area to sell their products to the soldiers. Farmers brought their **crops** to the area to sell. Crops are plants that are grown for food and other uses. Crops and other products could be loaded onto boats and brought to London to sell. The river made good transportation possible.

After a while, the soldiers left. But the people who had moved to the area stayed. They went on buying and selling products. More and more people moved to the London area. They made all kinds of things, from tables and chairs to beads and rings. Boats carried products all along the Thames River. Larger boats carried products from London's port to other countries.

Above is a medal that shows part of London many hundreds of years ago. Below is a picture of London today.
■ What is alike about these two pictures of London?

This buying and selling of products is also called *trade*. Trade helped London grow into a big, busy port city.

Philadelphia   More than 300 years ago, a man named William Penn came from England to America. He started a town he called Philadelphia (fil ə del' fē ə) between two rivers in what is now the state of Pennsylvania. Find Pennsylvania and Philadelphia on the map on pages 254–255.

Penn wanted Philadelphia to be a community where people could live without having to belong to one particular religion or church. At that time there were not many places in the world where people were allowed to do this. But Penn believed in **religious freedom.** He believed that everyone should be free to belong to any religion.

Philadelphia grew quickly. People moved there for religious freedom. Many of these people were good workers. There were good candle makers, shoemakers, bakers, and many others. People opened stores and sold food and other products. Soon the fine wide streets of Philadelphia were lined with stores and other businesses.

The top picture shows Philadelphia's river port in 1800. The bottom one shows Philadelphia today.
■ How do the pictures themselves tell you which one is older?

85

One of the most important parts of Philadelphia was its river port. Oceangoing ships were loaded in Philadelphia and sailed down the Delaware River and right on into the Atlantic Ocean. From there, the ships carried Philadelphia's products to cities all over the world.

Religious freedom, good transportation, and trade all helped Philadelphia grow into a big city.

Honolulu   There are still other natural resources that have helped some cities grow. One resource is climate. As you learned in Chapter 2, climate is the kind of weather that a place has over a long period of time. A second resource is the great beauty of a place.

The island state of Hawaii is world famous for its climate and beauty. Each year millions of people visit Hawaii. They like the fact that

Hawaii is famous for its climate and beauty. Visitors enjoy sunshine and warm temperatures year round. They admire the sandy beaches, flowers and palm trees, and green countryside.
■ If you were to visit Hawaii, what would you like to see?

Betsy Ross (1752–1836)

A legend tells us that Betsy Ross made the first American flag. A legend is a story that has been told over and over again for many years. The story may or may not be true.

We do not know for sure whether Betsy Ross made our first flag. But we do know a little about a real person named Betsy Ross. She and her husband, John, had a shop in Philadelphia, Pennsylvania. During the War for Independence, John was a soldier in the American Army. He was killed in a gunpowder explosion. After his death, Betsy Ross ran the shop. She was a seamstress, skilled at sewing.

Long after Betsy Ross died, her grandson told the story of the first stars and stripes. He had been told the story by his grandmother. One day in 1776, as Betsy Ross was tending the store, three men walked in. The very tall man was George Washington. Her visitors asked her to make an American flag.

They gave her a drawing of what they thought the flag should look like. The drawing showed a flag with stripes and six-pointed stars. Betsy Ross thought that the stars should have only five points. The men agreed.

Did Betsy Ross go ahead and make the flag? Her grandson believed that she did. Whether true or not, the legend of Betsy Ross has become part of the story of our country.

the temperature in Hawaii changes very little between summer and winter. It is warm the year round. There is lots of sunshine and lots of rain. Visitors also enjoy the flat, sandy beaches, the deep blue seas, the steep green mountains, and the colorful flowers.

Honolulu (hon əl ü′ lü) is the capital and largest city in Hawaii. Find Honolulu on the map on pages 254–255. Many people have moved to Honolulu to work in businesses that serve visitors to the state. Visitors like the big hotels, the

stores, and places to eat. Climate and beautiful scenery have helped Honolulu become a big city.

A third reason for Honolulu's growth is its location in the middle of the Pacific Ocean. Honolulu was a small island village when an English sea captain sailed his ship into its **harbor** in 1794. A harbor is a protected body of water, safe for ships. Other ships began to use the harbor. They stopped to take on food and fresh water for their long voyage across the Pacific Ocean. In time Honolulu became an important port.

Santa Fe   Santa Fe (sant ə fā′), New Mexico is one of the oldest cities in our country. It was started in 1610 by a man from the country of Spain. His name was Pedro de Peralta (pā′ drō   də   pə räl′ tə).

This city was built to be the center of **government** for what is now the state of New Mexico. Government is made up of the leaders of a group who make the laws and see that these laws are carried out.

Food and other supplies had to be brought to Santa Fe. At first everything came all the way from Mexico City on the backs of mules

Pearl Harbor, near Honolulu, is a big harbor. It is used as a United States naval base.
■ **How can you tell that the naval ships are quite large in size?**

and horses. Later, the Santa Fe Trail was opened. This trail, or path, started in the community of Independence, Missouri. It ran for 780 miles (1,255 km) to Santa Fe. Find Independence and Santa Fe on the map on this page.

Traders then began to bring supplies to Santa Fe over the trail. By the end of the 1860s more than 5,000 wagons were traveling over the Santa Fe Trail every year. Santa Fe became a trading center as well as a center of government. People who wanted to open stores and start businesses moved there. Others moved there to work for the government.

Today many of the people in Santa Fe have jobs taking care of visitors. Thousands of people visit Santa Fe because it is a beautiful city with a good climate. Visitors enjoy seeing Santa Fe's fine old buildings. They like walking through its winding streets.

In this old picture, travelers are shown nearing the end of the Santa Fe Trail. The town lies below.
■ What physical feature can you see?

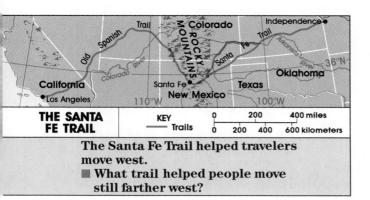

THE SANTA FE TRAIL

KEY
— Trails

0   200   400 miles
0   200   400   600 kilometers

The Santa Fe Trail helped travelers move west.
■ What trail helped people move still farther west?

CHECKUP

1. Why did cities first begin to form?
2. What are some important natural resources that have helped cities grow?

3. **Thinking Critically** Why is transportation important to the growth of cities?

Living and Working in Cities

Where do people live and work in cities?

VOCABULARY

apartment	goods
factory	service

Homes in Cities   All people need a home. Our homes give us shelter. They protect us from the weather. They also give us a safe place to live.

There are several kinds of homes in large cities. Some people live in tall buildings where other people also live. Some of these buildings are very large. They might have more than a hundred families living in them. A single person or a family lives in a group of rooms called an **apartment.** Apartment buildings are homes for many people.

These single houses in Baltimore, Maryland, are joined together to form a solid row.
■ How many families are likely to live in each house?

The tall apartment buildings on the left and the single houses on the right are located in large cities.
■ Why are all the buildings so close together?

Other people in cities live in single houses. Usually only one family lives in each single house. Some of these houses have a yard around them. Other single houses may be joined together to make a row of houses. The pictures on these pages show apartment buildings and single houses in different cities.

Apartment buildings and single houses may also be found in smaller communities. But in large cities the apartment buildings are often much bigger. Single houses in cities are often much closer together than they are in small towns.

Work in Cities Cities need many workers. These workers have many different jobs. Some work in stores, some in airports, and some in hospitals. Some workers drive trucks and deliver products. There are other workers who make products such as clothes, shoes, toys, and computers. They work in big buildings called **factories.**

Factories have machines that help the workers make the products. Some factories are very large. Several thousand people may work in one factory. The men and women who work in factories have special kinds of jobs.

Visiting a factory   There are hundreds of factories in and near the city of Fort Worth, Texas. One of these factories produces airplanes. Find Fort Worth on the map on pages 254–255.

Let us imagine that we can visit the factory where airplanes are made and see how the people work together. The airplanes made in this factory are very special. They are made for our country's air force and navy. These airplanes must fly very fast.

Some of the parts of these planes are made in different places inside the factory. Some are even made in other factories and brought to Fort Worth. The parts of the plane are assembled, or put together, in a huge *assembly building*. This building is so large that many planes can be put together there at one time. This is the part of the factory that we will see on our imaginary visit.

We see that there are many workers in the assembly building. We can tell that each worker has a special job to do in order to assemble an airplane.

Some workers put together the three parts of the airplane's frame. The frame is the body of the plane.

The assembly building of the Fort Worth airplane factory is shown above. One of the new planes is shown below.
■ Why is this new plane being flown before it leaves the factory area?

It holds the airplane together. Once the frame is put together, other workers help join the wings to the body of the airplane. Next, workers place a thin metal covering over the wings.

The engine must be put into the plane, and there are workers who do this important job. Then more workers help put the seats for the pilot and crew into the plane. Next the wheels are put into place.

After all the parts needed to fly the airplane are in their proper places, the plane is painted. Then it is tested to make sure there are no leaks. If everything is just right, the finished airplane is rolled out of the building. However, the work is not yet done.

Outside, the engine is tested. If the engine is in good running order, there is still another worker who must do an important job. A pilot flies the new plane to make very sure that everything works correctly. Now the airplane will be flown from the factory to an airport used by our air force or navy.

Goods for Sale   An airplane is just one product that is made in cities. Many factories make **goods** that anyone might buy. Goods are things that are made for sale. You can find just about anything you might want to buy in city stores.

Some stores are small. They are owned by one or two people who work in them. A small store usually sells only a few kinds of products. Other stores, such as department stores, are large. They have hundreds of different goods for sale. You can buy clothes, shoes, toys, and even furniture in a department store. Large stores need many workers.

Two friends are choosing a sweater in a department store.
■ What other clothes might they buy in this store?

The fire fighter on the left and the telephone company worker on the right both wear clothes that help protect them.
■ What clothes are they wearing to help keep them safe?

Providing Services You have learned that people in cities make, buy, and sell goods. People also provide **services.** A service is a kind of work that helps people. A bus driver helps people who want to go somewhere. A sales person in a store helps people who want to buy something. A teacher helps children learn. A man or woman who repairs roads helps drivers get where they need to be. These people are paid for their services.

They use the money they earn for their services to buy the goods and services they need.

Look at the pictures on this page. What kinds of services are these people providing?

CHECKUP

1. How is an apartment building different from a single house?
2. How is an airplane put together?
3. **Thinking Critically** Explain the difference between goods and services and give examples.

Having Fun in Cities

How do people have fun in cities?

VOCABULARY

longhouse

Enjoying Cities People live and work in cities, but they also have fun. Large cities have many interesting places to visit and things to do. Let us meet some students who live in five large cities. These students will tell you about some of the things they enjoy doing where they live.

Larry's City Larry lives in Boston, Massachusetts. Find Boston on the map on pages 254–255.

"Boston is a great place to live," says Larry. "There are so many things to do. The things that I like change with the season of the year. In the summer I like to go to the Hatch Memorial Shell. This is an outdoor stage along the Charles River. We can go there to hear music played. And it doesn't cost anything!

"For Thanksgiving each year, my family drives to Old Sturbridge Village. This community has been made to look like a small town of more than 150 years ago. We eat a meal that is like the meals eaten by the people in Sturbridge at Thanksgiving long ago. It's great to see how people lived back then.

"I go with my mom and dad and sister to Faneuil (fan′ yəl) Hall in downtown Boston. Mom said that Faneuil Hall is a famous place. Some of the people who helped our country win its freedom from England used to meet there. In the big meeting room is a huge painting of one of their meetings.

One way to have fun in Boston is to sail on the Charles River.
■ Can you find some older buildings in this picture?

95

"In the spring I like to watch the Boston Marathon. The marathon is a long footrace. Thousands of people run in it each April. My dad said that they run more than 26 miles (42 km). Each year they run close to my house and my school. I usually get to watch all of the men and women run by. They look really tired from running so fast and so far."

Carmen's City   Carmen lives in New Orleans, Louisiana. She will tell you about her city. Look at the map on pages 254–255. Can you find New Orleans?

"My favorite place in the whole city is the French Quarter. It was named after the French people who first settled here in the 1700s. It is the oldest part of New Orleans. I love to walk around the quarter with my family.

"Jackson Square is in the French Quarter. It faces the Mississippi River on one side. On the other three sides, there are many old buildings. One of these buildings is the oldest apartment building in the United States.

"One of the best times of the year is Mardi Gras (mär′ dē grä). This big celebration in New Orleans

takes place during February or March and lasts for several weeks. At Mardi Gras you can see parades during the day and night. My favorite is the Rex Parade. More people see this parade than any other. Last year I dressed up as a teddy bear and rode in the parade. I threw candy, necklaces, and toys to the people who were watching the parade."

A float in New Orleans's colorful Rex Parade is shown below.
■ What would you like to dress up as in a Mardi Gras parade?

Bernard's City   Bernard lives in Seattle, Washington. It is the largest city in the state. Find Seattle on the map on pages 254–255.

Bernard tells us about his city and his favorite place. "Seattle is named for Chief Sealth. He was a Native American. Native Americans are also called American Indians. Chief Sealth was helpful in keeping peace between the Native Americans and the early white settlers.

"I like living in Seattle. In winter my brothers and I go skiing in the nearby mountains. In summer my grandfather takes us fishing. Sometimes we go to the waterfront and watch the big ships dock.

"My favorite place near Seattle is Tillicum Village. It is part of a state park on Blake Island. To get there, you take a boat from Seattle. The village has a famous place to eat. This restaurant is called a **longhouse.** Longhouse is the name of one kind of house that American Indians built. As a family grew, the house was made larger by adding on to each end. This made the house longer.

"About 1,000 people can eat at one time in the longhouse at Tillicum Village. The food at dinner

This salmon is being baked by a Native American in Tillicum Village.
■ **How are the pieces of fish held?**

is salmon (sam′ ən). These fish come from the waters around Blake Island. The fish are cooked like the Native Americans cooked them long ago. They are placed on wood sticks over a fire.

"There is a stage, or raised place, in the longhouse, where Native Americans sing some of their songs. They also perform some of their dances.

"As we return to Seattle on the boat, I feel that I have learned more about Native Americans."

Jennifer's City Jennifer lives in Asheville, North Carolina. Find Asheville on the map on page 56.

"There are always things to do in Asheville," explains Jennifer. "We are in the center of the Blue Ridge Mountains, which are part of the Appalachian Mountains.

"When we have company stay with us," Jennifer continues, "we take them to see the huge house built by George Vanderbilt. It was built almost 100 years ago. The house and land around it are called the Biltmore Estate. The house has 250 rooms, and we can see at least 35 of them. Besides the house, we can walk through beautiful gardens.

"Another place near Asheville that I like to show people is Chimney Rock. To get to the top of this giant rock, you take an elevator up through the rock. From the top you can see for 75 miles (121 km)!"

Chie's City Chie is a young boy who lives in Tokyo in the country of Japan. Tokyo is the seventh largest city in the world and the largest in Japan. Find Tokyo on the map on pages 258–259.

Chie says, "There are several places in my city that are my favorites. One of these places is the Imperial Palace. This is where the emperor of Japan lives. For hundreds of years, emperors ruled our country. We still have an emperor, but Japan's government is now much like that of the United States. We elect the people we want to be our country's leaders.

"Each year on January 2, the emperor's palace is open for everyone to visit. There are several buildings there, but what I like the most are the gardens. Japanese gardens are beautiful, even in the

Visitors to Asheville like to see the Biltmore Estate.
■ Can you guess how many rooms are in this house?

winter when there are no flowers blooming.

"Another of my favorite places is Ueno Park. Each spring the cherry trees bloom there and make a beautiful sight. There is also a large building in the park, where concerts are given. At the concerts I can hear all kinds of music. The part of the park I enjoy most, though, is the zoo. There are hundreds of animals in the zoo. It is really fun to watch all the different animals.

"Two or three times a year, I go with my family to Korakuen Stadium. There we see my favorite team, the Tokyo Giants, play baseball. I really like baseball. Next year I will play Little League baseball.

"My older brother knows someone who played on the Little League team that went to the United States. There they played in the Little League World Series. The World Series is played to see which Little League team is the best in the world. I hope to play in the Little League World Series someday."

You have read about the things five boys and girls like to do in and around their city. They each have

These students and teachers had their picture taken in front of the Imperial Palace gardens in Tokyo.
■ Who, do you think, lives in the palace?

some special things that they enjoy. All of our communities have special things to do and ways in which to have fun. What are some things you especially like to do in and around your community?

CHECKUP

1. List at least five different things that the boys and girls you read about like to do in their cities.
2. In what country is Tokyo located?
3. **Thinking Critically** Why are there some differences among the things that the children in this lesson enjoy doing?

99

Reading a Schedule

USING A BASEBALL SCHEDULE

Most of our large cities have major league baseball teams. The teams play baseball from April through October.

At the start of each season, the teams make up schedules (skej′ əls). The schedules show information about the games. Below is part of a baseball schedule for the New York Mets.

This schedule shows the games the Mets will play in August. It tells if the game will be played at home in Shea Stadium or away in the other team's city. It tells which team the Mets will play and what time the game will begin. The name of each team is abbreviated, or shortened, on the schedule. But you can see what the abbreviation stands for below the schedule. For example, CIN is the abbreviation for the Cincinnati Reds. The schedule also shows other kinds of information.

SKILLS PRACTICE

Use the schedule to answer the questions below. Write your answers on a separate sheet of paper.

1. How many games will the Mets play in New York in August?
2. Which team will the Mets play on August 12?
3. Will the Mets play any doubleheaders in August? If so, whom will they play? Where will the game be played?
4. What time will the game on August 28 begin?
5. In which city will the game be played on August 7?

□ Home Games   **Mets Schedule**   □ Away Games

AUGUST

SUN.	MON.	TUES.	WED.	THURS.	FRI.	SAT.
1 1:35 PITT	2	3 2.35 CHI	4 2:35 CHI	5 2:35 CHI	6 7:35 PITT	7 7:05 PITT
8 1:35 PITT	9 7:35 STL	10 7:35 STL	11 7:35 STL	12 7:35 CHI	13 8:05 CHI	14 4:05* CHI
15 1:05 DH CHI	16	17 7:35 CIN	18 7:35 CIN	19 7:35 CIN	20 7:40 ATL	21 7:40 ATL
22 2:10 ATL	23 8:35 HOUS	24 8:35 HOUS	25 3:05 HOUS	26	27 8:05 ATL	28 7:35 ATL
29 1:35 ATL	30 7:35 HOUS	31 7:35 HOUS				

PITT - Pittsburgh Pirates
CHI - Chicago Cubs
STL - St. Louis Cardinals
CIN - Cincinnati Reds
ATL - Atlanta Braves
HOUS - Houston Astros

DH - Doubleheaders
* - Oldtimers Day

ALL GAMES ARE LISTED AS NEW YORK TIME

CHAPTER 4 REVIEW

MAIN IDEAS

1. The first cities began when people learned to grow more than enough food for their own needs.
2. Natural resources, such as good soil, water, and a good climate helped many cities begin and grow.
3. Good transportation and trade helped cities grow.
4. Some cities grew because they were centers of government.
5. People in cities live mostly in apartment buildings and single houses.
6. In large cities many people work in factories making goods. Other people work by providing services.
7. Cities provide a number of places and activities for recreation.

VOCABULARY REVIEW

Write the numbers 1 to 5 on a sheet of paper. Read each sentence below. The underlined words are vocabulary words. Write **T** if the sentence is true and **F** if it is false.

1. A factory is a place of work where machines are used to help people make products.
2. Transportation is the means by which people and products move from place to place.
3. Goods are those things that people do to help others.
4. A valley is an island between hills or mountains.
5. A bus driver provides a service.

CHAPTER CHECKUP

1. Why did each of the following communities grow to be a large city? (**a**) London (**b**) Santa Fe (**c**) Honolulu
2. List some jobs that service workers might do in a community.
3. What are some of the things that people living in cities do for fun?
4. **Thinking Critically** What do you think would have happened to early communities if people had never learned to specialize and divide the labor?
5. **Thinking Critically** Explain why you think it is important for communities to provide ways for people to enjoy themselves.

APPLYING KNOWLEDGE

Choose one of these cities to learn more about. Prepare a travel brochure or booklet. The brochure should tell people why they should visit the city and what they can see and do there. Draw a picture or two to show something of interest in the community.

1. Rio de Janeiro, Brazil
2. Paris, France
3. Mexico City, Mexico
4. Montreal, Canada
5. Cairo, Egypt
6. Nairobi, Kenya
7. Tel Aviv, Israel
8. Melbourne, Australia
9. Rome, Italy
10. New Delhi, India

5 Learning About Smaller Communities

A Small Town Grows and Changes ▪

Where do people live and work in a smaller community?

VOCABULARY ▪

spring	boundary	pesticide
profit	house	grain elevator
survey	raising	

Small Towns In Chapter 4 you learned about large cities. In this chapter you will learn about smaller communities, many of which are called towns.

There are a great many towns and smaller cities in the United States. Some of them are in the mountains. Some are along rivers or near oceans. Other smaller cities and towns are located near farmlands. Many Americans live and work in smaller communities across the country.

One of these communities is called Hannibal, Missouri. It is a town on the Mississippi River. Find Hannibal on the map on page 106.

Hannibal, Missouri, is a river town.
■ **Do you think that Hannibal is a small community? Why?**

Hannibal's Early History   The first people who lived in the area around Hannibal, Missouri, were Native Americans. They paddled their canoes along the mighty Mississippi River. They fished in its waters and hunted along its shore. The area was rich in fur-bearing animals, such as black bears, beaver, deer, and mink.

People from France first traveled through this part of Missouri more than 300 years ago. In 1673, French explorers, led by Father Jacques Marquette (mär ket′) and Louis Joliet (zhô lyā′), came to the area. They explored the Mississippi River past what would later become Hannibal.

Soon French trappers began to spend part of each year around Hannibal. They trapped animals for their skin and then sold the skins at trading posts.

One of these trappers reported finding a salt **spring.** A spring is water that bubbles up from under the ground. The water in this spring was salty. Salt was hard to find, and it was costly to buy. So as word spread about the salt spring, some people came hoping to make a **profit** in salt. When people sell something for more money than it cost them to produce it, they make a profit.

To make salt, people first dug a trench or long narrow ditch. Into

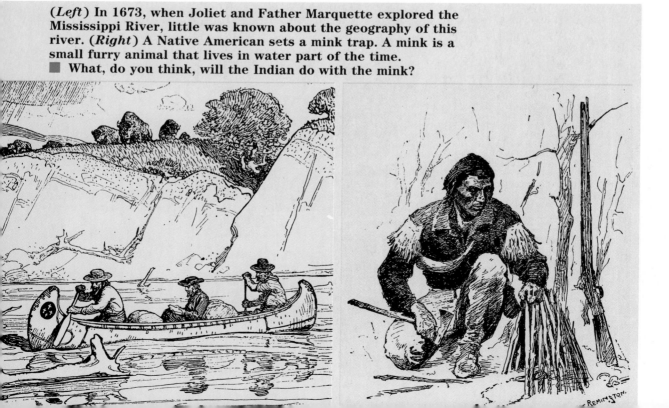

(*Left*) In 1673, when Joliet and Father Marquette explored the Mississippi River, little was known about the geography of this river. (*Right*) A Native American sets a mink trap. A mink is a small furry animal that lives in water part of the time.
■ What, do you think, will the Indian do with the mink?

In the 1800s, trading posts gave Indians and Europeans a place to exchange goods. The Indians brought their furs to trade.

■ **What goods might the Indians have received for their furs?**

this trench they placed trees cut from the surrounding woods. On top of the wood the salt makers placed big metal pots filled with the salty spring water. Then they burned the wood in the trench to boil the water. They boiled the water until only the salt was left in the bottom of the pots. The ashes from the burnt wood, the trench, and pieces of the pots can still be seen on a farm near Hannibal.

Founding a Town   Until 1803 a large part of our country was claimed by France. In that year,

however, President Thomas Jefferson bought their land, including all of Missouri, for the United States. A group of people was sent by the United States government to **survey** the new land. They measured the land and made maps to show its physical features. They also surveyed the land to set up its boundaries. A **boundary** is a line that separates one community, state, or country from another.

One of the people surveying the land was Moses Bates. He liked the area that became Hannibal.

105

Bates thought that it was an excellent place for a trading post. He and a friend built the first log house in Hannibal. Bates helped some people from St. Louis move into the house. They became the first permanent settlers in Hannibal.

As a result of the survey, a plan for the streets in Hannibal was drawn up. Hannibal officially became a town in 1819. Its name came from the survey work done by Don Antonio Soulard. He named the stream on the edge of town Hannibal Creek. No one knows exactly why he gave the creek that name. Today the creek is called Bear Creek, but the town kept the name of Hannibal.

Many communities in the United States have been named for places near the community. Others have been named for certain people or for faraway places. How did your town or city get its name?

Important Resources You learned in Chapter 4 how natural resources helped some cities grow. Natural resources also helped many smaller communities grow. The area that became Hannibal had several important natural resources.

People were first attracted to Hannibal for the salt and the many fur-bearing animals. Moses Bates built a storehouse and began to trade with the Native Americans and trappers in the area. He bought furs, deer skins, honey, and a variety of other goods and took them to St. Louis. There Bates sold them for a profit. Eventually he built a trading post near what is today Hannibal High School.

Later, Moses Bates used another of Hannibal's important

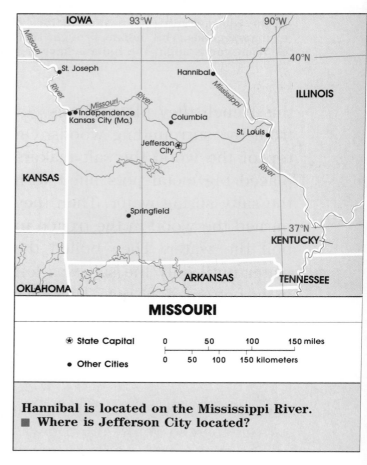

Hannibal is located on the Mississippi River.
■ Where is Jefferson City located?

This is a painting of Hannibal, Missouri, in the 1840s. It shows one reason why the community grew from about 30 people in 1830 to more than 1,000 people by 1840.
■ What is that reason for Hannibal's growth?

resources—the Mississippi River. He built boats to provide transportation along the river.

In the early 1800s, steamboats began to appear on the Mississippi River. A steamboat burned wood to boil water and make steam. The hot steam turned the engine that powered the boat through the water. By 1830, steamboats were a familiar sight in Hannibal. They brought supplies to the people living in the area and carried the products grown or made in Hannibal to markets along the river. The steamboats also brought new people to Hannibal.

At first Hannibal grew slowly. Records show that in 1830 there were about 30 people living in the town. However, Hannibal's location as a river port and the area's natural resources led to the town's rapid growth. By 1839 the population had grown to more than 1,000.

A Town Changes   In 1856 the Hannibal and St. Joseph Railroad was built. It connected Hannibal to the important trading centers of St. Joseph, Missouri, and Chicago, Illinois. Now people in Hannibal could easily trade with other communities.

In Hannibal's historic district, older buildings have been restored.
■ **Is there an historic district in your community?**

New industries began to develop. Factories that made shoes, cement, and railroad equipment were built. New businesses opened and people came to Hannibal for jobs. More people moved into the area for the good farmland.

Hannibal has changed since the days of the early settlers. The town has grown from a few people in the 1830s to about 19,000 people today.

Houses in a Small Town The first settlers, like most of the people in Hannibal today, lived in single

houses. Most of the early homes were made from logs.

When a family needed to build a house for themselves, they announced a **house raising.** The family gathered logs from the nearby forests. Their neighbors then came to help build the house. The logs were lifted into place. The ends of the logs were notched or cut out so that they would fit together. The logs were placed one on top of another until they were between 5 and 6 feet ($1\frac{1}{2}$ and 2 m) tall. Then the roof was built. Openings were left for the fireplace, door, and windows.

The house was finished by filling in the cracks between the logs with a mixture of mud and straw or grass. The fireplace was made from stones or sticks and mud. Mud lined the inside of the fireplace to help keep the sticks from catching on fire. The windows were covered with glass or a cloth. The opening for the door was small. A door measuring 3 feet (1 m) wide by 5 feet ($1\frac{1}{2}$ m) high was usually built to cover the opening.

A few homes were built from brick. Others were made from large stones found in the area. The stones were fitted together to form the walls of the house. The Old Stone House, built in 1839, is still standing in Hannibal. Today most of the homes in town are built from brick or wood.

Like many other small towns in the United States, Hannibal has some apartment buildings. These apartment buildings are not as big as the ones you might see in large cities. Most of the apartment buildings in Hannibal are one or two stories high.

Working in a Small Town   The people who live in a small town work in many different places. More people from Hannibal work at a factory owned by the American Cyanamid Company than at any other place in town. About 520 workers make substances that are added to animal feed. These substances help prevent disease and promote the growth of animals. The workers also make **pesticides**. Pesticides are chemicals used to control or destroy insects and other pests that are harmful to farm crops.

Another place in Hannibal where people work is along the Mississippi River. Several people work at the **grain elevator** located along the river front. A grain elevator is a tall building in which grains, such as wheat and corn, are stored. The grain is brought to the elevator by trucks and trains.

When there is enough grain in the elevator, the grain is loaded on a barge. This is a flat-bottomed boat. Most barges do not have a motor and cannot move by themselves. Often several barges are tied together and pulled or pushed down the Mississippi River by a tugboat. This small boat has a powerful engine, so the tugboat can tow several barges at once. Along the river there are many tugboats. Each

Grain from a grain elevator is being loaded onto a barge.
■ What, do you think, will happen to the grain next?

A tugboat pushing several barges is a common sight along the Mississippi River. Look at the map on page 106.
■ Name another river that carries boat traffic.

tug has someone who steers the boat and some deckhands who do the work aboard the tugboat.

People in Hannibal also work in stores and businesses. Hannibal has two shopping centers and many office buildings. It also has libraries, museums, and a hospital. It has banks, schools, and places of worship. It has offices for doctors and dentists. There are jobs for people at all of these places.

Mark Twain's Hometown Some people in Hannibal have jobs taking care of visitors. Each year thousands of people come to see the Mark Twain Museum and Boyhood Home on High Street. Mark Twain was a very important writer who grew up in Hannibal.

Mark Twain, whose real name was Samuel Clemens, wrote a book called *The Adventures of Tom Sawyer*. The book describes the adventures of a boy in a small Missouri river town about a hundred years ago. The town he wrote about was Hannibal, but he changed the name in the book to St. Petersburg. Perhaps there are books by Mark Twain in your school or community library.

CHECKUP

1. Why did people first move to the Hannibal area?
2. What is a house raising?
3. **Thinking Critically** Why, do you think, did the early settlers in Hannibal use logs and stones to build their houses?

Small Towns Are Special

What is the main difference between towns and cities?

VOCABULARY

sightseeing

Small Towns and Large Cities Towns and cities are alike in many ways. They all have homes and places of business. They have streets, schools, and places of worship. The main difference between towns and cities is size. Towns have fewer people and fewer buildings and businesses.

You have read in Chapter 4 about interesting places to visit and things to do in cities. People living in towns enjoy doing many of the same things. They like to visit parks and museums. They play baseball and ride bicycles. Sometimes they go to a nearby city and spend a day **sightseeing,** or seeing places of interest.

Some towns are very small. If your family has lived in such a town for a long time, you may know almost everyone there. When people have known other families for years, they usually feel close to them.

People in small towns often feel proud of their community because they feel that they are an important part of it. Most people also know the leaders of their community. Some leaders might have grown up in the town. Who are the leaders in your community?

Planning a Visit Cindy is proud of her town. She lives in Hannibal, Missouri, and she thinks it is a special place. Cindy's cousin is coming to visit her. Cindy wrote Jason a letter. She told him about some of the things to do and see in and around Hannibal.

In 1839 Samuel Clemens and his family moved to Hannibal.
■ Why might the State of Missouri put up this statue in Hannibal?

October 1, 1988

Dear Jason,

Mom just told me that you are coming for a visit. I've thought of lots of things for us to do. To help make our plans, I want to tell you about some of the places that we can see and some things we can do.

Since you haven't been to Hannibal before, you might like to take a ride on the Mark Twain Clopper. This is a horse and wagon that takes people on a sightseeing tour of Hannibal. The tour will start and end near the home where Mark Twain lived as a boy. If you visit his home, you can see how he and his family lived.

Pilaster House

Mark Twain Clopper

You can also visit the Pilaster House. An old drugstore has been rebuilt in it. Drugstores a long time ago were sure different from ours today. The Pilaster House also has a rebuilt doctor's office and kitchen that you can visit. You can learn a lot about how people in Hannibal lived long ago.

Another fun thing to do is take a boat trip on the Mississippi River. As you can probably guess, the name of the riverboat is the Mark Twain. The trip takes an hour. Be sure to bring your camera so you can take pictures.

Let me know what you would like to do. I've sent some pictures to help you decide.

Your cousin,
Cindy

Tom and Huck Statue

Riverboat Mark Twain

113

Mark Twain (1835–1910)

Samuel Clemens was one of America's greatest writers. He is better known as Mark Twain. He used that name to sign his writings.

Sam was born in the state of Missouri in 1835. He grew up in Hannibal, a town beside the Mississippi River. This was a wonderful place for growing up. Sam could swim in the river. Or he could watch the big river steamboats go by. Then there were the woods and caves at the edge of town. Every day Sam could look forward to an exciting adventure that just might happen to him in these mysterious places. But mostly Sam loved the great Mississippi River.

When Samuel grew up, he became a river pilot. His job was to guide a steamboat up and down the Mississippi River. Clemens said that being a river pilot was the finest job he ever had.

Clemens started to become known as a writer when he wrote a funny story about a jumping frog. It was about this time that he started signing his writings with the name Mark Twain.

Twain's best stories are based on his Mississippi River days. Someday you will want to read his books about Tom Sawyer and Huckleberry Finn. Tom Sawyer is a fun-loving boy, probably much like young Samuel Clemens was. Huck Finn is a homeless orphan. They have many adventures that are still fun to read about today.

When Mark Twain died in 1910, he was the country's best-loved writer.

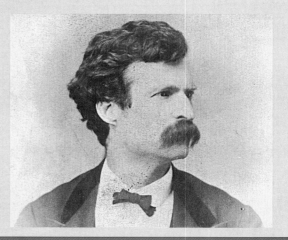

For National Tom Sawyer Days, girls and boys dress up as people from Mark Twain's books (*top left*) and pose in front of his boyhood home. Other children take part in contests such as frog jumping (*bottom left*) and fence painting (*right*).

■ Does your community, or a nearby one, have special days?

There are more interesting things to do and places to see than Cindy could tell about in her letter. One special event is held each year in July. It is called National Tom Sawyer Days. That is when boys and girls dress up as characters from Mark Twain's books and take part in different contests. One is the fence painting contest. Boys and girls are judged on the speed of their painting, on how well they paint, and on their costume. Other events during National Tom Sawyer Days include a frog jumping contest, a volleyball game in the mud, and raft races on the river.

CHECKUP

1. How are cities and towns alike?
2. What is the main difference between towns and cities?
3. **Thinking Critically** Why might people like to live in a small town?

115

Indio: A Special Town

What makes Indio special?

VOCABULARY

desert	date
well	irrigation

A Proud Past   Indio is a small town in southern California. Find Indio on the map on page 14.

Indio is located in a **desert.** A desert is a very dry area that receives little rain. Indio receives less than $3\frac{1}{2}$ inches (9 cm) of rain a year. There are few trees and plants in a desert.

The first people to live in the area that is now known as Indio were Native Americans. In their search for water, these American Indians dug **wells.** A well is a hole dug in the earth to get water. Sometimes the Indians found water a few feet below the surface of the desert. The wells provided enough drinking water for the small groups of Indians living in the desert.

Some people from Spain explored the area in the 1500s. But the first permanent settlers did not arrive until the 1870s. The Southern Pacific Railroad was being built. The railroad would connect Los Angeles, California, with New Orleans, Louisiana, and other cities in the United States.

This photograph shows the desert around Indio. Notice the different kinds of plants and land formations in the desert.
■ What might be a reason why some plants can grow in a desert?

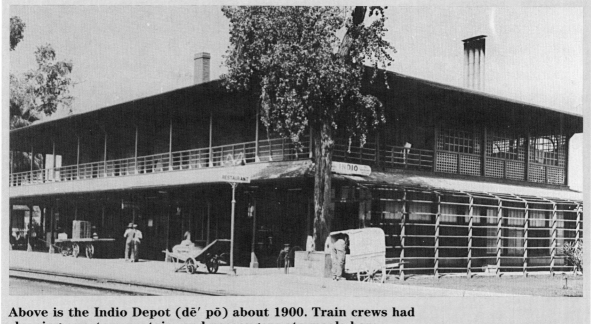

Above is the Indio Depot (dē′ pō) about 1900. Train crews had sleeping quarters upstairs and passengers ate meals here.
■ What do you think the word *depot* means?

A large train station was built at Yuma, Arizona. Another large station was at Los Angeles. The railroad company wanted to build a third station halfway between Los Angeles and Yuma. Indio was chosen as the best place for the new station. The first permanent settlers came to help build the railroad and the station.

At this time, Indio was known as Indian Wells. Its name came from the many water wells that Indians had dug in the area. Maps of the day showed hundreds of places called Indian Wells. The railroad needed a name for the town that was different from the name of other places. So the name was changed to Indio, in honor of the many Indians living in the area.

The railroad finally reached Indio in May 1876. With the railroad came people to operate the trains, run the station, dig more wells, and clear desert sands from the railroad tracks. Many of the early workers on the railroad were Indians and people from Mexico. Find Mexico on the map on page 256.

Indio has changed since these early days. The people of Indio are proud of their past. They like to show their town to visitors.

Visitors Enjoy Indio Many people from California and other states visit Indio and the surrounding area. They like the warm climate. They ride horses along miles of special trails. They play golf on the golf courses.

The Hot Air Balloon Rally draws thousands of people to Indio. Some visitors fly in the balloons. Others watch the colorful balloons sail across the desert sky.

Irrigation makes it possible to grow date palms and grapefruit trees in the area around Indio.
■ **How would you describe the land around Indio?**

A Big Celebration Each year Indio holds the National Date Festival. A **date** is a fruit that grows on date palm trees. The area around Indio is one of the world's leading date-producing areas.

In 1886, C. P. Huntington, president of the Southern Pacific Railroad, brought some date palm plants to Indio. The plants grew. By 1920, Indio was the date capital of the United States.

Max Drain is one of many retired people living in Indio. Although he no longer works at a paying job, he freely gives his time to the Indio Chamber of Commerce and other groups in town. Mr. Drain wants Indio to be an even better place to live.

Mr. Drain tells us about dates and the National Date Festival.

"Thanks to **irrigation**, farmers can grow crops in the desert. Irrigation is carrying water through pipes, ditches, or canals to lands that are dry. Today, dates are our most famous crop.

"A lot of work is required to produce the dates. In the past someone had to climb each tree seven different times before the dates were ready to be picked. The trees had to have their old branches cut off. The dates needed protection from the rain and birds, so paper bags were placed over each bunch of dates while it was on the tree. Today, most date growers use special machines to help them. One of these machines raises a person up to the top of the palm tree. This helps speed the work in the tree, since the trees no longer have to be climbed.

"These same machines are used to help workers pick the dates. The dates are ready to be picked between August and December of each year. People are lifted to the top of the trees where they cut the ripe dates from the tree.

"The National Date Festival is held each year in February. We plan every day to be a special one. The festival is held at the Riverside County Fairgrounds in Indio. There are seven large buildings and an arena or stadium.

"The arena is where some of the most popular events take place. It is also where some special races are held every day. These are the camel and ostrich races. Camels are big four-legged animals that live in parts of Africa and Asia. An ostrich is a big bird that cannot fly. It can run faster than any other

Growers put paper bags over the dates to protect them from birds and rain.

■ What color are the dates while hanging on the trees?

bird in the world. Ostriches live in Africa. People try to ride on the camels while small carts are tied to the ostriches and people ride in the carts.

"Every night of the ten-day festival, there is a play given on an outside stage. The stage is made to look like a street in a city in North Africa. Costumed actors and

At the National Date Palm Festival, visitors enjoy events such as a play (*left*) and an ostrich race (*right*).
■ Imagine that you are riding a cart in the ostrich race. Can you think of some words to describe how you might feel?

actresses from the Indio area perform dances and songs on the stage.

"A very special parade is held during the festival. This parade takes place on President's Day. That is the day in February when we celebrate the birthdays of two Presidents—Abraham Lincoln and George Washington. The parade winds through Indio. In the parade are decorated floats, marching bands, horse riders, and marching groups.

"There is always something going on during the festival. One day is known as Fiesta Day. On that day we honor the Mexican people. There are bands, dancers, and singers performing Mexican music. And there are delicious Mexican foods to taste.

"The Date Festival helps bring the whole community together to celebrate our present and our past. It helps us have pride in ourselves, our families, and our history."

CHECKUP

1. How did Indio get its name?
2. What can people do for fun in Indio?
3. **Thinking Critically** What, do you think, might have happened to Indio if the railroad had not built a station there?

Finding the Main Idea in a Paragraph

WHAT IS A PARAGRAPH?

Writing is an important skill. When you write, a paragraph can help you express your ideas clearly.

A paragraph is a group of sentences that tell about a certain thing. A paragraph usually begins with a topic sentence that tells what the paragraph is about. Other sentences in the paragraph explain the main idea. These sentences are called supporting sentences.

A NEWSPAPER ARTICLE

Newspapers provide us with information about people, places, and events. The paragraph below is from a newspaper article. Read the paragraph carefully and find the topic sentence and the supporting sentences.

Officials at the Staten Island Zoo had said that they will again have a Zoo Olympics in June. The huge New York zoo's Olympics will once again involve hundreds of children in contests with zoo animals. Children will find out whether they can stand on one leg as long as a flamingo can. They will also see whether they can jump as far as a frog can. Some children will discover whether they can eat sunflower seeds as fast as a parrot can. Those interested in taking part in the fun and activities of the Zoo Olympics should call the Staten Island Zoo for more information.

Now look at the paragraph closely. What is the main idea of the paragraph? The first sentence tells the main idea. That is, the Staten Island Zoo will have another Zoo Olympics. The other sentences tell what activities will be part of the Olympics, who will take part, and whom to call for more information. The supporting sentences explain the topic sentence.

SKILLS PRACTICE

Now it is your turn to write a paragraph. Read each of the sentences below. Write the topic sentence on a sheet of paper. Indent the first sentence. Then write the supporting sentences in the best order.

Zoo officials hope people who have never visited the zoo will come for the Olympics.

They hope that by attracting children to the zoo for the first time and by teaching children about some animals, they will want to return to the zoo often.

There are several reasons why the zoo holds the Zoo Olympics.

CHAPTER 5 REVIEW

MAIN IDEAS

1. One reason that smaller communities, as well as cities, begin and grow is that there are natural resources in the area.
2. Towns change over a period of time.
3. Towns, as well as cities, provide their citizens with a variety of homes, jobs, services, and places and activities for recreation.
4. The main difference between towns and cities is size—towns are smaller and have fewer people, buildings, and businesses.
5. People in smaller communities take pride in their town and in their town's past.
6. All our communities benefit from the influence of people who have come from different countries and who have different ways of life.

VOCABULARY REVIEW

Write the numbers **1** to **5** on a sheet of paper. Match the words with their meanings below.

    a. spring   **d.** desert
    b. survey   **e.** well
    c. pesticide

1. A very dry area that receives little rain
2. Water that bubbles up from under the ground
3. A chemical used to control or destroy pests harmful to crops
4. A hole that is dug in the earth to get water
5. Measure the land for size, shape, boundaries, and physical features

CHAPTER CHECKUP

1. Who were the first people to live in both Hannibal and Indio?
2. How did the railroad help both Hannibal and Indio grow?
3. What is a grain elevator?
4. **Thinking Critically** Do you think it would be easier to feel like an important part of your community in a small town or a large city? Explain why you feel that way.

APPLYING KNOWLEDGE

1. Pretend that you are going to Hannibal. Write a letter to Cindy, telling her what you would most like to see.
2. What would you want people to know about your community? Draw a picture of one place or activity that you think visitors might like. Write three or four sentences about your picture.
3. Most communities have special celebrations during the year. Select a celebration in your community or another community. Find information about the celebration and write a paragraph describing it.

SUMMARIZING UNIT 2

REVIEWING VOCABULARY

1. port A port is a place where ships can be safe from the winds and waves caused by ocean storms. They are also places where different products are loaded onto or unloaded from ships. How might a port help a community to grow?

2. citizen A citizen is someone who is a member of a community, state, or nation. What are some of the things that a good citizen tries to do?

3. government A government is made up of the members of a group that makes the laws for a community, state, or country. The leaders of a state government work in the capital city of their state. Use the map on pages 254–255 to find at least six state capitals.

4. goods Goods are things that are usually made to be sold. People make, buy, and sell goods every day. List ten things that you or your family have bought.

5. religious freedom The freedom to practice any religion is called religious freedom. What other freedoms do all Americans have?

EXPRESSING YOURSELF

1. Which would you use? Every day, ships, trains, trucks, airplanes, buses, and cars move people and products. Which kinds of transportation would you use to (a) move the furniture in your house from one city to another? (b) take your class to a picnic in a nearby park? (c) move oil from oil wells on another continent to the United States?

2. Thinking like an explorer Pretend that you are an explorer sent to find some land on which you will build a new town. What are some of the things that you would like the area around your new town to have?

3. What might have been? The city of Philadelphia has a fine port. What might have happened to Philadelphia if the two rivers between which it was built dried up shortly after William Penn started the town?

4. What would life be like? There are many people who provide valuable services. Describe what you think life would be like without police officers, truck drivers, or teachers.

5. Where would you live? If you could choose a community to live in, where would you live—in a large city or in a smaller community? Explain your decision.

Our Country's Farms and Resources

Your family may buy food in a store. But where does this food come from? It probably comes from different kinds of farms. The natural resources of good soil, clean air, rain, and warm sunshine help farmers to raise food for the people in our communities.

Farmers depend on other natural resources, too. They depend on the gasoline that comes from oil. They need it to run their farm machines and to get their crops to market. In Unit 3 you will learn more about our farms and the natural resources of our country.

These children live on a wheat farm. Wheat raised here goes by train and truck to a flour mill. There it is ground into flour.
■ Can you name some foods that are made out of flour?

(*Top*) This cattle ranch in Texas supplies some of our communities with food. (*Bottom*) Some of our food comes from other countries. This banana farm is in Brazil in South America.

What kind of food comes from the cattle ranch?

Forests are one of our important natural resources. Forests supply products that we use every day. People like to visit forests. In Unit 3 you will learn how our country cares for our forests.

Workers cut down trees and take them out of the forest. The wood will be used for many purposes.
■ Can you name some things you use that are made of wood?

If forests were to disappear, so would the beautiful creatures who live there. We would have no more wood to make tables and chairs and buildings. We could no longer hike or camp among the trees. So we must be very careful of our forests. We must not cut down too many trees. And we must be sure to plant new ones.

These friends are planting new trees.
■ Why is what they are doing a good thing?

Oil is one of the world's most important resources. It is found deep under the surface of the earth. Some oil is found under the bottom of the ocean. Workers pump the oil up from under the ocean floor. Workers are brought to their job by helicopter. Strong winds and high waves make their job hard and dangerous.

(*Top*) Workers drill for oil underneath the ocean floor. (*Bottom*) Some coal is found close to the earth's surface.
■ Can you see some coal here?

Coal too is an important natural resource. It can be burned to make heat and power. Some coal, like oil, is found deep underground.

127

6 Farm Products for Our Communities

Farms Yesterday and Today

How has farming changed?

VOCABULARY

income	harvest	planter
fertilizer	tractor	plantation
plow	harrow	cultivator

Farming Has Changed   Years ago most of the people in our country lived on farms. They worked very hard. They did almost everything for themselves. These farmers

made their own clothes. They made most of their own tools and the things they used in their homes. Farmers also grew their own food. They planted their own fruits and vegetables. They raised cows, chickens, and pigs. Sometimes they were able to grow only enough food to feed their family. At other times they grew more than they needed for themselves. Then they would sell their extra food. They used the money they were paid to buy things they could not make for themselves.

The big picture shows a modern farm. One of the smaller pictures shows farm work long ago and one shows farm work today.
How can you tell which picture shows farm work today?

Over the years, farming has changed. Farmers are now able to grow large amounts of food and other crops. They sell these crops to earn **income**, or money. They use part of their income to buy different goods they need.

Most Americans on farms today no longer make their own clothing, tools, or household goods. Instead, they buy most of these goods in stores. Many farmers even buy much of the food that they eat from supermarkets or grocery stores. They buy what they do not grow on their own farm.

Not as many people in our country live on farms today. Most Americans live in towns or cities. But even though there are fewer American farms, the people who live on these farms grow more food than ever before.

New Ways of Farming　There are several reasons why farms produce more food today. One reason is the use of **fertilizer** (fėr´ tə lī zər), or plant food. Farmers put fertilizer in the soil to make the crops grow bigger and stronger. They also use better kinds of seeds.

This family owns a large farm that can grow food for a great many people.
■ Why, do you think, are they buying food in a store?

The plants that grow from these seeds are healthier and produce more food.

Years ago the kinds of work that farmers had to do made it hard for them to grow large amounts of food. It once took farmers days to prepare the soil for planting. To do this, they used a **plow**. A plow is a tool used to turn over the soil and shape it into rows. Horses pulled the plow. After the rows of soil were prepared, the farmers of long ago planted seeds by hand. Farmers then spent much time taking care of the growing plants. More time was also spent during the **harvest**, or the gathering in of the ripe crops. Most farmers could only take care of small farms.

Another reason why American farmers produce more food today is because they use modern farm machines. With these machines, farmers can plow their fields and plant and harvest their crops much faster. They can farm much more land. Farms are much larger than they once were.

One of the most important farm machines is the **tractor**. Tractors are used to pull tools and other machines on the farm. Tractors have very powerful

This farmer is using a kind of harrow to break up and smooth the soil.
■ What machine is being used to pull the harrow?

motors. Some tractors are very large. Tractors have taken the place of horses in pulling the plow. Much land can be plowed in a short time when a tractor is used.

The **harrow** is another tool pulled by the tractor. The harrow is used to make the field smooth. It breaks up the large piles of dirt left by the plow. The harrow helps prepare the soil for planting.

Crops like corn and wheat can be planted by a machine called a **planter**. The planter is also pulled by tractor. The planter makes a small hole, drops a seed, and covers

131

Thomas Jefferson (1743-1826)

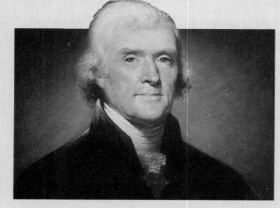

Thomas Jefferson was born in 1743 in what is now the state of Virginia. He grew up on a **plantation** with six sisters and a brother. A plantation is a very large farm. Tom did not go to school. Instead, he was taught by special teachers hired by his parents. Tom liked his studies, but he also loved hunting and fishing. He enjoyed riding a horse across the beautiful Virginia fields and paddling a canoe through the clear streams near his home.

Jefferson went to college and became a lawyer. He also became a leader in our country's struggle for freedom from Great Britain.

For 17 days in June 1776, this tall, redheaded young man sat down at a desk each morning. He was at work writing the most important paper in our country's history. We call it the *Declaration of Independence*. It said that America was free of British rule. On July 4 a group of American leaders meeting in Philadelphia, Pennsylvania, accepted what Jefferson had written. From that day, the United States has been an independent country. Later, Jefferson became the third President of this new country.

One of Jefferson's lifelong interests was farming. He knew a great deal about seeds and plants. He even invented a special plow. Jefferson's plow helped farmers to lift and turn the soil more easily in order to plant their crops.

Jefferson died on July 4, 1826. It was exactly 50 years after the Declaration of Independence had been accepted.

This Maryland farmer is using a planter to plant soybean seeds. The seeds are being planted among the remains of a barley crop.
■ Can you find the containers that hold the seeds?

These farm children are putting young plants into the plowed soil.
■ How can you tell the soil is plowed?

it with soil. Using this machine, a farmer can plant seeds quickly.

Tractors also pull machines called **cultivators**. Cultivators break up the soil between the rows of plants. This kills any weeds growing there. Weeds hurt crops by using up the food in the soil that is needed for growth.

In the rest of this chapter you will learn about some different kinds of farms. These farms supply food for all of our communities.

CHECKUP

1. How did the horse help farmers long ago?
2. Name four machines used by farmers today.
3. **Thinking Critically** Why are there fewer people living on farms today than there were long ago?

Dairy Farms

What is produced on a dairy farm?

VOCABULARY

dairy farm	creamery
pasture	hay

Dairy Products for You Today's farmers raise many different crops and animals in different parts of the United States. In states such as Wisconsin, California, New York, Minnesota, and Pennsylvania, many farmers have **dairy farms**.

The main work of a dairy farm is raising milk cows. The graph on this page shows the number of milk cows in the five leading dairy states. Some milk from these cows is made into products such as butter, cheese, and ice cream. Of course, some of the milk is used for drinking, too. These products are all called dairy products.

Wisconsin is sometimes called America's Dairyland. It is our leading dairy state. Almost 2 million milk cows *graze* in Wisconsin **pastures**. A pasture is a fenced field where milk cows eat grass and other plants. The dairy farms in Wisconsin produce more milk than any other state does. These farms also produce much of our country's cheese and butter. Find Wisconsin on the map on pages 254–255.

Now let us find out what it is like to live on a dairy farm.

Visiting a Dairy Farm "Hi, my name is Sara. I live in Wisconsin. My mom and dad own a dairy farm. We have about 500 cows.

"Most of our cows are called Holsteins (hōl'stīns). They have black-and-white coats. Holsteins produce more milk than other types of cows do. One of our cows—we call her Bessie—produces about 55 quarts (52 l) of milk a day.

"We also have some Jersey cows. They are a different type of

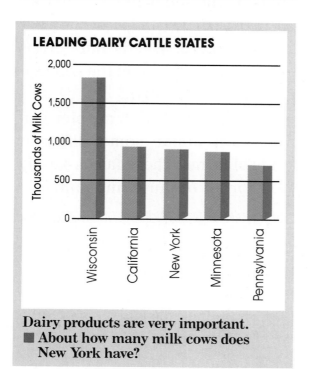

LEADING DAIRY CATTLE STATES

Thousands of Milk Cows

(y-axis: 0, 500, 1,000, 1,500, 2,000)

(states: Wisconsin, California, New York, Minnesota, Pennsylvania)

Dairy products are very important.
■ About how many milk cows does New York have?

This picture shows dairy cows in a modern milking room where they are milked by machine. Everything in a milking room has to be very clean.
■ Why, do you think, must everything in the milking room be clean?

cow than Holsteins. Jersey cows produce less milk than Holsteins, but their milk has more natural fat in it. The fat, called *butterfat*, is used to make butter.

"My dad says that dairy farms have really changed since he was a boy. He used to milk the cows by hand. Dairy farms needed many workers then.

"Today our cows are milked by machine. We take the cows to our milking room. The room is very clean. My job is to help wash and brush the cows before they are milked. We milk the cows early in the morning and late in the afternoon, so I have to work twice a day. This means I am up every morning before the sun comes up.

135

(Top) The truck keeps milk cool and clean. (Center) It's fun to feed the gentle cow. (Bottom) Cheese is an important dairy product.
■ What is the scale in the cheese store used for?

"As the cows are milked, the milk passes through pipes to the milk house. There it is cooled. The milk is kept there until it is put into a tank truck. The truck takes the milk to a **creamery**. At the creamery the milk is made into butter and other dairy products.

"In the summer the cows go out to the fields during the day. They graze on the grass in the pastures. In the winter we keep the cows in a barn. This protects them from the cold weather. The cows feed on **hay** in the winter. Hay is grass that has been cut and dried. It is often used as food for cows.

"Our cows are always eating. Mom says that each cow eats from 10 to 60 pounds (4½ to 27 kg) of food a day. Each cow drinks about 8 gallons (30 l) of water a day.

"Mom also told me that people in our country use dairy products every day. Our dairy farm supplies many communities with the dairy products they need."

CHECKUP

1. Name four dairy products.
2. What are the five leading dairy states?
3. **Thinking Critically** Why would a dairy farm want to have both Holstein and Jersey cows?

Vegetable Farms

How are vegetables raised?

VOCABULARY

greenhouse

Growing Fresh Vegetables for You   The parts of plants that people eat are called vegetables. Potatoes, carrots, corn, and beans are all vegetables. Can you name some others?

Our bodies need vegetables. They are one of our most important foods. Vegetables give us vitamins and minerals. We need these vitamins and minerals to grow and to stay healthy. Eating many different vegetables is a good way to get enough vitamins and minerals. It is important for us to eat vegetables every day.

Some vegetable farms are found far from cities. These farms are usually large, covering many acres of land. Often only one or two kinds of vegetables are grown on these farms.

These healthy vegetables are raised all over our country. Cabbages grow low and close to the ground. Corn can grow taller than you.
■ What other differences are there between cabbage and corn plants?

137

Southern California, southern Florida, Arizona, and Texas have some of our country's largest vegetable farms. These places have a warm climate all year. So farmers can grow vegetables all year round.

Besides a warm climate, vegetables need water to grow. Many farmers have a special way of watering called irrigation. They use ditches, canals, or pipes to carry water to land that is dry. In southern California, for example, there is almost no rain in the summer. The farmlands become very dry. So farmers irrigate the soil. That way they do not have to depend as much on rainfall.

Danny will tell you about a special kind of vegetable farm. As you read, think of the ways in which Danny's farm is different from the farms you have just learned about.

A Special Vegetable Farm "My family has a vegetable farm in New York," says Danny. "It is near New York City. Our farm is small. We have only a few acres of land, but we grow many different kinds of vegetables. We grow most of our vegetables outside during summer months.

"We raise some vegetables in our **greenhouse** during the winter. The greenhouse is a very large

These tomato plants are growing in a large greenhouse in the winter. The tomatoes on the left are not yet ripe enough to be picked and eaten.
■ How can you tell that the tomatoes on the right are ripe?

It's hard work to grow and pick vegetables, but it's fun to have a farm stand.
■ What is being sold at this vegetable stand?

building. It has windows in the top and sides. This lets in the light that the plants need to grow.

"We heat the greenhouse in the winter and keep it cool in the summer. The greenhouse lets us grow vegetables all year round. Even when there is snow on the ground, the plants in the greenhouse are warm. We grow mostly tomatoes in our greenhouse. We have fresh tomatoes all year long.

"Almost all of our vegetables are carried by trucks to stores in New York City. Every summer, though, my sister and I set up a vegetable stand. We put some tables by the road that goes past our farm. We have some signs that tell people what we are selling. Many people stop. They like our vegetables because they are fresh. My sister and I pick the vegetables for our stand each morning so that they are always fresh."

CHECKUP

1. Why is it important for us to eat vegetables?
2. Why are greenhouses important?
3. **Thinking Critically** Do you think that vegetables grown in greenhouses are more expensive than those grown in open fields?

A Cotton Farm

How is cotton grown?

VOCABULARY

cotton boll	crop duster
lint	cotton gin
insecticide	

Cotton   Cotton touches you every day. Many of your clothes have cotton in them. The sheets on your bed are probably made with cotton. The towels you use to dry your hands are made with cotton. Cotton can be made into more products than can almost any other crop grown. Each person in our country uses about 13 pounds (6 kg) of cotton each year. Almost 4 million Americans earn at least part of their income from cotton. How might cotton help people make money?

Look at the table on page 32. It gives the names of the five leading cotton-growing states. Now look at the map on this page. It shows where cotton is grown in the United

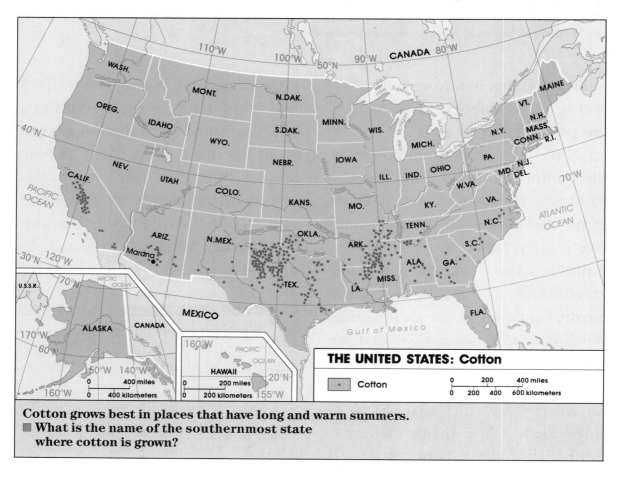

THE UNITED STATES: Cotton

Cotton grows best in places that have long and warm summers.
■ What is the name of the southernmost state where cotton is grown?

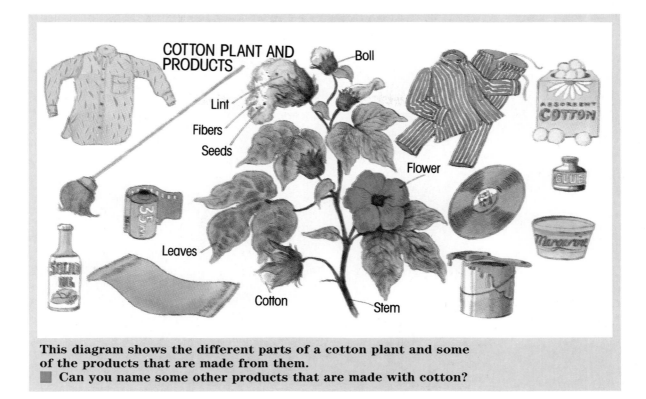

COTTON PLANT AND PRODUCTS

Boll

Lint

Fibers

Seeds

Flower

Leaves

Cotton

Stem

This diagram shows the different parts of a cotton plant and some of the products that are made from them.
■ Can you name some other products that are made with cotton?

States. As you can see, these places are all in the South. This is because cotton needs a long and warm summer to grow.

Every part of the cotton plant is useful. The **cotton boll** contains the soft, fluffy part of the plant. This part is called the **lint**. The lint is made up of *fibers*. These are like thin, strong, white threads. The long fibers of the cotton plant are used for making cloth and many other products.

The boll also holds the seeds of the cotton plant. These seeds are crushed to make cottonseed oil. The oil is used in cattle feed, paint, soap, fertilizer, and margarine.

The short fuzz found on the cottonseeds is used in making glues, mattresses, mops, paper, plastics, and other goods.

After the cotton bolls are picked, the leaves and stems of the cotton plant are cut down and mixed with the soil. This helps to put food into the soil for growing new cotton plants.

Now that you know about cotton, you are ready to learn about a cotton farm.

This is a cotton farm near Marana, Arizona. Today, machines harvest almost all of the cotton in the United States.
■ How, do you think, was cotton harvested before machines?

A Visit with Roy "My name is Roy. I live on a cotton farm near Marana, Arizona. My own great grandfather was the first to farm this land. That was in the 1920s. My grandfather and grandmother have told me about all the changes that have taken place in cotton farming since that time. They said that today it takes my father about 23 hours of work for every acre of cotton he farms. In the 1920s, it took my great grandfather more than ten times as many hours.

"Growing cotton keeps us busy all year. As soon as we have finished harvesting one crop, we begin preparing for the next. We cut down the old cotton plants and leave them on the ground. This keeps the soil from washing away during a heavy rain. Later we plow the field and mix the old plants into the soil. In the early spring we prepare the soil for planting by making beds, or low ridges, in the fields.

"The cotton seeds are planted in these beds in late April or early

May. We plant enough seeds to grow over 40,000 cotton plants on each acre of land. Our tractor is used to pull a planter that can plant six rows of seeds at one time.

"Once the cotton starts to grow, we work to keep insects and diseases from hurting our plants. We usually lose one plant to insects and one to disease for every ten that we plant. We spend a lot of money to save as much cotton as possible. We use **insecticides**. These are special insect-killing chemicals. We hire **crop dusters** to spray our plants with these insecticides. Crop dusters are people who fly special airplanes that spray insecticides on our fields.

These planes must fly very low to do their job well. Dad says that you can always tell if someone is a good crop duster. He says that when a good crop duster lands a plane, there will be lint on the wheels from touching the tops of the cotton plants!

"As the cotton grows, we irrigate our fields. Marana doesn't get much rain. Most of the rain we do get usually comes in the summer. But this rain is not enough to grow our cotton. We must also use irrigation. Large pumps bring up water from far below the ground. This water allows our cotton plants to stay healthy. Dad says that we must use this underground water

This cotton field is being irrigated by a large machine that can be moved from place to place.
■ **What tells you that this machine can be moved?**

These children are looking at a label inside a shirt. The label tells them that the shirt is made of cotton.
■ **Are any of your clothes made of cotton?**

with care. We must make sure that there is enough water left for farming in future years.

"In the fall the cotton is ready for picking. Grandma says that years ago, people picked the cotton off each plant by hand. Today we use a *cotton picker*. This is a huge machine that moves through the fields and picks the cotton from the plant.

"The cotton picker has a large cage in which to store the cotton. When the cage is full, a big truck pulls it to another machine called a **cotton gin**. This machine removes the seeds from the cotton. Then it shapes the clean cotton into

bales. In Chapter 2 you learned that bales are large packages of cotton. Each bale weighs about 500 pounds (227 kg).

"We sell the bales of cotton to companies that make the cotton into clothing. Who knows? Maybe the shirt or sweater you are wearing was made with cotton from our farm!"

CHECKUP

1. Name each part of the cotton plant and how it is used.
2. What two sources provide water for cotton farmers near Marana?
3. **Thinking Critically** What things do cotton farmers spend money for in order to have good crops?

A Rice Farm

How is rice grown?

VOCABULARY

dike   mill

Feeding the People of the World

Some farm crops are of great importance to large numbers of people. Grains such as wheat, oats, and rice are three of these crops. Perhaps the most important of these is rice. Rice is the main food for about half of the world's people.

In Asia, millions of people eat rice three times each day. Many of these people have little else to eat. In India, for example, each person eats about 1/2 pound (1/3 kg) of rice every day. In the United States, many people eat rice and gravy, rice pudding, and rice cereal. Each American eats about 7 1/2 pounds (3 kg) of rice each year.

The map below shows where rice is grown in the United States.

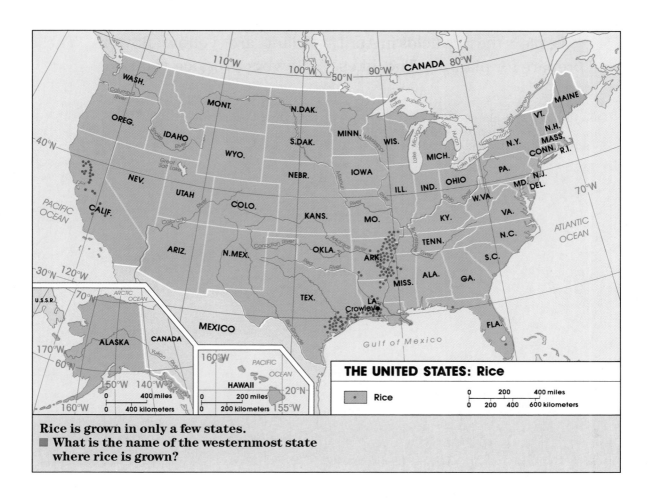

THE UNITED STATES: Rice

Rice

Rice is grown in only a few states.
■ What is the name of the westernmost state where rice is grown?

Visiting a Rice Farm Molly lives on a rice farm in Louisiana. It is near a town called Crowley.

"Rice farming is different from other types of farming," explains Molly. "Rice plants need a lot of water to grow. They also need warm temperatures. We grow rice in fields that we flood with water from irrigation ditches. The rice fields are divided by **dikes**. These dikes are banks of earth. They are 1 or 2 feet (1/3 or 2/3 m) high and 4 or 5 feet (1 or 1 1/2 m) wide. The dikes hold the water in the field.

"We plow the rice fields in April and prepare for planting. The dikes must be examined and repaired or rebuilt. We also must check the irrigation ditches and the water pumps to be sure that they are ready for flooding.

"The rice seeds are planted in late April or early May. This is done by airplane. A low-flying airplane spreads the seeds evenly over our flooded fields. When the rice begins to grow, these fields look like beautiful green lakes.

"The rice plants grow to be about 4 feet (1 m) tall. They look like tall grass. At the top of each plant are yellow flowers. These flowers produce the rice.

This photograph shows large rice fields near Crowley, Louisiana. The fields have been flooded with water.
■ **What is holding the water inside the fields?**

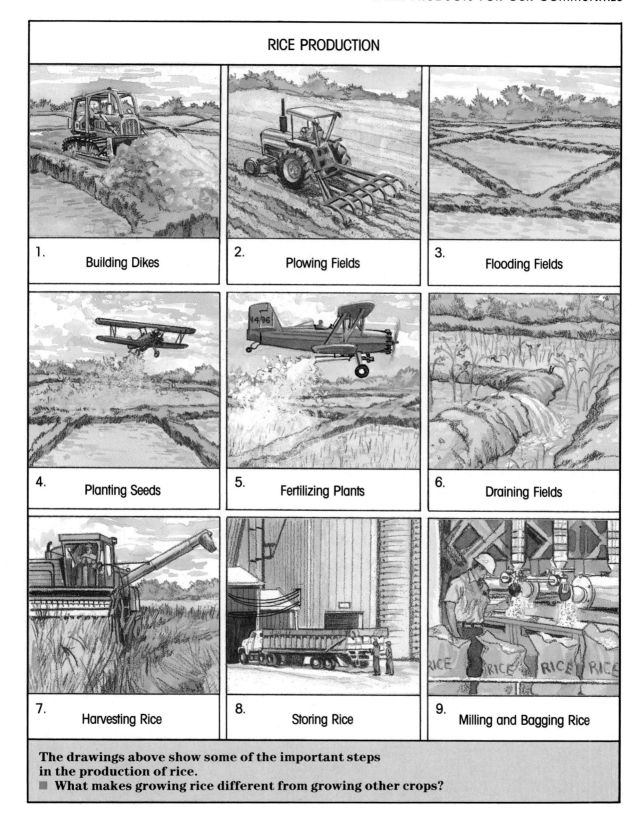

RICE PRODUCTION

1. Building Dikes

2. Plowing Fields

3. Flooding Fields

4. Planting Seeds

5. Fertilizing Plants

6. Draining Fields

7. Harvesting Rice

8. Storing Rice

9. Milling and Bagging Rice

The drawings above show some of the important steps in the production of rice.

■ **What makes growing rice different from growing other crops?**

Rice can be part of a healthy school lunch.
■ **What else is on these students' lunch trays?**

"We harvest our rice in late September. This is about 5 months after it is planted. About 2 weeks before harvest, we drain each field. When the fields are dry, a huge machine called a *combine* cuts the rice plants. The combine also separates the rice from the rest of the plant. The rice is then dried with heated air. Each year, we harvest more than 5,000 pounds (2,270 kg) of rice from each acre.

"After we have harvested the rice, it is **milled**. Mill means 'to remove the *hull*, or hard outer shell, of the rice.' If just a little of the hull is removed, the rice will be brown. If all of the hull is removed, the rice will be white.

"We go to a rice festival each year in Crowley. This takes place after the harvest. Last year I saw a display of the many ways that rice can be used. I learned that rice is used to feed cattle and to make such products as soap, starch, margarine, and makeup. I learned that farmers in parts of Asia burn rice hulls to heat their homes."

CHECKUP

1. Why is rice such an important crop?
2. Airplanes are used to plant rice. In what other way are airplanes used in rice production?
3. **Thinking Critically** Why, do you think, is most rice grown in the United States in areas that have a short winter?

Ranches

What are two types of cattle ranches?

VOCABULARY

ranch	windmill
livestock	veterinarian

Raising Livestock You have probably seen a **ranch**. You may have passed by a ranch when you were traveling. You may have seen one on a television show or in a movie. Maybe you even live on a ranch.

The dictionary tells us that a ranch is a large farm for raising cattle, sheep, or horses. These animals are called **livestock**.

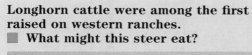

Longhorn cattle were among the first raised on western ranches.
■ **What might this steer eat?**

Livestock need a lot of grass to eat. A ranch has to have many acres of grassland to feed animals. This is a problem on ranches in dry areas where little grass grows. Places such as this may need 50 acres (20 ha) of land to feed one cow.

Earlier in this chapter you read about milk cows. These cows live on dairy farms. Ranches are the home of another type of cattle, called beef cattle. Beef cattle are raised for their meat. We eat the meat of cattle as roast beef, hamburger, and beef hot dogs. Texas produces more beef cattle than any other state does.

The King Ranch One of the largest ranches in the United States is the King Ranch in southern Texas. This ranch has 823,000 acres (333,000 ha) of land. This is more land than the entire state of Rhode Island has. The 60,000 cattle on this ranch could provide enough beef to give half the people in our country a hamburger. The ranch has more than 2,000 miles (3,000 km) of fence. If set in a straight line, this fence would reach from the ranch headquarters in Kingsville to Boston, Massachusetts.

Many busy ranchers in Texas are Mexican Americans. Here workers are roping a calf.
■ **What protects these ranchers from the hot sun?**

There are many **windmills** on the King Ranch. Windmills are machines that use the power of the wind to pump water to the surface from far under the ground. The land on the ranch is often dry. So the windmills are important. They provide the water that the cattle need for drinking.

Hundreds of people work on the ranch. In the 1850s, Richard and Henrietta King started the ranch. They needed many workers to make the ranch a success. To get these workers, they hired almost an entire village of people from Mexico. These workers moved with their families to live on the ranch.

Many of the people who live and work on the ranch today still belong to these same families.

Life on a Cattle Ranch   All ranchers have busy days. They fix broken fences. They check the water supply to be sure that there is enough water for the animals. In many areas, they also put out blocks of salt for the cattle to lick. The animals need salt in their diet.

In some places, winters can be very cold. In these areas, ranchers plant and care for crops of hay in the summer. As you have learned, hay is often used as winter food for livestock. When snow covers the ground, the cattle cannot find food on their own. Then ranchers spread hay on the ground for them to eat.

Ranchers care for their cattle in other ways, too. Sometimes a calf, or baby cow, becomes sick. When this happens, the calf and its mother may be moved from the fields to the barn. Here the ranchers can give the sick animal special care. A **veterinarian** (vet ər ə nãr′ ē ən), or animal doctor, might give the calf some medicine.

The horse is still a cowhand's best friend. However, newer ways of transportation are also used on

many ranches. Cars, trucks, and jeeps now carry cowhands and cattle. There are also motorcycles and helicopters on some ranches.

A Different Type of Ranch

The land on many ranches is used mostly for grazing cattle. There is another type of ranch, one that uses most of its land for growing food for cattle. In addition to hay, the rancher plants and grows corn and other cattle food. These crops are harvested and stored in tall storage tanks. As food is needed, it is taken from the storage tanks to machines which mix and prepare the food.

The cattle do not graze in fields. They are kept in a building most of the time. Their mixed food is placed in the building for them, and there are special water tanks. Because of the special diet, many cattle on these ranches grow large very quickly.

These cowhands use horses to help them herd cattle. A helicopter hovers above.
■ How might a helicopter help on a big ranch?

CHECKUP

1. Why do ranches like the King Ranch need a lot of land for their cattle?
2. What are some of the things that ranchers do?
3. **Thinking Critically** In what ways may the new means of transportation used on ranches today be better than horses?

A County Fair

VOCABULARY

county fair	**rodeo**
auction	

Why People Go to County Fairs

Ranchers and farmers are always trying to raise better animals and crops. **County fairs** help them do this. These fairs are held in many counties in the United States. A county is a political division within a state.

At a county fair, ranchers see prize-winning animals and can talk with the owners. The ranchers can compare ways of feeding their livestock. Sometimes the animals are sold during a livestock show that is held at the fair. **Auctions** are held each day. At an auction the animals are sold to the people who will pay the highest price.

At a fair farmers can see prize-winning farm products and talk with other farmers. They can compare ways of raising crops.

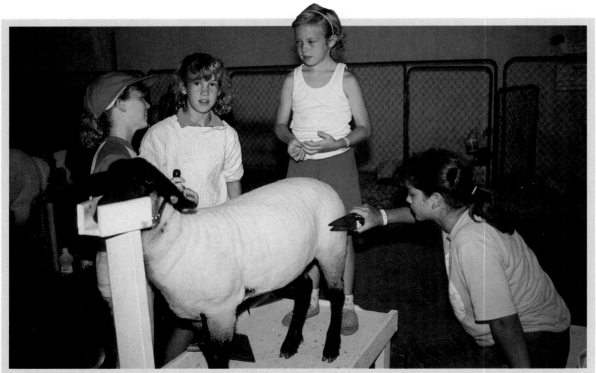

Girls and boys can belong to special clubs like the 4-H Club, and raise farm animals that win prizes at a county fair.
■ What animal are these 4-H members getting ready to show?

Sometimes there are shows of farm machinery and equipment. There may even be special classes to teach new ways to care for animals and crops.

A county fair is a fun place to spend a day. There may be a children's pet parade. Boys and girls can march in the parade with their pets. Marching bands from the schools in a county may play each day at a fair. There may also be contests to see who bakes the best cake and the best pie or who can eat the most watermelon.

Fun at a Rodeo   Still another attraction at a county fair is a **rodeo**. A rodeo is a group of contests that show the skills of cowgirls and cowboys. Rodeo comes from the Spanish word *rodear* (rō de är'), meaning "to surround," or "to round up." The word rodeo has become part of our language.

There are many different events in the rodeo. An event such as bull riding tests a cowhand against an animal. The cowhand must stay on the bull for a certain number of seconds.

Other rodeo events test a person against time. One such event

People enjoy watching a rodeo at a county fair.
■ What is this rider doing?

is steer wrestling. The cowhand jumps from a horse onto a running steer. Then the cowhand grabs the horns of the steer and tries to wrestle the animal to the ground. The person who wins this event is the one who brings the steer down in the least amount of time. Other timed events include steer roping and barrel racing.

CHECKUP
1. How does a county fair help ranchers and farmers raise better animals and better crops?
2. What is an auction?
3. Where did the word *rodeo* come from?
4. **Thinking Critically** Why do people go to a county fair?

Reading a Diagram

A MILK-PRODUCTS DIAGRAM

In this chapter, you have learned about a dairy farm and dairy products. About half of the milk from dairy farms is used for drinking. The rest is made into a number of products.

The diagram below shows some of the products made from milk. Diagrams like this one help you to see a lot of information quickly. Notice that this diagram shows two main kinds of milk products. One is food products. These are the products that people or animals eat. The other is nonfood products. These products are used for many other purposes.

SKILLS PRACTICE

Use the diagram to help you answer the following questions. Write on a sheet of paper.

1. What is a nonfood product that you might eat or drink?
2. Which of the food products shown would you not eat?
3. Are plastics a food or a nonfood product?
4. Would you use a food or a nonfood product to stick two pieces of paper together?
5. Would you keep food or nonfood products in your freezer or refrigerator?

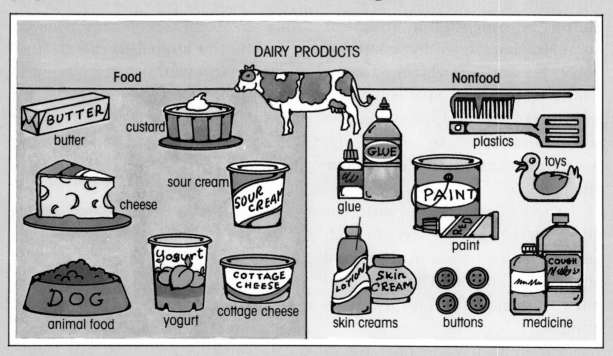

DAIRY PRODUCTS

Food — butter, custard, cheese, sour cream, animal food, yogurt, cottage cheese

Nonfood — glue, plastics, toys, paint, skin creams, buttons, medicine

CHAPTER 6 REVIEW

MAIN IDEAS

1. There are fewer American farms today than there were long ago. But these farms of today produce far more crops because of better seeds, fertilizer, and modern machines.
2. Dairy farms produce milk and milk products, such as butter, cheese, and ice cream.
3. Many vegetable farms in the United States use modern methods, such as greenhouse farming and irrigation.
4. Cotton is grown in the southern United States on farms that use modern methods of planting, caring for, and harvesting the crops.
5. Rice is grown in the United States in fields into which large amounts of water are pumped.
6. Many ranches raise livestock in fields where the animals graze on grass for food. Other ranches keep their livestock indoors, and special mixed food is brought to them.
7. At county fairs ranchers and farmers have an opportunity to exchange ideas.

VOCABULARY REVIEW

Copy the sentences in the next column and fill in the blanks with the right vocabulary term.

a. county fair	f. livestock
b. greenhouse	g. dikes
c. dairy farm	h. income
d. cotton gin	i. plantation
e. hay	j. rodeo

1. Holstein and Jersey cows are found on a _____ .
2. The seeds are removed from the cotton by a _____ .
3. Rice fields are divided by banks of earth called _____ .
4. Vegetables can be grown all year long in a _____ .
5. Prizes are given to the best livestock at a _____ .
6. Farmers buy the things they need with the _____ they get from the sale of their crops.
7. During the winter cattle may be given _____ as food.
8. Cattle, horses, and sheep are called _____ .
9. A _____ is a large farm.
10. Steer roping and barrel racing are two events at a _____ .

CHAPTER CHECKUP

1. What are some changes that have taken place on farms and ranches over the years?
2. How are greenhouses used?
3. Why are county fairs held?
4. **Thinking Critically** Farmers sometimes have very serious problems. What might they be?

APPLYING KNOWLEDGE

Make a farm products booklet. Choose one crop such as cotton. Find out all of the products made from this crop. Cut out or draw pictures of these products. Glue and label them in your booklet.

7 Resources for Our Communities

Petroleum, a Valuable Resource

Why is oil an important resource?

VOCABULARY

mineral	fuel	electricity
petroleum		

Earth's Resources   You have learned that our country is very large and has many natural resources. One natural resource is **minerals**. A mineral is a substance most often buried below the earth's surface. People must take the minerals from the earth in order to use them.

This picture shows part of a large oil field.
What shows you where each oil well is located?

Petroleum   One of the resources that we call a mineral is **petroleum** (pə trō′ lē əm). Petroleum is a dark liquid that we usually call *oil*. Oil is very valuable because we use it in so many different ways.

Oil is an important **fuel.** A fuel is anything that is burned to make heat. A fuel can also be burned to make power for running machines. The gasoline that makes our cars, buses, trucks, and airplanes run is made from oil. We can burn oil in our furnace to heat our homes and places of business.

The heat from burning oil can also run large motors that make **electricity.** Electricity is a kind of energy that gives light and heat. We use electricity when we turn on a light, or watch television.

People use oil or products made from oil every day. Oil is used to make asphalt (as′ fôlt) or blacktop roads. Oil is used in the ink that prints the letters on this page. Your plastic trucks and dollhouses may also contain oil products. So may some of your clothes, medicines, and records.

A Nonrenewable Resource Another reason why oil is so valuable is that it is a *nonrenewable* (non ri nü′ ə bəl) resource. This means that once oil is taken from the earth, it cannot be replaced. There is only a certain amount of oil in the world. After it is used up, there will not be any more. We cannot make or grow oil.

Where Is Oil Found? Most oil is found deep under the ground. However, there have been places around the world where oil seeped

This chart shows some of the many products that are made from petroleum.
■ Which product would be used more in cold weather?

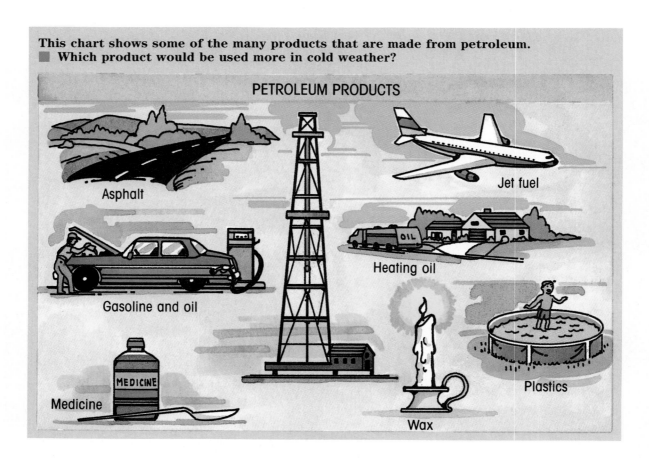

PETROLEUM PRODUCTS

Asphalt

Jet fuel

Gasoline and oil

Heating oil

Medicine

Wax

Plastics

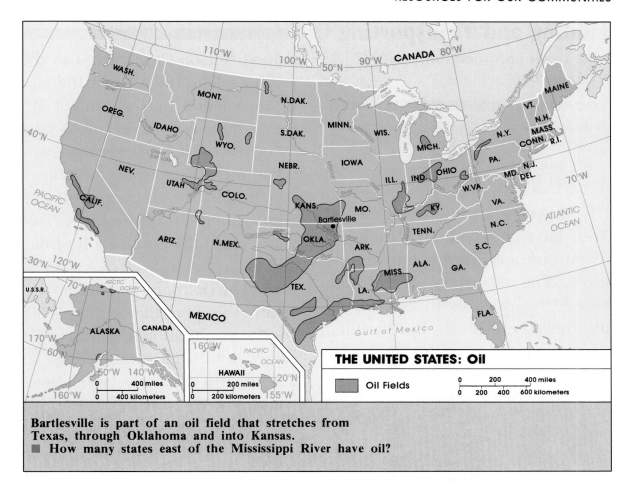

THE UNITED STATES: Oil

Oil Fields

| 0 | 200 | 400 miles |
| 0 | 200 | 400 | 600 kilometers |

Bartlesville is part of an oil field that stretches from Texas, through Oklahoma and into Kansas.
■ How many states east of the Mississippi River have oil?

up from below the earth's surface. So some people long ago knew about oil. They burned it in lamps to make light. They used it to seal cracks in wooden ships.

Today a great deal of the world's oil has been found. Much of it has already been used. People are always looking for more oil. Look at the map on this page. It shows where oil has been found in the United States. Which states have large oil fields?

Turn to page 276. Look at the two bar graphs that show oil production. Which five of these states produce the most oil? Which five countries produce the most oil?

CHECKUP

1. Why is oil an important natural resource?
2. Name three ways in which we use electricity.
3. **Thinking Critically** Why is oil sometimes called black gold?

Finding and Transporting Oil

How is oil obtained and transported?

VOCABULARY

derrick	refinery
bit	pipeline
offshore oil platform	

Oil Makes a Community Grow

You have learned that natural resources help cities and towns to grow. The discovery of oil has caused many cities to grow. One of these cities is Bartlesville, Oklahoma.

Only Native Americans lived in the area until 1868. Then a trader named Nelson Carr moved to the area to sell products to the Indians. In 1875 Jacob Bartles bought Mr. Carr's business and set up a post office. Soon Mr. Bartles's name was taken for the name of the town.

In 1897 the first major oil well was drilled in Bartlesville. Two years later, the Santa Fe Railroad arrived in town. Now oil could be loaded on railroad cars and carried to other parts of the country. With good transportation at hand, people drilled more and more wells. At one time in the early 1900s, there were more oil wells in Bartlesville than there were houses.

The oil boom caused Bartlesville to grow rapidly. Today the city's population is about 35,000. Other businesses have come to Bartlesville, but oil remains an important industry.

Visiting a Derrick

Mrs. Turner lives in Bartlesville. She works for an oil company. As part of her job, she visits the places where the company is searching for oil. Mrs. Turner will take us with her to one of these places. She will also tell us about other places where her company looks for oil.

In the early 1900s, Bartlesville was a booming oil town
■ What other kinds of businesses might have come to Bartlesville to serve the oil industry?

160

"You know that we take oil from under the ground. We do this by drilling wells. The first place that you will learn about is a few miles from Bartlesville. There are no paved roads to the place where we are drilling. The deep holes in the dirt road were made by the big trucks that carry all our tools.

"There's the **derrick.** It holds the drilling equipment. The derrick is a steel tower. Most derricks are between 80 and 200 feet (24 and 61 m) tall.

"You can see the workers placing a drill **bit,** or cutting tool, on the end of a piece of pipe. The bit is very strong. It will cut and break up rocks as it drills deep into the earth.

"The large motor next to the derrick will turn the pipe and the bit. As the bit drills deeper, more pipe will be added. Some of our wells go down several miles. Most of our oil comes from wells like this one.

"After the well is drilled, and if we have found oil, another tool will be brought here. This tool is a special kind of pump. The derrick will be taken down. The pump will be put in its place to bring the oil to the surface of the earth."

These men are working at an oil well near Bartlesville, Oklahoma.
■ Why, do you think, are they wearing hard hats and heavy gloves?

Offshore Oil Wells "Most of our oil comes from wells like this one. But we also have oil wells in Lake Texoma between Oklahoma and Texas. There are even some wells in the ocean.

"To reach that oil, workers have to drill wells in the lake or ocean floor. They work from an **offshore oil platform.** This is a large structure made of steel or concrete. It has a derrick like the one that we have just seen. It also has living space for the workers. Some of our platforms are many

161

miles from land. The wells are drilled in very deep water.

"I hope our tour of a derrick has helped you understand how we get oil from below the surface of the earth."

Petroleum Products At the start of this chapter, you read about some of the products that are made from petroleum. The oil taken from the wells must be changed into these products to be useful to people.

Once oil is taken from the ground, it goes to a **refinery.** At the refinery, machines make the oil pure. Then the oil is changed into products that people can use.

The huge ship, called a tanker, carries millions of gallons of oil.
■ How might the many storage tanks be used?

The big picture shows an offshore oil platform. The small one shows workers being lowered onto a platform.
■ What might they be lowered from?

Moving the Oil Oil has to be moved from the oil well to the refinery. Oil and oil products have to be moved from the refinery to your community. Railroad tank cars, trucks, and ships called tankers are all used to transport petroleum.

Another way that oil is transported is through **pipelines.** A pipeline is made by welding, or joining, many pieces of pipe together. Some pipelines are more than 3,000 miles (5,000 km) long. Usually a pipeline is placed about

(Left) The Trans-Alaska Pipeline is 800 miles (1,300 km) long.
(Right) This huge oil refinery is in Saudi Arabia.
■ What tells you that this is not an American refinery?

3 feet (1 m) under the ground. Sometimes a pipeline is built above the ground. Pumps push the oil through the pipeline.

The Trans-Alaska Pipeline crosses Alaska, our largest state. It was one of the most difficult pipelines to build. It had to cross rivers, streams, and mountains. More than half of this pipeline is built above the ground.

Overseas Oil   The United States uses more petroleum than any other country does. We do not produce all the oil we need, so we buy oil from other countries.

The oil that we buy from other countries comes to the United States in tankers. These huge ships carry millions of gallons of oil to the United States.

Much of the oil we buy comes from Saudi Arabia (soud′ ē ə rā′ bē ə). Find Saudi Arabia on the world map on pages 252–253.

Saudi Arabian oil is pumped from wells and sent through pipelines to port cities. At the ports the oil is placed in large storage tanks. The oil is held in these tanks until it is sent through other pipelines to the tankers. The tankers then carry Saudi Arabian oil to the United States and to other nations in the world.

CHECKUP

1. How do we get oil from under the surface of the earth?
2. Why does the United States buy oil from other countries?
3. **Thinking Critically** How would your life be different without petroleum?

Coal, a Valuable Resource

How is coal obtained?

VOCABULARY

mine shaft

What Is Coal? Coal is a valuable natural resource. Coal, like oil, is called a mineral resource. It is a black rock that will burn. Also like oil, it is a very important fuel that can make heat and power.

Coal is found on every continent of the world. It is also mined in 26 of the 50 states in the United States.

Producers of Coal There are two bar graphs on page 276 that show coal production. Look at the graph that shows the leading coal-producing countries in the world. Which country produces the most?

Coal production in the United States is shown on the second bar graph. This graph shows that more

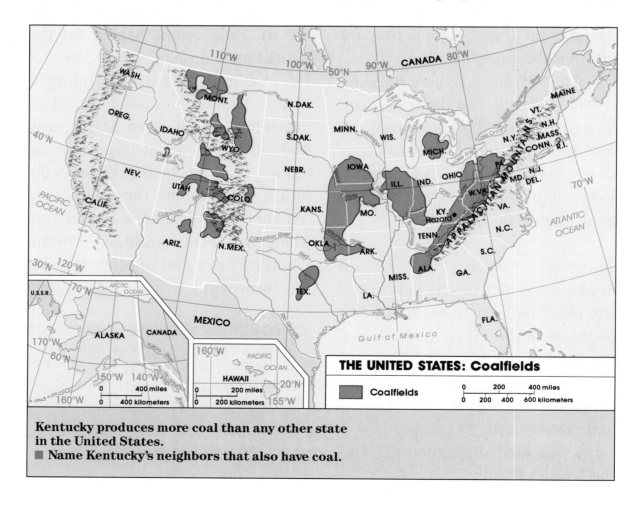

THE UNITED STATES: Coalfields

Coalfields

Kentucky produces more coal than any other state in the United States.
■ Name Kentucky's neighbors that also have coal.

Electricity in the mines provides more light than miners had long ago. But mines can still be dark and sometimes dangerous places. This Kentucky miner uses a machine to remove the coal.
■ **How do you think miners of long ago dug out the coal?**

coal is produced in Kentucky than in any other state. Find Kentucky on the map on page 164. There are large coalfields in both eastern and western Kentucky.

A Coal-Mining Town There are a number of coal-mining towns in Kentucky. Many of these towns began and grew because coal had been found in the area. Hazard is a coal-mining town in Kentucky. Find Hazard on the map on pages 254–255.

You can see that Hazard is in the southeastern part of Kentucky.

It is located on the edge of the Appalachian Mountains. Today many products are made in Hazard, but it is also known as a coal-mining community.

Some of the people of Hazard work in coal mines or for mining companies. The coal is located deep under the ground. The mines have been dug far below the earth's surface to reach the coal. Miners must travel down a **mine shaft** on an elevator. A mine shaft is a kind of tunnel that has been dug downward from the surface of the earth to where the coal is found.

165

All the miners wear special shoes and caps, or helmets. The helmets and shoes are hard and strong. They protect a miner from getting hurt by falling pieces of rock or coal. Often the helmets have lights on them. These lights help the miners see in the dim mine. The miners also wear special glasses to protect their eyes.

Years ago, coal miners used picks and shovels to dig out the coal. Today, machines do most of the work in coal mines. Miners must know how to run these machines.

One machine digs out the coal and loads it onto a conveyor, or moving, belt. The conveyor belt takes the coal to the mine train. The train carries the coal to the mine shaft. At the shaft, the coal is placed in an elevator and lifted to the surface.

Once the coal reaches the surface of the ground, it is sorted into different-sized pieces. Then it is washed and dried. Finally the coal is loaded onto trains, trucks, or barges. It is then shipped all over the country. Much of the coal goes to electric power companies. These companies burn the coal to make heat for running the machines that make electricity.

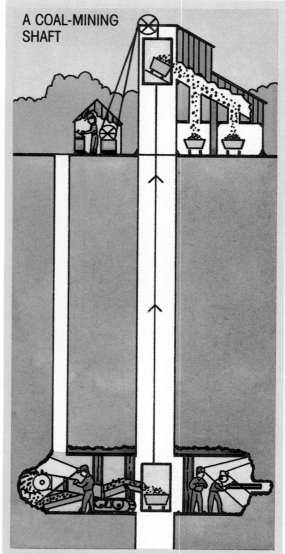

A COAL-MINING SHAFT

This diagram shows how a mine shaft is used.
■ What work is the machine at the bottom doing?

CHECKUP
1. Why is coal valuable?
2. What do miners wear to help keep them safe in the mines?
3. **Thinking Critically** How has the work of miners changed?

Food from the Sea

How do we obtain fish and other seafood?

VOCABULARY
lobster

Fishing Communities   Among our important resources are oceans, lakes, and rivers. From them we get many different kinds of seafood. People all over the world eat fish and other seafood.

These fishing boats are in a California harbor.
■ Look at the map on pages 254–255 to see where they go to catch fish.

Many communities began as fishing communities. They usually have a good harbor. A harbor is a protected body of water. It helps to keep boats safe from storms.

Fishing is still important in many communities along our coasts. Many people in or near these communities earn their living by fishing. Most mornings they go out in boats to the fishing grounds and return to the harbor at night with the fish they have caught. If it was a good day, there will be plenty of fish to sell.

Some fishing boats go far out into the ocean. They go where the ocean water is very deep. These boats are very large and can stay out at sea for weeks. They use big nets to catch many different kinds of fish.

Maine Lobsters   One kind of fishing is **lobster** fishing. Many people like to eat lobster meat.

Have you ever been in a grocery store or fish market and seen a glass tank filled with water and some sea animals? The animals are dark green or dark blue in color. They have a hard shell and two big claws. They are called lobsters.

They may have been caught along the coast of Maine. Look at the map on pages 254–255. Find the state of Maine. Maine has a long coastline with many harbors.

Lobsters are caught in traps called pots. A trap is made of wood or metal. Pieces of fish are put in the trap. Rocks are placed in the trap to make it sink to the bottom of the ocean. A rope is tied to the trap before it is put into the water. A small block of painted wood is tied to the other end of the rope. The wood block floats on the water. This float, as it is called, shows where the lobster pot is placed. The lobster goes into the pot to eat the fish. Once inside, the lobster cannot get out.

On a Lobster Boat   Margie lives near Rockland, Maine. Her father has a boat that he uses to help catch lobsters. Sometimes on Saturdays or during the summer, Margie helps her father on the boat.

Margie often goes with her father to Monhegan Island. It is about 25 miles (40 km) from their home. They have some lobster pots in the water near the island.

This man lives in a community near the coast of Maine. He catches lobsters to sell in order to make his living.
■ Where is the lobster pot in which the lobster was caught?

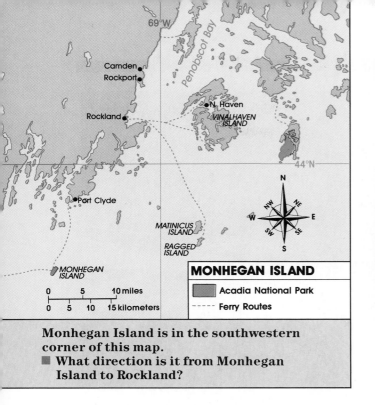

Monhegan Island is in the southwestern corner of this map.
■ What direction is it from Monhegan Island to Rockland?

A lobster boat heads for the spot where traps were sunk the day before.
■ Why must this Maine worker keep the boat in good running order?

Margie says, "Monhegan Island is famous for its lobsters. It takes our little boat more than two hours to reach the island. But it is worth the long trip. We always have lobsters in our traps. My father has to make this trip every day to check the traps.

"When we get to the island, our work really begins. We have to pull each trap out of the water. If there is a lobster in the trap, we carefully take it out so that it won't pinch us with its claws. Then we put another piece of fish in and lower the trap back into the water. I put each lobster in a big tank of water to keep it alive.

"When we return to Rockland, a company buys all our lobsters. The lobsters are put into special boxes to keep them alive. Then they are sent to stores all over the country. When you see a big lobster in a store or a restaurant, it might be one that we caught at Monhegan Island."

CHECKUP

1. Why is a good harbor important to a fishing community?
2. How are lobsters caught?
3. **Thinking Critically** Laws have been passed that limit the places where people are allowed to catch lobsters. Why, do you think, do we have such laws?

Using Natural Resources Wisely

Why should we learn to use and care for the earth's resources wisely and well?

VOCABULARY

pollute	national forest
conservation	ranger
Congress	fish hatchery

Cutting down trees and preparing the logs to be sold is called lumbering.
■ Do you think there has been too much lumbering here?

Saving for the Future   We use the earth's natural resources every day. Because these resources are so important, we have to be careful how we use them.

If we cut down too many trees, the forests will disappear. Then there will be no trees to use to build houses or to make paper. There will be no place for wild animals and wild birds to live and hide. People will not have forests to camp in.

If we dump trash and garbage into the rivers and oceans, the waters will become **polluted,** or dirty. Dirty water is unhealthy for people to use. We cannot drink it or swim in it. It is also harmful to the fish and other animals that live in and around water.

If we let factories pour smoke into the air, our air will become polluted. Polluted air hurts almost everything it touches. It can make our eyes sting and fill with tears. It can make paint on buildings fade and peel off. It can eat away metal. It can kill trees and other plants.

Trees, water, and air are some of our most important natural resources. We need to take care of them so that they will not be spoiled and wasted. We need to save our great natural resources for the future. This good use of natural resources is called **conservation** (kon sər vā′ shən).

170

Rachel Carson (1907–1964)

When Rachel Carson was a little girl, she did not have playmates. But she did have beautiful woods and fields to wander in. Rachel learned a great deal about trees and birds and flowers.

When she was older, she spent a summer at the seashore. There she learned to love the sea and its creatures, just as she loved her woods and fields. Rachel went on to study about science and living things in college.

Rachel Carson had always wanted to be a writer. When she was only 10 years old, she wrote a little story that was printed in a magazine. When she was grown up, she began to write about the sea. Her most famous book is called *The Sea Around Us*.

About 1950, Rachel Carson began to hear that all around the country great numbers of fish and birds were dying. She found out that they were being killed by pesticides. Rachel Carson knew that insects must not be allowed to destroy food crops. But she became very worried about the birds and animals.

She wanted to help them, so she wrote a book called *Silent Spring* in 1962. She wrote that if pesticides went on being used, one spring would come when there would be no birds left to sing. As time went by, it became clear that what she had said was true. So then our government made a law that stopped the use of harmful pesticides.

Responsible Citizens and Good Conservation We are all responsible for conservation. Every good citizen tries to use our resources wisely. Today many people are showing that they care about the earth and its resources. In many of our communities across our state and across our whole country, people have worked together to make the air we breathe cleaner. People have worked hard in our towns and cities to clean up polluted water. They have worked to get laws passed that protect our forests and certain kinds of wildlife.

People in all our communities have shown that they are good citizens. They have built parks and planted trees and flowers. They have worked hard to clean up their communities.

A Concerned Citizen and President Conserving our natural resources is not a new idea. Good citizens have worked for conservation for a long time. Years ago, President Theodore Roosevelt was interested in conservation. He was very sick when he was a young boy. He spent much of his time outside. He liked to walk through

(*Left*) The Hudson River, once heavily polluted, is cleaner today.
(*Right*) Teddy Roosevelt loved our forests and tried to protect them.
■ Why, do you think, is it important to protect our natural resources?

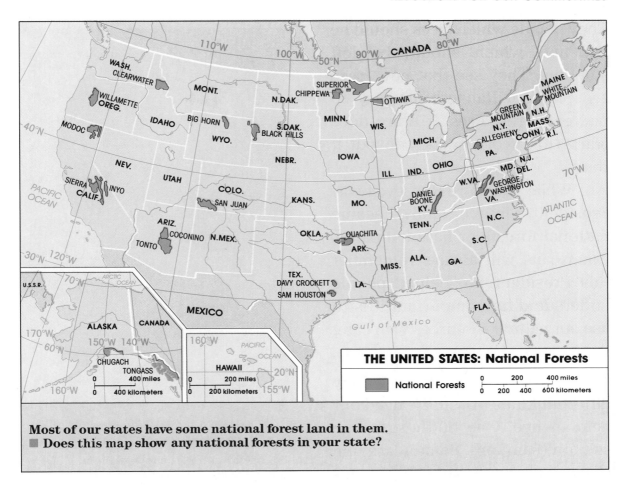

THE UNITED STATES: National Forests

National Forests

Most of our states have some national forest land in them.
■ Does this map show any national forests in your state?

forests filled with wildflowers, plants, and trees. He watched the birds and animals in the forests. He learned their names and saw how they lived. He learned that many animals need plants for food.

Life in the out-of-doors made Teddy Roosevelt healthy. It also taught him many things about nature. He cared about the land.

When he became President of the United States, Mr. Roosevelt wanted to protect our natural resources. He talked to members of **Congress** about the need for conservation. Congress is the group of people who are picked to make laws for the United States. Together the President and Congress made millions of acres into **national forests.** A national forest is a forest that belongs to us all. No one may buy or harm this land.

Rangers are people who help to take care of the national forests. Rangers work for the government.

They decide which trees should be cut and which should be left standing. They see that new trees are planted. Rangers also try to prevent forest fires. If a fire does start, they work quickly to put it out.

While Theodore Roosevelt was President, much land became national forests or national parks. Americans will always remember this President. He helped people understand how important it is to use our natural resources with care.

Protecting the Salmon Many different kinds of wildlife need our help to live. One of these is the salmon (sam′ ən). Salmon are one of our most important fish. Millions of people cook and eat salmon every year.

Many salmon are born in the freshwater streams in the states of Oregon, Washington, and Alaska. After they are born, they swim to the Pacific Ocean to live. When they are ready to lay their eggs, they swim back up the rivers and streams to the fresh water where they were born. Here more salmon are born.

One of the largest salmon rivers in the country is the Columbia

The bright color of these salmon makes them easy to recognize.
■ How can you tell if they are in a river or an ocean?

River. It flows between Oregon and Washington. Find this river and the two states on the map on pages 254–255. Years ago, Native Americans known as the Chinook lived along the Columbia River. The Chinook ate salmon that they caught in the river. There were many salmon then.

Today there are fewer salmon in the Columbia River. Dams have been built across the river in the last 50 years. Dams such as the Bonneville Dam block the water of the Columbia River. As the water is let through the dam, it runs motors that make electricity. The electricity is used by the people of nearby cities, such as Portland, Oregon, and even faraway cities, such as Los Angeles, California.

Salmon cannot swim through the dams, so special fish ladders have been built. These ladders help salmon swim upstream to the fresh water where they lay their eggs.

Salmon move up the steps of the fish ladder by leaping from pool to pool.
■ **How else may they climb the ladder?**

A FISH LADDER

step

step

step

Fish Hatcheries Another way of protecting salmon is to use a **fish hatchery.** Thousands of salmon are born in hatcheries every year. The fish are raised at the hatchery until they are big enough to put into the rivers to swim to the Pacific Ocean.

Fish hatcheries are one part of salmon conservation. Another way to help save the salmon is sometimes used. The salmon are caught soon after they are born. They are placed in large water tanks on boats and trucks. The fish are then transported hundreds of miles and released into the river past all the dams. Then the salmon can easily swim to the ocean.

Many salmon are caught each year. Some are killed by polluted rivers. But many people are working to make sure that there are always salmon in our waters.

CHECKUP

1. Why is it necessary for people to be careful about how they use natural resources?
2. What did Theodore Roosevelt do to conserve our country's natural resources?
3. **Thinking Critically** How can good citizens show that they are interested in conservation?

Using the Index and the Glossary

THE INDEX

Your social studies book has a special section called the Index. The Index lists important people, places, and things found in the book. Words in the Index are listed in alphabetical order.

If you want to find information about oil you can turn to the Index and find the words beginning with the letter *O*. Then you can look at the list until you find the word *Oil*. The numbers after the word *Oil* are the pages on which you can find facts about oil.

The main words in the Index are called entry words. Sometimes there are other words listed just below an entry word. These words are called subentries. Find the word *Communities* in the Index. What is one of the subentries under *Communities*?

SKILLS PRACTICE

The index in this book begins on page 290. Use the Index to answer the questions below. Write your answers on a sheet of paper.

1. On what Index page are the words that begin with *O*?
2. On what pages could you find information about oil?
3. How many subentries are there under the word *Communities*?
4. On what Index page would you find the word *Ports*?

5. Where do you find the list of pages on natural resources, with the words beginning with *N* or with the words beginning with *R*?

THE GLOSSARY

Another important part of your book is the Glossary. The Glossary is like a dictionary. It lists important words in alphabetical order. The words in the Glossary are the vocabulary words at the beginning of each lesson in the book.

Suppose you have forgotten what one of the vocabulary words means. You can turn to the Glossary and find the word. There will be a definition, which is a sentence or two that tells you what the word means. A guide is provided to help you pronounce the word. There is also a page number listed for each word. The page number tells you the page on which the word is first used in your book.

SKILLS PRACTICE

The Glossary in this book begins on page 282. Use the Glossary to answer the questions below.

1. What is the meaning of *derrick*?
2. On what page of your book was the word *pasture* first used?
3. Look at the words listed under *C*. Find a word in which the letter *C* sounds like the letter *S*.
4. What is the definition of *greenhouse*?

CHAPTER 7 REVIEW

MAIN IDEAS

1. Petroleum is a valuable natural resource. People use oil and oil products every day.
2. Oil is obtained by drilling deep into the earth and pumping it to the surface.
3. Oil is transported by rail, truck, ship, and pipeline.
4. Coal is a valuable natural resource that is obtained by mining.
5. Coal and oil are important fuels.
6. The oceans, lakes, and rivers supply fish, lobsters, and other seafood, which are obtained by fishing.
7. If our natural resources are not to disappear, we must all learn to use and care for them wisely.

VOCABULARY REVIEW

Copy the sentences below and fill in the blanks with the right vocabulary word. Write your answers on a separate sheet of paper.

a. coal	**f.** conservation
b. derrick	**g.** pollute
c. refinery	**h.** fuels
d. pipelines	**i.** lobsters
e. hatchery	**j.** petroleum

1. A _____ helps to drill for oil.
2. People _____ the water when they throw garbage into it.
3. A rock that burns is _____ .
4. Much of our oil is carried across the country through _____ .

5. Young salmon are often raised at a fish _____ .
6. At a _____ , machines make petroleum pure.
7. Traps are placed in the ocean water to catch _____ .
8. Oil is also called _____ .
9. Taking care of natural resources so that they will not be spoiled or wasted is called _____ .
10. Coal and oil are _____ that provide power.

CHAPTER CHECKUP

1. Where is oil found?
2. How is coal mining today different from mining in the past?
3. How are lobsters caught?
4. What has been done to protect salmon?
5. **Thinking Critically** Name two renewable and two nonrenewable resources.

APPLYING KNOWLEDGE

1. Collect pictures that show natural resources found in or near your community. Place the pictures on a poster.
2. Choose one natural resource that has helped your community. Write a short report about that resource. Use the library to find information. Ask the librarian to show you how to locate the information you need.

8 Connecting Our Communities

People Need Transportation

Why is transportation so important for Americans?

VOCABULARY

raw materials   invent

A Big Country   In this book you have read about people and communities throughout the United States. As you know, we live in a very large country. People on the West Coast of the United States live about 3,000 miles (4,800 km) from people on the

East Coast. Yet no matter where they live, most Americans know a good deal about people in other parts of their country.

One reason for this is transportation. In Chapter 4 you learned that transportation is the carrying of people and products from one place to another.

Why People Travel   People move from one place to another for many reasons. Some transportation covers short distances. Inside their communities, many people travel to work. They travel to shop in stores. They go to

There are many different kinds of transportation.
■ Can you name the ones that you see in these pictures?

church or temple and to school. They go to the post office, to parks, and to many other places.

Other people make longer trips. Many men and women have jobs outside the communities in which they live. They may visit friends and relatives in other areas. They may take vacation trips to the seashore or the mountains.

Moving Goods

We need transportation to move goods as well as people. **Raw materials** must be carried to factories. Raw materials are things found in nature that can be made into finished products. For example, iron ore is a raw material that is mined in Minnesota. It may be carried to Gary, Indiana, to be made into steel. The steel made in Gary may be shipped to North Carolina, Utah, Ohio, or Oregon to be used in constructing tall buildings. Or it may be used in Detroit, Michigan, to build trucks and automobiles.

The products of farms and factories must also be carried to different places. They go to markets and stores to be sold. Your shirt or skirt might have been made in a factory hundreds of miles from the store in which it was bought.

Transportation—Then and Now

People have always been on the go, moving from one place to another. But in earlier times, transportation was much different from what it is today. If people went to another community, they may have had to walk. Perhaps they rode on a horse or in a wagon pulled by

This picture shows transportation in the mountains of California in 1865. ▪ What provided the power to move the wagons and the stagecoach?

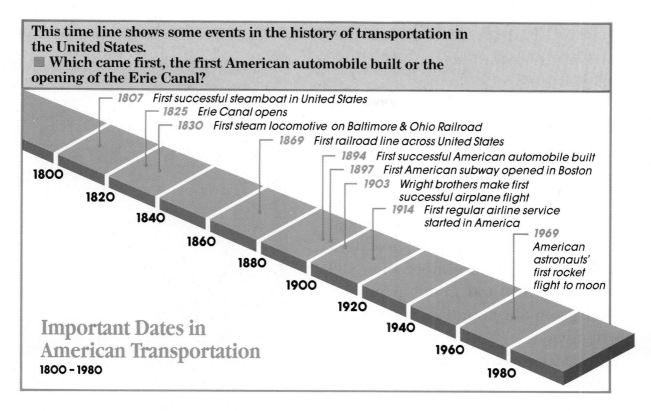

This time line shows some events in the history of transportation in the United States.

■ Which came first, the first American automobile built or the opening of the Erie Canal?

1807 First successful steamboat in United States
1825 Erie Canal opens
1830 First steam locomotive on Baltimore & Ohio Railroad
1869 First railroad line across United States
1894 First successful American automobile built
1897 First American subway opened in Boston
1903 Wright brothers make first successful airplane flight
1914 First regular airline service started in America
1969 American astronauts' first rocket flight to moon

1800
1820
1840
1860
1880
1900
1920
1940
1960
1980

Important Dates in American Transportation
1800 – 1980

horses. It took much longer to make a trip than it does today.

If someone crossed the ocean 200 years ago, he or she had to go on a sailing ship. The force of the wind on the sails moved the ship through the water. If there was no wind, the ship could not move. Voyages sometimes lasted for many weeks.

There were no automobiles, steamships, or airplanes until someone **invented** them. To invent means to make something that no one else has ever made. Look at the time line above. It shows the years in which some important

things have happened in the field of transportation.

The inventions and events shown on the time line have resulted in faster transportation by land and on water. And they have also added a new means of transportation—air travel.

CHECKUP
1. Why is good transportation needed in our country?
2. When was the first railroad line across our country completed?
3. **Thinking Critically** Compare the ways that people traveled in the early days of our country with the ways they travel today.

How People and Goods Are Moved

What different kinds of transportation are there?

VOCABULARY

taxicab	subway	cargo
suburb	canal	

Cars and Buses Carry People

The automobile is the most common means of transportation on land. There are more than 130 million cars and about 6 million buses on our country's streets and highways.

More than eight out of ten workers in our country go to work by car. Some join in *car pools*. In a car pool, several automobile owners ride together. Each takes a turn driving his or her own car and carrying the others.

On city streets, **taxicabs** carry people. A taxicab is a car for hire. Passengers must pay the taxi driver to take them where they want to go.

Another way of moving people is by bus. A bus has many more seats than a car and is used to carry large numbers of people. Most buses run in cities, but others run between cities. Some even travel all the way across the country. There are also special kinds of

These people travel by bus in their city. The bus is often crowded.
■ Why, do you think, is the time important to bus riders?

buses, such as those that carry pupils to and from school. Today there are more than 330,000 school buses in the United States.

Trucks Carry Goods

In our country there are 40 million trucks that carry goods. They carry bread from bakeries, milk from dairies, and wood from lumber mills. They bring goods to supermarkets and gasoline to service stations. When a family moves from one part of

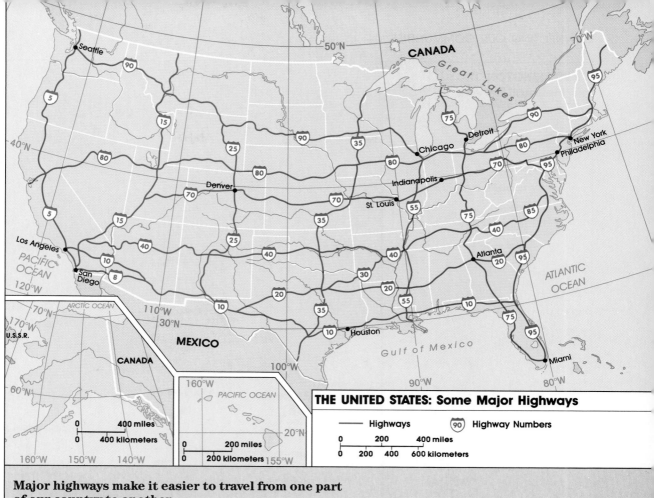

THE UNITED STATES: Some Major Highways

—— Highways   (90) Highway Numbers

Major highways make it easier to travel from one part of our country to another.
■ What highway connects St. Louis and Denver?

the country to another, trucks carry their belongings from their old home to their new one.

Trucks are the most common means we have of carrying goods. Sometimes you might count the number of trucks you see in one day. You will see many more trucks than trains or airplanes.

Railroad Trains Another form of transportation is the railroad train. Automobiles may travel wherever there are streets or highways, but trains can run only on rails. There are rail lines between hundreds of cities in our country.

Railroad trains carry both people and goods. Many people in **suburbs** go to work by train. A suburb is a smaller community near a large city. People who have jobs in the city often live in the suburbs.

Inside some large cities, people may use the **subway**. A subway is a train that runs under the ground.

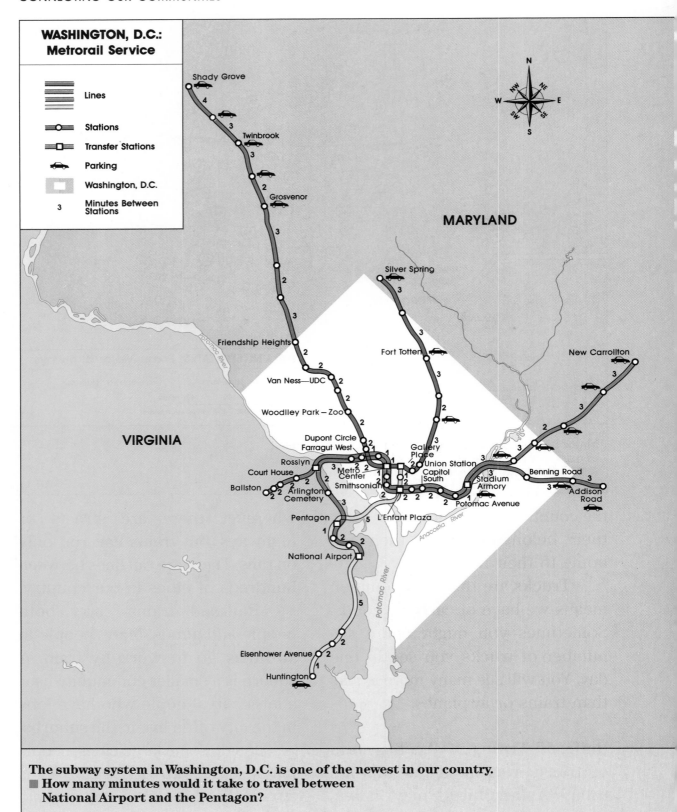

WASHINGTON, D.C.: Metrorail Service

Legend:
- Lines
- ○ Stations
- □ Transfer Stations
- Parking
- Washington, D.C.
- 3 Minutes Between Stations

Stations: Shady Grove, Twinbrook, Grosvenor, Friendship Heights, Van Ness—UDC, Woodley Park—Zoo, Dupont Circle, Farragut West, Rosslyn, Court House, Ballston, Arlington Cemetery, Pentagon, National Airport, Eisenhower Avenue, Huntington, Metro Center, Smithsonian, L'Enfant Plaza, Silver Spring, Fort Totten, Gallery Place, Union Station, Capitol South, Stadium Armory, Potomac Avenue, Benning Road, Addison Road, New Carrollton

MARYLAND

VIRGINIA

The subway system in Washington, D.C. is one of the newest in our country.

■ How many minutes would it take to travel between National Airport and the Pentagon?

Railroads bring us many of the goods we need and want. The biggest and heaviest goods are often carried on railway cars rather than on trucks.

Kinds of Railway Cars   There are special kinds of railway cars for carrying different kinds of goods. One kind is the boxcar. This car has closed sides, a roof, and sliding doors. It looks like a big box on wheels. Goods in boxcars are protected from the weather. Boxcars carry many kinds of goods, from machinery to wheat.

Trains that carry products are often made up of very many different kinds of railroad cars.
■ **Can you name some cars below?**

Another railroad car is called a refrigerator car. It keeps the products inside cold, just as the refrigerator in your home does. Refrigerator cars carry such products as meat and fresh fruit.

The flatcar is another kind of railroad car. It does not have sides or ends but has only a floor. It carries goods that do not have to be protected from the weather. Flatcars are often fitted with metal racks on which new automobiles and trucks are carried from factories where they were built.

A tank car is shaped like a huge bottle lying on its side. The tank car carries different kinds of liquids. Tank cars carry such products as oil and chemicals.

Water Transportation   Look at the map on pages 254–255. Notice how many cities in the United States are located along oceans, lakes, and rivers. In Chapter 4 you learned that transportation by water has caused some cities to become big, busy ports. Even some cities that are located at a distance from natural bodies of water can be reached by **canals**. A canal is a waterway that people have dug out of the land.

Amelia Earhart (1898–1937)

Amelia Earhart was a famous pilot in the early days of flying. When almost all pilots were men, she proved that a woman could fly as well as a man.

As a girl in Kansas, Amelia liked to roam the cliffs and explore the caves along a river near her home. In 1921, as a young woman, she had her first airplane ride. In those days, airplanes were small, light machines made of wood, canvas, and wire around an engine. But Amelia Earhart was thrilled to ride in a machine that could fly like a bird. It was a new way to explore.

Soon she took flying lessons, and in 1928, she became the first woman to cross the Atlantic Ocean in a plane. But she was not satisfied. She wanted to be the first woman to pilot a plane across the Atlantic.

A few years later she got her wish and flew across the ocean alone. She went on to make other record-breaking flights.

In 1937, Amelia Earhart was the pilot of a plane that set out to fly around the world. With only 5,000 miles (8,000 km) to go, she and her helper headed for an airfield on a small island in the Pacific Ocean. But they never arrived. No trace of the plane or the two people aboard was ever found.

Amelia Earhart has not been forgotten. Daring flyers like her prepared the way for the day when millions of people would travel by air.

Once, many more people traveled by ship than they do today. They traveled on big, beautiful steamships called *ocean liners*. Now, however, it is mostly goods that travel by steamship. You have learned about some of the goods that are found along the docks in Wilmington, North Carolina.

The goods that ships carry are called **cargo**. The cargo of a ship may be made up of many different kinds of products—for example, bags of flour, boxes of chinaware, and machinery.

Air Transportation   Airplanes travel at much higher speeds than do automobiles, trains, and ships. They can move people and goods over long distances a great deal faster than the other kinds of transportation.

The place where airplanes take off and land is called an *airport*. Airports need much more space than train and bus stations. The airports must have long runways on which airplanes take off and land. A runway must be smooth and flat. For the largest planes,

This big, busy airport is in Baltimore, Maryland. Large airplanes take off from and land on the long runways.
■ Can you find other kinds of transportation in the picture?

187

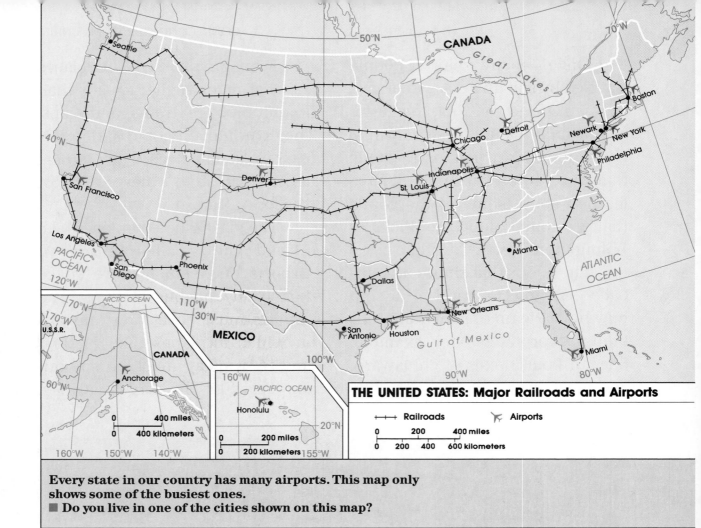

THE UNITED STATES: Major Railroads and Airports

Railroads ⊢⊣   Airports ✈

0   200   400 miles
0 200 400 600 kilometers

Every state in our country has many airports. This map only shows some of the busiest ones.
■ **Do you live in one of the cities shown on this map?**

runways have to be more than 3 miles (4 km) long. For this reason, airports have to be built outside of cities and towns.

The Dallas-Fort Worth Airport in Texas is the largest airport in the world. The world's busiest airport is the Chicago-O'Hare International Airport. It is just outside of Chicago, Illinois.

Airlines earn most of their money from carrying passengers. The kinds of goods they carry are those that need quick delivery, such as cut flowers, fruits, and medicine.

CHECKUP

1. What special kinds of railroad cars are there?
2. How may inland cities be reached by water?
3. **Thinking Critically** If you were to make a trip across the United States, what kind of transportation would you choose and why?

188

People Need Communication

Why must people have ways of communication?

VOCABULARY

communication	satellite
cable	antenna

Learning About Our World No matter where Americans live, most of them today know a good deal about life outside their own community. One reason for this is transportation. As you learned earlier in this chapter, automobiles, airplanes, and even ships, carry people to communities nearby and far away. In this way, they learn firsthand about other people and places.

Communication (kə myü nə kā′ shən) is another reason why people know more about the world they live in. *Communication* means "the giving and receiving of information and ideas." We communicate when we talk and listen. We also communicate through reading, writing, and drawing.

Communication helps us learn about what is happening in our community, our country, and other parts of the world. We can learn about some events as soon as they

Sometimes it's fun to tell a secret to a friend.
■ How are the friends in this picture communicating?

take place. For example, we can see and hear the President of the United States speaking on television. We can hear on the radio about a traffic jam on the highway. We can use the telephone to talk with people here in our own community—or in another country. Communication helps us know and understand the world we live in.

Communication—Then and Now Long ago, people had only a few ways to communicate. They could talk with each other and write letters. But there were no radios, television sets, or telephones until people invented them. Before those inventions, it took weeks for news to travel from one side of the country to the other.

However, some people searched for new and better ways to share information. Their inventions changed the ways in which we communicate today. Look at the time line on page 191. It shows when some important events that improved communication took place.

These young boys worked as telephone operators around 1900.
■ **Would you like to be an operator?**

The Telephone One of the most important inventions in the field of communication was the telephone. From the time line on the next page you can see that the telephone was invented in 1876. However, it had taken Alexander Graham Bell, the inventor, many months of trying and failing before he got the telephone working successfully.

Many improvements have been made on the telephone since 1876. For a long time, someone who made a call had to give a person called the *operator* the name of the person that was being called. The operator then connected the proper phone lines. Today we can call almost anywhere in the world without the help of an operator.

Cables and Satellites About 30 years ago, a telephone line, or **cable**, was placed on the bottom of the Atlantic Ocean. A cable is a bundle of wires protected by a strong covering.

The cable ran all the way to Europe. It let Americans call people in Europe for the first time. Other

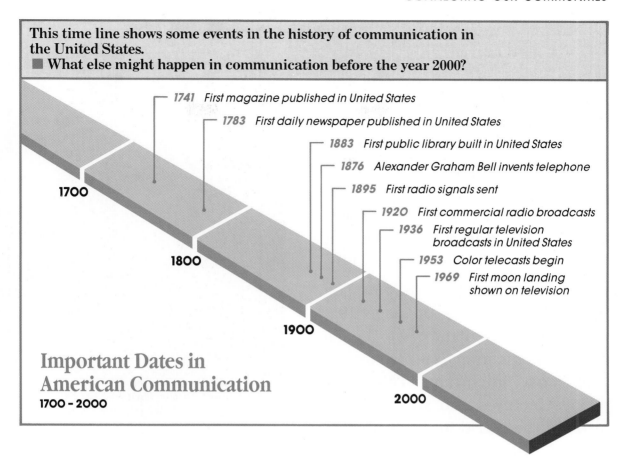

This time line shows some events in the history of communication in the United States.
■ What else might happen in communication before the year 2000?

1741 First magazine published in United States

1783 First daily newspaper published in United States

1883 First public library built in United States

1876 Alexander Graham Bell invents telephone

1895 First radio signals sent

1920 First commercial radio broadcasts

1936 First regular television broadcasts in United States

1953 Color telecasts begin

1969 First moon landing shown on television

1700

1800

1900

2000

Important Dates in American Communication
1700 - 2000

cables were placed in the Pacific Ocean. These cables allow us to call such distant places as Japan and South Korea.

Within the past 25 years, **satellites** (sat′ ə līts) have been used to communicate with people in other countries. A satellite is an object that circles the earth, carrying special communication equipment. Giant rockets have lifted the satellites thousands of miles into space.

On the ground, special stations send signals to a satellite. From out in space, the satellite sends the signals back to stations in another country.

The radio   Unlike a telephone, a radio is not connected by a wire to an office or to a radio station. A radio has a special **antenna** (an ten′ ə). This is a wire or a metal rod that picks up radio waves or signals. The signals are sent from radio stations. The radio changes these signals that we cannot hear into sounds that we can hear and understand.

Many people helped to bring about the invention of the radio. One was Guglielmo Marconi (gü lyel' mō mar kō' nē), who lived in Italy. In 1895, Marconi invented a way of sending radio signals through the air.

The radio was the first invention that let people hear about events as they took place.

Television   As you can see from the time line on page 191, television is one of the newer means of communication. It is also one of the most important. Television brings pictures and sounds from around the world into our homes.

In many ways, television is like radio. A television set uses an antenna to receive the signals sent out by the television station. The television set changes the signals into pictures that we see and sounds that we hear.

Today most Americans have a television set. Of every 100 homes in the United States, 98 homes have television. In each of these homes, people watch television for an average of 6 hours a day.

Television helps us to learn about faraway places. We can see and hear the leader of another

There is a television set in almost all of the homes in the United States.
■ What is your favorite television program?

country on a news program. We can watch a special show about life in Mexico, France, or China. We can watch a movie or see a ball game. There are many different shows to enjoy.

CHECKUP
1. What is communication?
2. How did people communicate long ago?
3. **Thinking Critically** Which event shown on the time line on page 191 do you think was most important? Why?

Words on Paper

In what different forms can words on paper serve as means of communication?

VOCABULARY

print	**reporter**
newspaper	**ZIP code**
magazine	

The Printed Word   **Print** is a very old and important means of communication. *Print* means "the words stamped in ink on paper." Whenever people read a **newspaper**, a **magazine**, or a book, they are getting information through print.

Information from Newspapers

More than 65 million newspapers are sold every day in the United States. A newspaper is made up of sheets of paper on which news stories are printed. Newspapers carry other useful information. They also carry ads telling people about certain goods or services. These ads are paid for by stores and other businesses.

Most newspapers are printed every day. They are called daily newspapers. There are more than 1,700 daily newspapers in the United States. A daily newspaper tells us what is happening in the world, in our country, and in our community. The most important news is given on the front page.

Some large communities have more than one daily newspaper. Sometimes one paper in a large community is printed in the early morning and another paper is printed in the afternoon.

Some newspapers are printed once a week. They are called weekly newspapers. They are usually printed in the suburbs of large cities or in small towns. A weekly paper has news of special interest in one community.

This family has divided up the Sunday newspaper so that everyone has part of it to read.
■ Which part are the girls enjoying?

One of the most important steps in producing a newspaper is gathering the news. This is the job of a **reporter**. A reporter interviews people to gather information for a news story.

Sometimes a reporter must research, or search out, facts for a story in other ways. The reporter does this to be sure the information is true. The facts must be correct. This is because millions of readers depend on newspapers for information.

Information from Magazines

A magazine is a collection of stories or articles. Most magazines have pictures and a bright cover. The cover shows the name of the magazine and usually has a picture on it. The cover may also list some of the stories in the magazine.

Each year several thousand different magazines are printed in the United States. Some are printed every week. Others are printed every month or every few months.

Magazines give us information and ideas about many different things. Some weekly magazines give us the news. Articles in magazines may tell more about an event than newspaper articles do.

These children want to buy some magazines. There are many interesting and colorful magazines that are just for children.
■ How can you tell that these children probably want to buy the magazines that they are looking at?

Some magazines are written for one group of people. There are magazines written for boys and girls in elementary schools. Some of these magazines are *Children's Digest, Boys' Life, Jack and Jill, Ranger Rick, Highlights for Children, and National Geographic World*. Have you seen any of these magazines?

Many magazines have articles on one or two special subjects. What would you learn about if you read *Flying, Golf Digest, Field & Stream, Skiing,* or *Better Homes and Gardens*?

Information from Books All books, including your schoolbooks, are a form of communication. By reading this social studies book, you have learned about many different communities. You have probably read other books at home. From each book, you get information and ideas. Sometimes you learn something new. Other times you learn more about a subject.

Books are one way that a person can communicate with many other people. Authors can share their ideas with people they probably will never see.

Interesting information and pictures can be found in magazines. This young reader enjoys his colorful magazine. ■ What is your favorite magazine?

Information From Letters The writing of letters is one of our oldest forms of communication. When you write a letter, you share your ideas with someone else.

It is the job of the United States Postal Service to deliver the mail that people send. There are about 30,000 post offices in our country. At a post office, a person can mail a letter or package and buy stamps. The money that people pay for stamps is used to run the postal service. A stamp shows that a person paid for a letter to be delivered.

Other countries also have post offices. As in our country, the post offices sell stamps that are put on mail. Many people like to collect stamps from faraway places.

Sending a Letter Let us imagine that you have written a letter to a friend in a community a thousand miles away. You put the letter in an envelope. On the front of the envelope, you write the name and address of your friend. You also put your own name and address in the upper left-hand corner.

Then you put a stamp on the envelope and drop the letter in a mailbox. What do you think happens to your letter then?

A postal service worker collects your letter along with others from the mailbox. The worker takes the mail to a post office. There other workers sort the mail. They put envelopes of the same size together.

The envelopes then go to a machine. On the envelopes the machine prints the name of the community where the letter was mailed. It also prints the date.

Writing a letter is a good way to communicate with a friend who lives in another community. Your letter stays safely in the mailbox until a letter carrier takes it out.
■ Have you ever mailed a letter to a friend?

The machine *cancels*, or marks, the stamp. This means that the stamp cannot be used a second time.

Another machine reads the **ZIP code** on the envelope. The ZIP code is a group of numbers that are part of the address. From the numbers, postal workers can tell where each letter is going.

Letters going to the same area are put together. Then a truck carries the mail to an airport. At the airport your letter is put on an airplane going to the city where your friend lives.

In that city a mail truck meets the airplane. Workers unload the bags full of mail. The truck carries the mailbags to a post office in the community where your friend lives. There the mail is sorted according to ZIP code again. If your friend lives in a large city, the ZIP code will show to what part of the city the letter should be sent.

At the post office in that part of the city, a letter carrier picks up the mail. The letter carrier sorts the mail according to address, and then delivers it. Your letter is delivered safely to your friend.

These postal service workers are sorting the mail according to ZIP code in a Denver, Colorado, post office. It is very important to put a ZIP code on the envelope.

■ How would you feel if you got a letter from a friend?

A space station like the one above is a satellite in which people can live and work as they circle the earth.
■ Would you like to live in space?

An Ever-Changing World In this chapter you have read about some very important means of transportation and communication. You have also learned how transportation and communication bring people together.

By traveling to other places, we can see how other people live. By sharing ideas and information with them, we begin to know them better. We can better understand what is going on in the world.

The world as we know it is always changing. People are always trying to invent new products. They try to figure out new ways of doing things in order to make our lives better. Doctors are working to make us healthier. They are discovering new medicines and ways of treating diseases.

New ways of building houses, offices, and stores will be developed. More and more buildings may be heated by *solar energy*, or power from the sun. Solar energy may be one way to conserve on our use of oil.

There will be changes, too, in transportation and communication. In the future we may be able to move from place to place and communicate in ways that we have not yet thought of.

Soon you will have come to the end of this book. But the world will go right on changing. And you will go on asking questions and searching for answers. Maybe you will be one of those great inventors who find the kind of answers that helps the whole world.

CHECKUP

1. Can you name three examples of communication through print?
2. How do ZIP codes help the delivery of mail?
3. **Thinking Critically** Which kind of reading do you think is the best way to get information: newspapers, magazines, books, or letters? Why?

Reading a Mileage Chart

MEASURING DISTANCE

A map scale is one way to find out how far one place is from another. A second way is to use a mileage chart. A mileage chart is usually found on a road map. It helps a map reader find the number of miles between places.

READING A MILEAGE CHART

Look at the chart below. Place a finger on Indianapolis on the side of the chart. Now place another finger on Milwaukee at the top of the chart. Move both fingers, one across and the other down, until they

meet. Did they meet at 268? That is about the number of road miles between the two cities.

SKILLS PRACTICE

Now do the same for the cities listed below. Number from **1** to **5** and write the correct number of miles between the two cities.

1. Jacksonville and Phoenix
2. Seattle and Chicago
3. Los Angeles and Milwaukee
4. Indianapolis and Memphis
5. Chicago and Jacksonville

MILEAGE CHART	Chicago	Indianapolis	Jacksonville	Los Angeles	Memphis	Milwaukee	Phoenix	Seattle
Chicago		181	980	2054	530	87	1713	2013
Indianapolis	181		799	2073	435	268	1698	2194
Jacksonville	980	799		2377	674	1067	2000	2924
Los Angeles	2054	2073	2377		1817	2087	389	1131
Memphis	530	435	674	1817		612	1442	2290
Milwaukee	87	268	1067	2087	612		1751	1940
Phoenix	1713	1698	2000	389	1442	1751		1437
Seattle	2013	2194	2924	1131	2290	1940	1437	

CHAPTER 8 REVIEW

MAIN IDEAS

1. Transportation enables people and goods to get from one place to another.
2. The major means of transportation are automobiles, trains, ships, and airplanes.
3. Communication enables people to share ideas and information and to learn more about the world in which they live.
4. The telephone, the radio, and television have brought about great changes in communication.
5. Newspapers, magazines, and books are important sources of information about the world.
6. Letter writing is one of the oldest forms of communication.

VOCABULARY REVIEW

Write the numbers **1** to **10** on a sheet of paper. Match the words with their meanings below.

a. communication	**f.** invent
b. newspaper	**g.** magazine
c. antenna	**h.** subway
d. reporter	**i.** ZIP code
e. satellite	**j.** suburb

1. One who gathers facts for a news story
2. To make something that no one else had ever made
3. An object that circles the earth carrying communications equipment
4. A smaller community near a large city
5. A train that runs under the ground
6. A collection of stories or articles that is usually printed each week or each month
7. Numbers used by the postal service to speed up mail delivery
8. The giving and receiving of ideas and information
9. A wire or metal rod that picks up radio or television signals
10. Sheets of paper printed with the news

CHAPTER CHECKUP

1. What is the most common means of land transportation for travelers in our country?
2. What different kinds of railroad cars are there?
3. **Thinking Critically** What do you think is the main difference between television and radio as means of communication?
4. **Thinking Critically** If you wanted to tell a secret to a friend in another community, what means of communication would you use?

APPLYING KNOWLEDGE

1. Make a booklet of pictures, showing different kinds of transportation. Label each picture.
2. Write a newspaper story telling about something that has happened at school or in your community.
3. Address an envelope to a friend. Be sure to include the ZIP code. Draw a stamp in the proper place.

SUMMARIZING UNIT 3

REVIEWING VOCABULARY

1. income   Income is the money people earn. Everyone needs some form of income so they can pay for the costs of daily living. What are some of the ways in which people earn an income?

2. insecticide   Insecticides are chemicals that farmers spray on their crops. For what purpose do farmers use insecticides?

3. fuels   Fuels can be burned to make heat or to make power for running machines. Name two important fuels. Can you think of any other kind of fuel?

4. conservation   Conservation is the wise use and protection of our natural resources. Give several examples of how people in our country help to conserve these resources.

5. communication   Through communication we share ideas and information. Name some ways in which people have been communicating for a very long time. Name some newer means of communication.

EXPRESSING YOURSELF

1. Who would you rather be? Imagine that you could choose between being a coal miner and being a worker on an offshore oil platform. Who would you rather be? Explain your decision.

2. Thinking like a farmer Imagine that you were a farmer and you could save your crop by using a certain kind of insecticide. However, that chemical would also kill the birds and small animals around your land. What would you do?

3. Doing something new What if you could be a famous inventor, like those mentioned in Chapter 8? What kind of invention would you like to make?

4. Old ways or new ways? Long ago the most common means of land transportation was the horse. Today it is the automobile. Think of the good things and the bad things about each means of transportation. Which do you like better—the old ways or the new ways? Explain your decision.

5. Getting the news If you were a reporter for a big city's daily newspaper, what kind of news story would you most like to work on?

The United States—
Citizenship and History

If you have muddy shoes, you clean them before you go inside. You are obeying a rule. Someone in your family made that rule. Cars stop when a police officer holds up a hand. The drivers are obeying a rule called a law.

You know who makes the rules in your family. In Unit 4 you will learn more about who makes the laws for your community, your state, and your nation.

These children have just come home from school on a rainy day.
■ **What rule are they obeying?**

The crossing guard is helping these students get to school safely.
- What rule must the students obey?
- What law must the drivers obey?

Sometimes a person might break a law and get arrested. Then a judge
must decide whether the law was really broken or not.
The judge also decides what the punishment should be if the
law was broken.
- What might the person sitting in front of the judge be doing?

Communities pay judges and police officers to do their work. These people are community service workers. Communities depend on service workers to do many things for them. You have read about some service workers in Chapter 4. In this unit you will learn more about service workers who work for a community and how the community pays them for their work.

These men are very important community workers. They help to keep their city clean.
■ What might happen if there were no workers to take away garbage and trash?

All of our community workers are important. Community workers help keep us safe and healthy. They keep our roads repaired. They keep our parks and playgrounds pleasant places to be. They see that we get clean water to drink and fair laws to obey. We could not live in our communities without the services of these workers.

Some community service workers take part in holiday parades. Everybody enjoys the flags and music and costumes of a parade. People in communities celebrate many holidays. Some holidays are celebrated in only one community. Others are celebrated by the whole country.

This community in Pennsylvania is celebrating a holiday called Laurel Day. All the beautiful laurel flowers are in bloom around the town.

■ Can you tell what service workers are taking part in this parade?

These community workers are marching in a holiday parade in New York City. They look fine in their uniforms.
■ What do you call these service workers?

9 Citizenship

Serving the Community

Why do communities provide services?

VOCABULARY

| tax | property | property tax |

A Fire Fighter   "My name is Al O'Brien. I work for my community. I am a fire fighter, but I don't ride on fire trucks. I work on a fireboat.

"My community has a large port where hundreds of ships come every year. There

This fireboat is helping to put out a dangerous fire at a dock in the Gulf of Mexico.
■ What do you think might have caused the fire?

is always a chance of a fire on a ship, on the docks, or in a warehouse. The fireboat that I work on is here to help put out these fires.

"The fireboat has large pumps. These pumps get water from underneath the boat. The water is then pumped through our hoses and onto the fire.

"I have to know how to put out fires. I have to know how to save people who might fall into the water. That means that I must be a good swimmer. I must also know first aid

so that I can quickly care for someone who has been hurt.

"I help to keep the water in the port clean, too. My fireboat has special equipment to help clean up anything that might spill into the water from the ships. Several times my boat has worked to clean up oil that was spilled from a ship. It is good to know that I can help protect the port and its water. It is good to know I am serving my community."

A Lifeguard "My name is Judy Rosales. I am a lifeguard here at the swimming pool. I work for the people of my community. My community's Department of Parks and Recreation pays me to be sure that everyone obeys the pool rules and swims or plays safely.

"I had to have special lifeguard training and pass the tests. I had to show that I can swim for a long time. I also had to show that I know how to help save people.

"Much of my day is spent in a chair high above the pool. From my chair I can see everyone in the water. I watch carefully to be sure that everyone in the pool is safe. Several times I have had to jump into the pool to save someone.

The lifeguard is helping a little girl learn how to swim in this community pool.
■ Do you think the little girl looks happy or a bit scared?

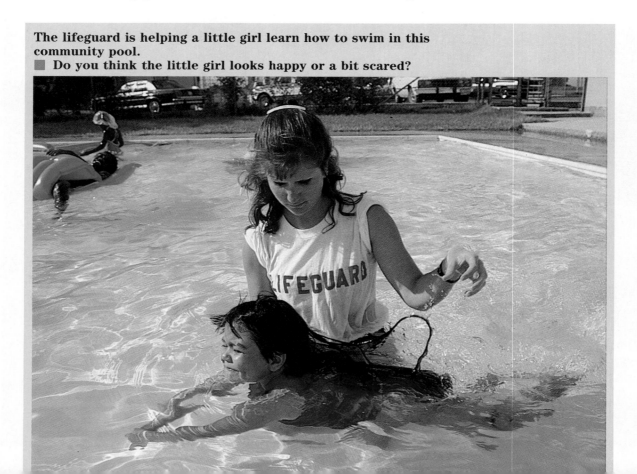

"I also watch to be sure that no one is running alongside the pool. Sometimes a person might slip and get hurt. And I have to see that people who jump off the diving board are not jumping too close to the swimmers.

"My favorite part of the job is the swimming lessons I give. It's fun to teach small children how to swim, enjoy the water, and follow safety rules. It is a good way to serve my community!"

A Road Planner "My name is Bill Schultz. I work for my community's Road and Highway Department. My community is growing. There are more and more cars and trucks using our roads. My job is to help plan and build new roads. I help decide where the roads should be built.

"You might have seen people in your own community who have jobs like mine. Much of our work is done close to busy roads. We wear brightly-colored hats and shirts or jackets. They help keep us safe. The bright colors make it easy for drivers to see us.

"We use special tools and equipment to be sure that new roads will be built correctly. We

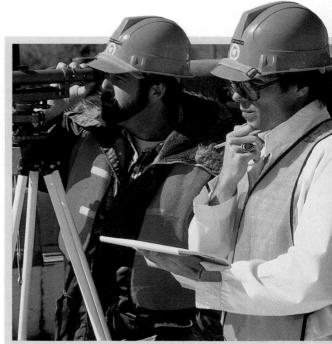

These workers are planning how to build a road in just the right place.
■ Why are they wearing bright vests and hard, colorful hats?

put some of this equipment on special poles and stands that we carry. This equipment helps us know if we are building the road in the right place and at the right height.

"It is nice to know that I play a part in building and improving the roads of my community."

A Doctor "My name is Rita Davis. I am a doctor. But I do not have an office like many other doctors. I help people who suddenly become very sick or get badly hurt. They need to get to a hospital quickly.

"The people in my community set up what we call 'Life Flight.' Life Flight uses a helicopter to carry people to the hospital. I ride in the helicopter so I can care for sick or hurt people right away. Sometimes fast care can save a person's life.

"A pilot, a special Life Flight nurse, and a doctor are always at the hospital. If a phone call tells us that we are needed, we run to a place on top of the hospital. This is where our helicopter lands and takes off. We can usually reach a person in trouble within a few minutes.

"Most of the people that we care for have been hurt in accidents. We carry all kinds of equipment and supplies on the helicopter. After finding out what is wrong, we can begin caring for the person right there. Next, we have to be sure that it is safe to move the person. Then we carefully place the person in the helicopter. While we are in the air, one of us calls the hospital. The people at the hospital have to know what is wrong right away. Then they can get ready to help. They can get the right medicines and equipment for us.

"The quick service that we provide has saved the lives of several people in my community."

Services for Everyone People in a community depend on certain things. They depend on good roads when they drive to work or to a store. They depend on police and fire fighters to help keep them safe. They depend on schools and teachers to help their children learn. They depend on many services.

Most people cannot pay for their own fire truck or police

A medical team helps a patient aboard a Life Flight helicopter.
■ Where has the helicopter landed?

A worker repairs the shiny red paint on a fire truck.
■ What parts of a fire truck do you think are most important to keep in good condition?

department. They cannot afford to build their own schools. They are not able to build and care for their own roads. That is why communities provide many needed services for their citizens.

In Chapter 4 you read that services are the kinds of work that help people. You know about the work that teachers, police officers, and other community service workers do. You have just read about some unusual service workers. You can understand why services are important to a commmunity.

Paying for Services A lot of money is needed to provide community services. The many people who work for your community have to be paid. Places such as parks and swimming pools have to be kept clean. Buildings such as schools and libraries must have heat and electricity. Roads have to be built and repaired. Fire trucks, police cars, and school buses must be kept in good condition. Who pays for all of these things? Everyone in the community does. We all pay because we are all helped by the services.

The people in this office are lined up to pay their property taxes. They are waiting in one of the offices of their community's government building.

■ **Do you know about other taxes that people pay?**

The money that we pay to our community is called a **tax**. Taxes are used to pay for community services. Most of the tax money comes from people who own **property**. They own land, houses, or other kinds of buildings in their community. The owners of land and buildings pay a **property tax**. The amount of the tax depends on how much the property is worth. If your house is worth more than your neighbor's house, then you must pay more property tax than your neighbor pays.

Serving your community and helping to pay for community services is an important part of being a good citizen.

CHECKUP

1. What are some services provided by communities?
2. Why are taxes important?
3. **Thinking Critically** Why do communites provide services?

Community Rules

Why do we need rules and laws?

VOCABULARY

council	vote	penalty
mayor	judge	fine
election		

Rules for Everyone   There are rules for the games we play. There are rules at home. There are rules at school. There are rules in every community. There are rules that everyone in the United States must follow.

Who makes all these rules? You may have made up rules for a new game you wanted to play. But most rules are made by parents and other adults.

Most of the rules at home are made to keep you and your family healthy and safe from harm. Some rules are made to protect property, or the things you own. One rule in most homes is that you should never play with matches. Why is this an important rule?

One of these pictures shows a child obeying a family rule. The other shows people obeying a community rule.
■ What rule is being obeyed in each picture?

School Rules   Some of the rules in your school may be like the ones below. Read each rule. Why do you think each is an important rule?

Rules of Our School

1. Remain in your seat while riding on the school bus.
2. Keep your classroom and lunchroom clean.
3. Put all books and papers away when you leave for lunch, recess, or at the end of the day.
4. Walk, do not run, in the halls.
5. Talk in class only when given permission.
6. Line up quietly and follow the teacher during a fire drill.
7. Keep quiet in the library so other people can study.

Rules in a Community   A community's rules are called laws. Wherever you go in a city or town, you see signs showing some of these laws. You probably have seen traffic signs that say Stop or One Way. You have also seen signs that say Do Not Litter or Keep Off the Grass.

These laws were made to help protect people and property in the community. All the citizens of a community are responsible for obeying its laws.

Community Lawmakers   The laws of a community are made by community leaders. These leaders are called by different names in different communities. In many

Members of a city council talk about plans and laws for their community.
■ What helps them get their voices heard in this big room?

The man in the voting booth is 18 years old. He is going to vote for the first time. Another man is signing his name before voting.
■ Can you guess why he has to sign before he can vote?

communities the leaders are members of the town or city **council**. A council is a group of men and women who are chosen by the people in a community to make laws and plans for the community. Most communities also have a **mayor**. The mayor's job is to help make the laws and to see that the laws are carried out. A mayor or a council are part of a community's government. People must choose their leaders wisely.

In the United States, people choose their government leaders in an **election**. In an election citizens can **vote,** or say whom they would like as leaders. The people who get the most votes win the election. These men and women become the government leaders.

The mayor and the council also must make sure that their community provides good services for its people. You have read about many of these services. But there are others for which a community's leaders are responsible. Some of these services depend on seeing that natural resources are used

Tom Bradley (1917–   )

As a small boy, Tom Bradley learned what hard work was. He was born on December 29, 1917 in Calvert, Texas. His parents were sharecroppers in the cotton fields. Sharecroppers work on farmland for the person who owns the land. In return for their work, they receive a share of the crops. Cotton farming is hard work.

When he was 7 years old, Tom and his family headed for a new life in California. Tom did very well in the Los Angeles schools and at the University of California. He got good grades and he was very good at games and sports.

In 1940, Tom Bradley became a police officer. While he was working for his community in the police force, he also went to school at night. He studied law. In 1961, Bradley left the police and went to work as a lawyer. But he still worked for his community. For 10 years he was on the Los Angeles City Council.

That is the group that helps the mayor run the city.

In 1973, Tom Bradley himself was elected mayor of Los Angeles and has held that job ever since. He still believes in hard work. By 7:30 A.M., Mayor Bradley is already at his desk in City Hall. For the next 12 to 15 hours, he is busy taking care of the community's business. One of the things he has worked hard at is cutting down crime. He has also worked to get cleaner air and water for Los Angeles. Tom Bradley has become one of the best and most popular government leaders in America.

wisely. For example, the government must make sure that the community always has enough good clean water. Providing good water is an important community service.

You can see that a community's government leaders are very important. They must make laws that help and protect the people of the community. They must plan well and wisely. Voting for government leaders is an important part of good citizenship.

Obeying Laws In Chapter 7, you learned that we are all responsible for conserving our natural resources. Good citizens use natural resources wisely. You know that good citizens try to serve their community. You read that paying for community services is part of good citizenship. You have learned that good citizens also help choose their community's leaders by voting in elections. All citizens have another important job. That job is to obey the laws of the community.

This water is going from the Colorado River to the cities of Los Angeles and San Diego through a kind of canal called an aqueduct.
■ How do the signs help keep the water clean?

People who may have broken a law come before a judge in a *court*. Courts and judges are part of our government.

■ **How can you tell that this picture shows an American court?**

Most people in a community do a very good job of obeying the laws. They want to help make their community a safe place to live and work.

A few people do not obey these laws. This is why communities need police officers. The women and men who work for the police department protect the people from those who break the laws.

When it appears that someone has broken a law, that person may have to appear in court before a **judge.** The judge listens to those who say a law was broken and to those who say that a law was not broken. The judge must be fair and hear all sides of the case. If the judge decides that the person disobeyed a law, then the judge also has to decide on a **penalty** for the person. A penalty is a punishment. There are different penalties for breaking different laws. A person may have to pay a **fine.** This is a certain amount of money that must be paid for not obeying a law. Sometimes a person is put in jail.

CHECKUP

1. What are laws?
2. Why do we need rules and laws?
3. **Thinking Critically** Name one law that you think is important in your community. Tell why you chose it.

State Governments

What is a state government?

VOCABULARY

capitol	Governor's
legislature	Mansion
governor	

Fifty States   You learned in Chapter 1 that your community is part of a state. You also learned that there are 50 states in the United States. Each of these 50 states has its own government. The people in each state elect their own leaders who make laws for that state.

You also learned in Chapter 1 that each state has a special city that is its state capital. The leaders of the state meet in the state capital to make laws to help and protect all the people of the state.

There are state traffic laws telling people how to drive their cars safely. There are laws telling boys and girls how many years they must go to school. The laws also tell the schools how many days they must be open each year. There are state laws telling people not to throw litter in state parks and on highways. There are state laws telling people not to pollute the air and water. People who are caught breaking these laws may be fined an amount of money or may even be sent to jail.

Each state has a law telling how many years boys and girls in that state must go to school.
■ What is the name of the school?

One State Capital   We will now look at one state's capital. Nashville is the capital of the state of Tennessee. But it was not always the state capital. In Tennessee's early history, four different towns served as the center of government. Nashville became the state capital in 1826.

STATE CAPITOLS

Honolulu, Hawaii

Hartford, Connecticut

Raleigh, North Carolina

Springfield, Illinois

Salem, Oregon

Juneau, Alaska

A state capitol is the government building where a state legislature meets and makes laws for the state.
■ Why, do you think, is there often a statue in front of the capitol?

(*Left*) The capitol in Nashville, Tennessee, was designed with many columns to look like a Greek temple. (*Right*) Within the capitol is the Senate Chamber where state senators meet.
■ What are the two flags in the Senate Chamber?

The Capitol Building   One of the most important buildings in any state capital is the **capitol** building. It is in the capitol that the **legislature** (lej′ ə slā chər) meets. The legislature is a group of elected government leaders who make the laws of the state. They also decide how the taxes paid to the state should be spent.

The present capitol building in Nashville, Tennessee, was built on Capitol Hill, the highest point in the city. Work was started on the capitol building in 1845 and completed in 1859. The capitol was built from marble that came from Tennessee.

The capitol building was designed by a famous architect (är′ kə tekt) named William Strickland, who lived in Nashville. An architect makes plans for buildings and sees that these plans are carried out by the people who actually put up the buildings. The capitol was designed with many columns to look like a Greek temple. During the building of the capitol, William Strickland died. He was buried within the walls of the capitol. The building was completed by his son. Tennessee's capitol has been in constant use since 1853.

When people visit Nashville, many of them drive by the capitol and admire its beauty. Some people take the free tour of the inside of the capitol. Among other things, visitors see the large rooms where the members of the legislature hold their meetings.

The Governor The **governor** of a state is the most important leader of the state government. He or she works with the state legislature to make laws for the whole state. The governor also makes sure that state laws are obeyed. The citizens of a state choose their governor by voting in an election.

The home used by a governor is known as the **Governor's Mansion.** These buildings are usually very large homes near the state capitol building. In Tennessee the Governor's Mansion is near Nashville. It was once a private home until the state bought the building and grounds in 1949.

State Offices The offices of the state government take up several large buildings in Nashville. The State Highway Department, the State Education Agency, and other parts of the state government all have their offices in Nashville.

Nashville's War Memorial (*center*) honors Tennessee's men and women who died in world wars.
■ Is there a war memorial in your community?

Many people in state capitals all over the country work in such offices for their own state governments.

CHECKUP
1. Why is a city that is a state capital important?
2. What is a governor?
3. **Thinking Critically** How are state and community governments different?

Our Nation's Capital

What is the purpose of Washington, D.C.?

VOCABULARY

White House
monument
archives
Declaration of
Independence

Constitution of
the United
States
astronaut

Washington, D.C.   You have seen that each of our states has a capital. Students in North Carolina have a different state capital from those living in California. But there is one capital that we all share. That is the capital of our country. This city is Washington, D.C.

Find our national capital on the map on page 255. Notice that Washington, D.C., is not in any state. You can see that Washington, D.C., is between Maryland and Virginia.

Washington, D.C., is built on land given to the United States by Maryland. Washington, D.C., was planned as a government city. It was named for George Washington, who was the first President of the United States.

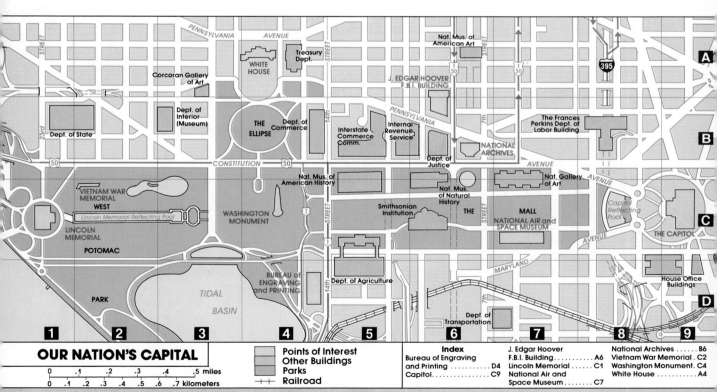

OUR NATION'S CAPITAL

0   .1   .2   .3   .4   .5 miles
0   .1   .2   .3   .4   .5   .6   .7 kilometers

Points of Interest
Other Buildings
Parks
+++ Railroad

Index

Bureau of Engraving
and Printing D4
Capitol C9

J. Edgar Hoover
F.B.I. Building A6
Lincoln Memorial C1
National Air and
Space Museum C7

National Archives B6
Vietnam War Memorial . C2
Washington Monument . C4
White House A4

This map of Washington, D.C., shows many interesting places to visit.
■ What Point of Interest is in box C-1?

223

OUR NATION
THE UNITED STATES OF AMERICA

The Pledge of Allegiance to the Flag of the United States

I pledge allegiance to the Flag of the
United States of America, and to the Republic
for which it stands, one Nation under God,
indivisible, with liberty and justice for all.

Flag of the United States

National Anthem
The Star-Spangled Banner

Oh, say, can you see, by the dawn's early light,
What so proudly we hailed at the twilight's last gleaming?
Whose broad stripes and bright stars, through the perilous fight,
O'er the ramparts we watched were so gallantly streaming?
And the rockets' red glare, the bombs bursting in air,
Gave proof through the night that our flag was still there.
Oh, say, does that star-spangled banner yet wave
O'er the land of the free and the home of the brave?

National Capitol Building

American Eagle

Great Seal of United States

Visiting Washington, D.C. There are many interesting places to visit in Washington, D.C. There are too many places to see in one day. To help you know more about the capital, let us take a tour. We will visit some of the famous and important places. Our guides are two high school students.

A Tour of Washington, D.C.

Bill: Washington, D.C., is a very beautiful city. Beth and I are proud to live here and go to school here.

Beth: The first place that we will visit on our tour is the **White House.** This is the building in which the President of the United States lives. The President's office is here, too. The President takes care of much of the country's business in the White House. The White House has 132 rooms. It also has a very large yard that covers 18 acres (8 ha).

Bill: We can see five rooms in the White House. These are the only ones open to visitors. We will not be able to see the rooms where the President lives and works.

Beth: Our next stop is a famous **monument** (mon′ yə mənt). It is the Washington Monument. It was built to help people remember George Washington. There is an elevator that we can take to the top of the monument. From there we can see most of the city.

Thousands of people come each year to visit the White House (left) and the Washington Monument (right).
■ **Find these places on the map of Washington, D.C., on page 223.**

Bill: We are going now to the National **Archives** (är′ kīvs). This is where records of our country's past are kept. These old books and papers are important to all of us. We never want to forget our nation's history.

Beth: In the National Archives are two very special things. The first one is the **Declaration of Independence**. This is a paper that was written more than 200 years ago. The Declaration of Independence gives the reasons why our country no longer wanted to be ruled by the government leaders of England.

The second important paper is the **Constitution of the United States**. The Constitution was also written more than 200 years ago. It set up the ways in which our government would work. Very wise people wrote the Declaration of Independence and the Constitution.

Bill: From here we are going to the Capitol. This is the building in which the men and women who are elected to Congress meet. It is here that the plans and laws for our whole country are made. The laws that are made by Congress must be obeyed by all the people in all the states of our nation.

The boys and girls on the left are looking at the Constitution of the United States. On the right is our national capitol building.
■ **Why, do you think, is there glass covering the Constitution?**

Interesting Notes About Our Presidents

George Washington became our nation's first President in 1789.

Woodrow Wilson was the first President to speak over the radio.

Franklin Delano Roosevelt was the first President to appear on television.

The first President to travel to a foreign country was Theodore Roosevelt.

Eight Presidents died in office: William Henry Harrison, Zachary Taylor, Abraham Lincoln, James Garfield, William McKinley, Warren G. Harding, Franklin D. Roosevelt, and John Kennedy.

Three Presidents died on the Fourth of July: John Adams and Thomas Jefferson in 1826; James Monroe in 1831.

Presidents Ulysses Grant, Dwight Eisenhower, and Jimmy Carter were graduates of United States military service academies. Grant and Eisenhower graduated from West Point and Carter graduated from Annapolis.

Courtesy of the Harvard University Portrait Collection

The first President to be sworn into office in Washington, D.C., was Thomas Jefferson.

Only one child of a President was born in the White House. That was Esther Cleveland, the daughter of Grover Cleveland in 1893.

There have been three sets of presidential relatives: John Adams and John Quincy Adams (father and son); William Henry Harrison and Benjamin Harrison (grandfather and grandson); Theodore Roosevelt and Franklin Roosevelt (cousins).

Beth: After our visit to the Capitol, we are going to the National Air and Space Museum. In here we can see the first airplane that ever flew. That was the airplane flown by the Wright brothers in North Carolina. Here also is the *Spirit of St. Louis.* This was the first airplane to fly across the Atlantic Ocean without stopping.

The pilot of the *Spirit of St. Louis* was a brave man named Charles Lindbergh.

Bill: You can also see different spacecraft used by **astronauts** (as′

trə nôts). An astronaut is a man or woman who is a pilot or a scientist. Astronauts travel and work in an American spacecraft. They try to learn more about outer space.

Some of these brave people have traveled to the moon. In this museum we can see and touch some of the rocks that they brought back from the moon.

Beth: A few blocks away is the Bureau of Engraving and Printing. This is where our money is designed, or drawn and planned. There are huge machines here. They print a lot of the paper money that we have in our pockets.

Bill: Now we are at the FBI building. *FBI* stands for Federal Bureau of Investigation. The men and women who work for the FBI are called special agents. They are carefully trained in their work. The FBI investigates, or looks into, more than 180 different kinds of crimes. Some of these crimes are kidnapping, bank robbery, and attacking the President.

Beth: We are going to leave the city of Washington to visit some important places just across the Potomac River in Virginia. The first

The Air and Space Museum is a favorite place for boys and girls to visit. ■ How can trees grow in this museum?

place we will visit is the Pentagon. It is the largest office building in the world. It covers 29 acres (12 ha). Almost 27,000 people work here. In the Pentagon are the main offices for the Army, Navy, and Air Force.

Bill: Not far from the Pentagon is Arlington National Cemetery. Thousands of people are buried here. Each of them has served in the United States Army, Navy, Air Force, or Marines. President John F. Kennedy is buried here. He once served in the Navy.

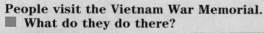
People visit the Vietnam War Memorial. What do they do there?

Many people come here and to the Vietnam War Memorial in Washington, D.C. On the stone of the Vietnam War Memorial are the names of people who fought and died for America in a terrible war. People visit these places because they want to remember the men and women who served America in the armed forces.

Beth: Our last stop in Virginia is Mount Vernon. This was the home of George Washington. His grave and many of his belongings are here. You can see some of the fields where Mr. Washington planted crops. Mount Vernon looks out on the Potomac River. You can see the rocking chair that Mr. Washington sat in as he looked across the river.

Bill: I hope that you have enjoyed your visit to our nation's capital. You should try to come back again someday. There are many more interesting places to visit here.

CHECKUP

1. What is the White House?
2. What is Mount Vernon?
3. **Thinking Critically** If you were to go to Washington, D.C., what place would you like most to visit? Tell why.

Understanding Cause and Effect

WHAT IS CAUSE AND EFFECT?

Cause and **effect** is when one thing happens that makes something else happen. For example, in the 1950s many people were concerned about the dangers of using pesticides carelessly. They expressed their concern by writing and speaking out on the matter. As a result of their concern, government leaders made a law that stopped the use of harmful pesticides. The **cause** was the concern shown by many people. The **effect** was the making of a new law.

Understanding cause-and-effect relationship helps you to see how some events cause other events.

SKILLS PRACTICE

Look at the Cause and Effect chart. Match an **EFFECT** picture with each **CAUSE** picture.

SKILLS PRACTICE

Write the numbers 1 to 5 on a sheet of paper. Match each **CAUSE** with the correct **EFFECT**.

CAUSE

1. Students ran in the school halls.
2. The community wanted to build a new zoo.
3. People in the state wanted everyone in a car to wear a seat belt.
4. More than half the voters in the country did not like the way the President was leading the country.
5. A driver parked in a No Parking area.

EFFECT

A. Taxes were raised.
B. A new person was elected as our country's leader.
C. Jill slipped on the floor and hit her head.
D. A new law was passed.
E. A police officer gave a ticket to a driver.

CHAPTER 9 REVIEW

MAIN IDEAS

1. People in a community need certain services for their health and well being that they themselves cannot afford. Therefore the community provides these services for its citizens.
2. The people in a community pay taxes. Tax money is used to pay for needed services.
3. We need rules and laws in order to protect people and property.
4. Laws are made by the leaders of a community, state, or nation.
5. A state government is made up of women and men elected by the people to make laws and plans for their state at the state capital.
6. Washington, D.C., the capital of the United States, is where laws and plans for the whole country are made by elected government leaders.
7. Good citizens serve their community, vote for its lawmakers, and obey its laws.

VOCABULARY REVIEW

Write the numbers **1** to **10** on a sheet of paper. Read each sentence below and decide whether it is true or false. The underlined words are vocabulary terms. Write **T** if the sentence is true and **F** if it is false.

1. A <u>fine</u> is an amount of money that must be paid for not obeying a law.
2. We <u>vote</u> to choose our leaders.
3. A <u>mayor</u> is the leader of a state.
4. We pay a <u>tax</u> to vote in an election.
5. A governor lives in the <u>White House.</u>
6. A <u>capitol</u> building is where a mayor lives.
7. A state <u>legislature</u> makes laws for a state.
8. A <u>judge</u> decides whether or not a law has been broken.
9. The amount of <u>property tax</u> a person pays to the community depends on how much the property is worth.
10. The National <u>Archives</u> is a place where bees are kept.

CHAPTER CHECKUP

1. Who makes the laws in most communities?
2. Who pays for community services?
3. Where does a state legislature meet?
4. Why is a judge important?
5. **Thinking Critically** How is the national capital different from state capitals?

APPLYING KNOWLEDGE

1. Make a list of the rules you follow at school. Beside each rule write the penalty for breaking the rule.
2. Prepare a chart on your state, giving the information listed below. You may draw pictures to illustrate some of the information.

Name	State flower
Size in square miles	State tree
Population	State animal
Largest city	State bird
Capital city	Year it became a state

10 Our Nation Celebrates Its Past

Communities Celebrate Holidays

Why do we celebrate holidays?

Vocabulary

tribe   custom

Special Days All of us enjoy holidays. Holidays are very special days. On some holidays we do not go to school. Grown-ups do not go to work. Parades or parties may be part of celebrating a holiday.

A parade on Independence Day is one way to celebrate the holiday.
■ On what date is Independence Day celebrated in our country?

Holidays to Remember Special People

Some of our holidays help us remember special people who are close to us. These people may be mothers or fathers or grandparents. We remember them and all of their help and care on Mother's Day, Father's Day, and Grandparents' Day. We may send cards or give presents to celebrate these days. Or we may do something helpful or pleasant for our special person.

Some holidays are celebrated to remember famous people. This kind of holiday takes place on the birthday of the person being remembered. Can you think of a famous person whose birthday we celebrate?

Festivals in Honor of Friendship

There are celebrations to help us remember special friends. One well-known celebration is the National Cherry Blossom Festival in Washington, D.C. It is held each spring when the cherry trees are covered with their flowers. The celebration reminds us of the friendship between the people of Japan and the United States.

In 1912, the city of Tokyo, Japan gave 3,000 cherry trees to the city of Washington. Helen Taft, wife of President William Howard Taft, planted the first of the cherry trees in our country's capital. Since then the trees have grown and thousands of people come each spring to enjoy their beautiful flowers.

Special events are planned for each day of the festival. Among them are the lighting of a 300-year old Japanese stone lantern, the playing of Japanese and American

Washington, D.C., is especially beautiful during cherry-blossom time. The white building is the Thomas Jefferson Memorial.
■ Why, do you think, was Jefferson honored with a memorial?

music, and shows of art and crafts from Japan. Have you visited Washington during this festival?

Another celebration in honor of a group of people is held each year in Bismarck, North Dakota. Find Bismarck on the map of the United States on pages 254–255.

This celebration is called the United Tribes International Pow-Wow. Native Americans from more than 40 **tribes** in Canada and the United States take part in the celebration. An Indian tribe is a group of families who share the same way of life. This pow-wow, or meeting, is the largest gathering of Native Americans in the nation.

In addition to thousands of Indians, many people who are not Indians also come to the pow-wow. Native Americans enjoy sharing their **customs**. A custom is the special way a group of people does something.

Many different events are held during the pow-wow. Among the events are Indian dances, shows of Indian arts and crafts, and an all-Indian rodeo.

This young Native American shows the traditional dress of his tribe.
■ Do you think he dresses this way when he goes to school?

Communities Have Special Holidays Every community has special days. One special day might celebrate when a community was first started. A holiday might celebrate an event in a community's past that it is very proud of.

In this chapter you will learn about several holidays that are shared by all of the communities in the United States.

CHECKUP
1. Why do we have holidays?
2. What is remembered during the celebration of National Cherry Blossom Festival?
3. **Thinking Critically** What are some holidays in your community?

Columbus Day

Why do we celebrate Columbus Day?

VOCABULARY

Indies

The East Indies Christopher Columbus was born in Italy, a country in Europe. Find Italy on the map on pages 258–259. As a boy, Columbus dreamed of sailing to faraway lands, and when he was 19 years old, he became a sailor.

On his voyages, Columbus heard much talk about the **Indies.** This was the name given to eastern and southern Asia. People in Europe wanted the spices, gold, and precious stones found in those far-off lands.

But it was hard to get to the Indies. Look at the map on pages 252–253. Ships from Europe had to sail hundreds of miles to reach the Indies. They went south along the coast of Africa and then east through the Indian Ocean. Often there were bad storms near the southern tip of Africa.

This old picture shows Columbus and his crew when they first sighted America after their long journey.
■ How can you tell that the crew were happy to see land?

Columbus's Idea   Columbus believed that there was an easier way to get to the Indies. The world is round, he thought. Maybe we could reach the Indies in the east by going west. We should sail west across the Atlantic Ocean.

This was a daring idea. In Columbus's day, people were afraid to sail far out into the Atlantic Ocean. Columbus set out to prove that his idea was right. The king and queen of Spain gave him three ships and supplies. Columbus hired sailors, and the ships left Spain in August 1492. Soon the ships headed out into the Atlantic.

Land at Last   For more than a month, the ships sailed westward, always out of sight of land. The sailors were afraid, but Columbus would not turn back. Then finally, on October 12, 1492, land came into sight. Columbus thought that the land he had reached was the Indies. So he called the people he found there Indians. But the world was much bigger than Christopher Columbus thought, and the Indies were still far away. It was not the Indies of Asia that lay directly across the Atlantic Ocean from Europe. It was America!

We often celebrate Columbus Day with parades.
■ Who is the man above dressed up as?

An October Holiday   We now celebrate Columbus Day on the second Monday of October. On that day we honor Christopher Columbus for sailing to America in 1492.

CHECKUP

1. Why did Europeans want to go to the Indies?
2. What was Columbus's idea?
3. **Thinking Critically**   What might Columbus have named the Indians if he had known that he had landed in America?

237

Thanksgiving Day

Why do we celebrate Thanksgiving Day?

VOCABULARY
Pilgrim

The Pilgrims The first Thanksgiving Day feast took place about 125 years after Columbus arrived in the New World. A group of people we call **Pilgrims** sailed from England on a ship named the *Mayflower*. They were seeking a place where they could live in peace and pray to God in their own way. In November 1620, after a voyage of 66 days, the Pilgrims landed in the New World. They landed on the coast of what is today the state of Massachusetts. There they started a community called Plymouth.

It was almost winter, and the Pilgrims set to work building huts for shelter. To get food, they fished, dug clams, and shot ducks and geese. But life was very hard that first cold winter. Many Pilgrims became sick. By spring, almost half of them had died.

A Thanksgiving Dinner Life became better with the coming of spring. Friendly Indians showed the

This picture shows an American artist's idea of what the Pilgrims' first Thanksgiving feast looked like.

■ Who was the Pilgrims' guest at this table?

"The Thanksgiving Feast" N.C. Wyeth. Courtesy of the Metropolitan Life Insurance Company. Photo by M. Varon 1985

Pilgrims how to prepare fields for growing corn. The fall harvest was plentiful. The Pilgrims were able to gather enough food from their fields for everyone. The leader of the Pilgrims declared that they would give thanks for their fine crops. They would celebrate with a thanksgiving feast.

Everyone in Plymouth joined in preparing for the feast. Some men went hunting. They brought back ducks and geese and wild turkeys. Some of the corn was ground to make a kind of flour called cornmeal. Then the women were able to bake cornmeal bread. The children picked wild berries and plums. The Pilgrims invited their Indian friends, who brought deer meat.

Much of the food was roasted over open fires. The Pilgrims and their guests ate at long tables that were set up outdoors. The feasting went on for 3 days.

As time went on, more and more people celebrated with prayer and feasting after the harvest. When the United States was formed and people moved west, they took the custom along with them. Now Thanksgiving Day is celebrated all across our country.

This family is celebrating Thanksgiving with a special dinner. What foods might the family eat?

A November Holiday We now celebrate Thanksgiving Day each year on the fourth Thursday of November. On that day, Americans give thanks to God for all the good things that have been given to them. People come together with families and friends to have a joyous feast.

CHECKUP

1. Why did the Pilgrims celebrate with a thanksgiving feast?
2. Who were the Pilgrims' guests at the 3-day feast in 1621?
3. **Thinking Critically** What might have happened to the Pilgrims without the help of friendly Indians?

239

Independence Day

Why do we celebrate Independence Day?

VOCABULARY

colony   delegate

The First Colonies   The first settlers from England arrived in the New World in 1607. During the next 100 years, the English set up several **colonies** along the Atlantic coast. A colony is a place that is located at a distance from the country that governs it.

In 1707 the countries of England, Scotland, and Wales joined to form the Kingdom of Great Britain. On the map on page 260, find the area called the United Kingdom. That is the name we use today for Great Britain. The people of Great Britain were called British. By 1733 there were 13 British colonies in America.

As time passed, many people in the colonies felt that they were not being treated fairly by Great Britain. They did not want to pay certain taxes that Great Britain asked them to pay. They felt that Great Britain really had no right to keep British soldiers in the American colonies.

Becoming Independent   In 1775, fighting broke out in Massachusetts between the colonists and British soldiers. The next month, each of the 13 colonies sent some people to speak for them at a big meeting in Philadelphia, Pennsylvania. Those people were called **delegates.** Their job was to decide what to do about the trouble with Great Britain.

Some colonists wanted to remain under British rule. But more and more colonists wanted to throw off the rule of Great Britain. So the delegates voted that the American

Delegates at the Philadelphia meeting read through the great Declaration of Independence.
■ How can you tell who wrote it?

colonies should become one free and independent country. This idea was set down in writing, in what we call the Declaration of Independence. You have read something about this important paper in Chapters 6 and 9.

The delegates signed the Declaration of Independence on July 4, 1776. Church bells were rung. Bonfires were lit. Cheering crowds filled the streets of cities and towns.

The War Goes on   Even though independence had been declared, the fighting went on. It was 7 years before the British gave up. The Americans had won the War for Independence.

The United States of America has now been independent for more than 200 years. During all those years the Fourth of July has been one of our biggest holidays.

A July Holiday   We celebrate Independence Day each year on July 4. It is the birthday of our country, the United States of America. On July 4, 1776, our country became free and independent.

Independence Day is also called the Fourth of July. People

Everyone enjoys watching firework displays on the Fourth of July.
■ **What did the boy do to celebrate the holiday?**

celebrate this holiday in many ways. Some communities have parades and games. In the evening there may be fireworks. Families join in picnics and cookouts. The American flag waves in front of public buildings, shops, and homes.

CHECKUP

1. Why did the American colonies want independence?
2. What is the Declaration of Independence?
3. **Thinking Critically**   What might have happened if the United States had lost the war?

Washington's Birthday

Why do we celebrate Washington's Birthday?

VOCABULARY

surveyor   militia

A Great Leader Our country became independent from Great Britain on July 4, 1776. But no one knew whether the United States could keep its independence. George Washington led his country through its early years. By the time he died, the United States was off to a good start as a free land.

Surveyor and Soldier George Washington was born on a plantation in Virginia on February 22, 1732.

Young George was good with numbers. By the time he was 15 years old, he was working as a **surveyor**. A surveyor measures land and makes maps.

By the age of 20, Washington was a captain in the Virginia **militia** (mə lish′ ə). The militia was a group of soldiers that a colony called upon in time of trouble. As a soldier, Washington made several trips into the unsettled country of the West. That land was claimed by France. Washington led his soldiers in battle against the French troops. He became known for his bravery.

A Fight for Freedom After Washington's marriage to Martha Custis, he and his wife lived on a large plantation called Mount Vernon. The peaceful life they lived there ended when Virginia and the other colonies fought for their independence from Great Britain. Washington was made the leader of the American army. He led the troops with great skill to win the War for Independence.

In 1787, delegates from the 13 states met in Philadelphia. George

George Washington was a great hero in the new nation.
■ How does this old picture tell you that people thought he was a hero?

These children wear clothes like those worn in Washington's time.
■ Why, do you think, are they dressed up like this?

Washington was chosen to run the meeting. The delegates wrote a set of new laws for the United States. It is known as the Constitution of the United States. It is still used today. You learned a little about our Constitution in Chapter 9.

Our First President   One of the new laws said that the United States should have a president. Everyone agreed that the person for the job was George Washington.

In 1789, Washington became our country's first President. After 8 years as President, he returned to Mount Vernon. He died in 1799.

A February Holiday   We now celebrate Washington's Birthday on the third Monday in February. No other American has been more admired than George Washington. It is said that he was "first in war, first in peace, and first in the hearts of his countrymen."

CHECKUP
1. What was Washington's earliest service as a soldier?
2. What part did Washington play in the writing of the Constitution?
3. **Thinking Critically** What might the United States be like if the new Constitution had said that our country should have a king instead of a president?

Memorial Day

Why do we observe Memorial Day?

VOCABULARY

Civil War   slavery

The Civil War   For more than 60 years after the great George Washington was President, our country grew bigger and stronger. Then a terrible war took place. On one side were the Northern states. On the other side were the Southern States. Memorial Day was first observed after this war.

The war that started in 1861 is known as the **Civil War**. It is also called the War Between the States. It began after the states in the Southern part of the country voted to leave the United States and set up their own government. Their aim in the war was to keep their independence under their own government. The aim of the Northern states was to keep the United States from breaking up.

Another aim of the North was to end **slavery**. When slavery is allowed, some people are permitted to own other people. For a time in our country, black people could be bought and sold to work for white people.

This old picture shows a regiment of black soldiers fighting for the North.
■ Can you find the Southern flag?

The Civil War was fought mostly in the South. The war ended in 1865 when the North won. All the states were again under a single government, that of the United States of America. Slavery was ended. There was peace at last.

Honoring the War Dead   About 1 million young men had been killed or wounded in the war. In the South many fine cities, towns, and plantations lay in ruins. In both the North and the South, families shed tears over the death of loved ones on Civil War battlefields. There was hardly a community that had not lost some of its young men.

These boys and girls have observed Memorial Day by placing flowers on the graves of members of our armed forces.
■ What uniform are some of the boys wearing?

In those communities, people promised that the war dead would not be forgotten. They set aside a special day for honoring those who had died in the war. On that day, people went into cemeteries and put spring flowers on the graves of both Northern and Southern soldiers.

A Spring Holiday In most of the states, Americans observe Memorial Day on the last Monday in May. Most southern states have their own day for honoring their dead. The date may be different in different states. But it is always in the spring, when flowers grow.

On Memorial Day we now honor not only the Civil War dead but also those who fell in later wars. On that day we remember all those who lost their lives fighting for our country. The graves of those who served in the armed forces of our country are decorated with flags and flowers. Another name for Memorial Day is Decoration Day.

CHECKUP
1. Why did the Civil War take place?
2. How did Memorial Day get started?
3. **Thinking Critically** Why do we use Memorial Day to honor all those who died for our country, not just those who died in the Civil War?

Dr. Martin Luther King, Jr.'s Birthday

Why do we celebrate Martin Luther King, Jr.'s, Birthday?

VOCABULARY
civil rights

Civil Rights Leader   The Civil War had ended slavery. The slaves became free American citizens. But in many places they were kept from having the same rights as other Americans. This unfair treatment changed very little in the years after the Civil War. Then in the 1950s and 1960s, Dr. Martin Luther King, Jr., set out to bring equal rights to all Americans.

Martin Luther King, Jr., was born on January 15, 1929, in Atlanta, Georgia. He was a **civil rights** leader. Civil rights are the rights that all Americans are given under the law. For example, all American citizens have the right to vote. All American citizens have the right to be treated fairly and equally in public places.

In 1955, Dr. King was the minister of a church in the city of Montgomery, Alabama. In that city and many others in the South, black people riding in city buses could sit only in the back seats. One day a black woman named Rosa Parks got on a bus and found the back seats filled. She had been working all day and was tired. She sat down in another seat and was arrested.

Dr. Martin Luther King, Jr., said that the woman had as much right to any seat as other citizens. With Dr. King as their leader, the black people of Montgomery refused to ride on the buses again until they had the same rights as the other riders. Dr. King told his people to be strong but never to use force or violence. They did as he said and finally won out.

Equal Rights for All   After that, Dr. King led meetings and marches in other cities to demand equal

Both black and white Americans march for civil rights with Dr. King.
■ Can you find Dr. King in the picture?

A special bulletin-board display honors Dr. King's birthday.
■ **What did the students do for this day?**

rights. A very important event in the fight for civil rights came in August of 1963. Dr. King led a march of more than 200,000 people to Washington, D.C. The purpose of the marchers was to ask our government's leaders for equality for all Americans. During the next 2 years, two new civil rights laws were made. Among other things, these laws made sure that black people were allowed to vote.

In 1968, Dr. Martin Luther King, Jr., was shot and killed. In 1983 his birthday was made a holiday by our government.

A January Holiday   Each year we celebrate Dr. Martin Luther King, Jr.'s, Birthday on the third Monday in January. On that day we honor the man who led the struggle for black people to have the same rights as other Americans.

CHECKUP
1. What are civil rights?
2. How did Dr. King become interested in civil rights in Montgomery, Alabama?
3. **Thinking Critically** Can you think of some civil rights that were not named in your book?

Reading a Time Line

WHAT IS A TIME LINE?

In Chapter 2 you learned that a time line, like a map, is a scale drawing. For example, on a map each inch can stand for a certain number of miles. On a time line each inch can stand for a certain length of time. A time line helps you see when certain events happened and the order in which they happened. Time lines help us to understand history.

SKILLS PRACTICE

The time line below is 6 inches long. Each inch stands for 80 years. This time line shows the dates of some important events in American history. Look at the time line and answer the following questions. Use a separate sheet of paper.

1. Which event came first, Washington's becoming our first President or the writing of the United States Declaration of Independence?

2. Would the Pilgrims have known about Dr. Martin Luther King? Why or why not?

3. Which happened first, Texas declaring its independence from Mexico or the Mexicans winning a battle against the French? Write down both dates.

4. The first Americans landed on the moon in 1969. Before what date would you place that event on the time line?

5. The hundredth birthday of the Statue of Liberty was in 1986. Could you place that event on the time line below?

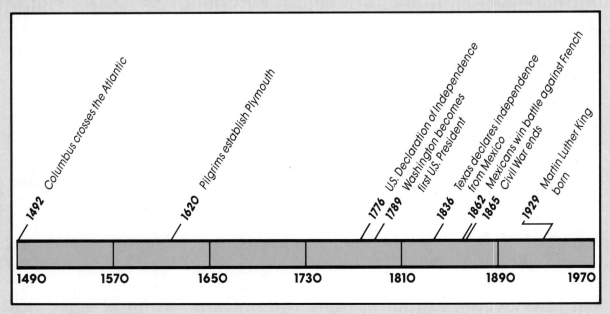

1492 Columbus crosses the Atlantic
1620 Pilgrims establish Plymouth
1776 U.S. Declaration of Independence
1789 Washington becomes first U.S. President
1836 Texas declares independence from Mexico
1862 Mexicans win battle against French
1865 Civil War ends
1929 Martin Luther King born

| 1490 | 1570 | 1650 | 1730 | 1810 | 1890 | 1970 |

CHAPTER 10 REVIEW

MAIN IDEAS

1. Holidays are special days.
2. Holidays help us remember important events and important people.
3. Holidays can be celebrated in many different ways.

VOCABULARY REVIEW

Write the numbers 1 to 10 on a sheet of paper. Match the terms with their meanings below.

a.	tribe	**f.**	Pilgrims
b.	civil rights	**g.**	militia
c.	Civil War	**h.**	slavery
d.	colony	**i.**	delegate
e.	Indies	**j.**	surveyor

1. Where Columbus thought that he had landed
2. A system under which some people are allowed to own other people
3. A group of families who share the same way of life
4. People who came to America to practice their own religion
5. Soldiers that a colony could call upon in times of trouble
6. A war that took place between the North and the South
7. A place that is located at a distance from the country that governs it
8. Rights that all Americans are given by law
9. Someone who measures land and makes maps
10. A person who represents a number of other people and speaks for them at a meeting or in a legislature

CHAPTER CHECKUP

1. What is a holiday?
2. What happens at the United Tribes International Pow-Wow?
3. What did Christopher Columbus do?
4. Why is George Washington honored with a holiday?
5. Why do we remember Dr. Martin Luther King, Jr.?
6. What great event happened on July 4, 1776?
7. On what holiday do we remember all those brave people who died for our country?
8. **Thinking Critically** Why, do you think, is it important that we have holidays?

APPLYING KNOWLEDGE

Use a clean piece of white paper to draw pictures of how different holidays are celebrated. First draw a line from the top to the bottom of the paper, dividing it into two equal parts. Then draw a line from one side to the other side of the paper, dividing it in half again. You should end up with four boxes on your paper. Each box should be about the same size. Label each of the boxes with the name of a different season of the year. For example, the top left box might be labeled *Spring*. Draw a picture in each box, showing a holiday that occurs during that season of the year. Be sure that you label each picture with the name of the holiday.

SUMMARIZING UNIT 4

REVIEWING VOCABULARY

1. tax   The money people pay to their community is called a tax. The community uses this money to pay for community services, such as schools, roads, and hospitals. Name one kind of tax that helps to pay for these services.

2. vote   People in the United States choose their government leaders by voting. Name two important community leaders who are chosen by vote.

3. capitol   The building in each state where state leaders meet to plan and to make laws for that state is called the capitol. There is another word that sounds the same and is spelled almost the same. That word is *capital*. What is the difference between a capitol and a capital?

4. monument   Monuments are built to honor a person, a group of people, or an event. The Washington Monument in our nation's capital honors George Washington, our first President. What are some other ways in which we honor people?

5. colony   A colony is a place that is located at a distance from the county that governs it. When did our country stop being a colony of Great Britain?

EXPRESSING YOURSELF

1. Who would you rather be? There are many ways in which people can serve their community. One is by being a community service worker. Fire fighters, teachers, librarians, road repair workers, and police officers are just a few of the people who serve our communities. If you wanted a job serving your community, what job would you pick? Why?

2. What laws do you want? Laws are made to protect people and property from harm. What are some car safety and traffic laws that you feel are good ones? What new law on car safety might we need?

3. Are you responsible? As a citizen in a free country, you have many freedoms. You also have many responsibilities. What are some of these responsibilities, and why should free people have them?

4. What if. . .? What if you were given the chance to declare a new holiday? What person, event, or time of year would you choose to honor? Explain your choice.

5. Whose community is best? You have learned about many communities this year. Most people think that their own community is the best. Explain why all of them are correct in their opinion.

AREA AND POPULATION OF THE FIFTY STATES

State	Area in sq mi	Area in sq km	Rank in area	Population (in thousands)	Rank in population
Alabama	50,767	131,487	28	4,083	22
Alaska	570,833	1,478,458	1	525	49
Arizona	113,508	293,986	6	3,386	25
Arkansas	52,078	134,883	27	2,388	33
California	156,299	404,814	3	27,663	1
Colorado	103,595	268,311	8	3,296	26
Connecticut	4,872	12,618	48	3,211	28
Delaware	1,932	5,005	49	644	47
Florida	54,153	140,256	26	12,023	4
Georgia	58,056	150,365	21	6,222	11
Hawaii	6,425	16,641	47	1,083	39
Idaho	82,412	216,432	12	998	42
Illinois	55,645	144,120	24	11,582	6
Indiana	35,932	93,064	38	5,531	14
Iowa	55,965	144,950	23	2,834	29
Kansas	81,778	211,805	14	2,476	32
Kentucky	39,669	102,743	37	3,727	23
Louisiana	44,521	115,310	33	4,461	20
Maine	30,995	80,277	39	1,187	38
Maryland	9,837	25,477	42	4,535	19
Massachusetts	7,824	20,265	45	5,855	13
Michigan	56,954	147,511	22	9,200	8
Minnesota	79,548	206,030	15	4,246	21
Mississippi	47,233	122,333	31	2,625	31
Missouri	68,945	178,568	18	5,103	15
Montana	145,388	376,555	4	809	44
Nebraska	76,644	198,508	10	1,594	36
Nevada	109,894	284,624	7	1,007	41
New Hampshire	8,993	23,292	44	1,057	40
New Jersey	7,468	19,342	46	7,672	9
New Mexico	121,335	314,258	5	1,500	37
New York	47,377	122,707	30	17,825	2
North Carolina	48,843	126,504	29	6,413	10
North Dakota	69,300	179,486	17	672	46
Ohio	41,004	106,201	35	10,784	7
Oklahoma	68,655	177,817	19	3,272	27
Oregon	96,184	249,117	11	2,724	30
Pennsylvania	44,888	116,260	32	11,936	5
Rhode Island	1,055	2,732	50	986	43
South Carolina	30,203	78,227	40	3,425	24
South Dakota	75,952	196,715	16	709	45
Tennessee	41,155	106,591	34	4,855	16
Texas	262,017	678,623	2	16,789	3
Utah	82,073	212,569	13	1,680	35
Vermont	9,273	24,017	43	548	48
Virginia	39,704	102,832	36	5,904	12
Washington	66,511	172,264	20	4,538	18
West Virginia	24,119	62,468	41	1,897	34
Wisconsin	54,426	140,964	25	4,807	17
Wyoming	96,989	251,202	9	490	50
Washington, D.C.	69	178	X	622	X
United States	3,539,295	9,169,762	X	243,399	X

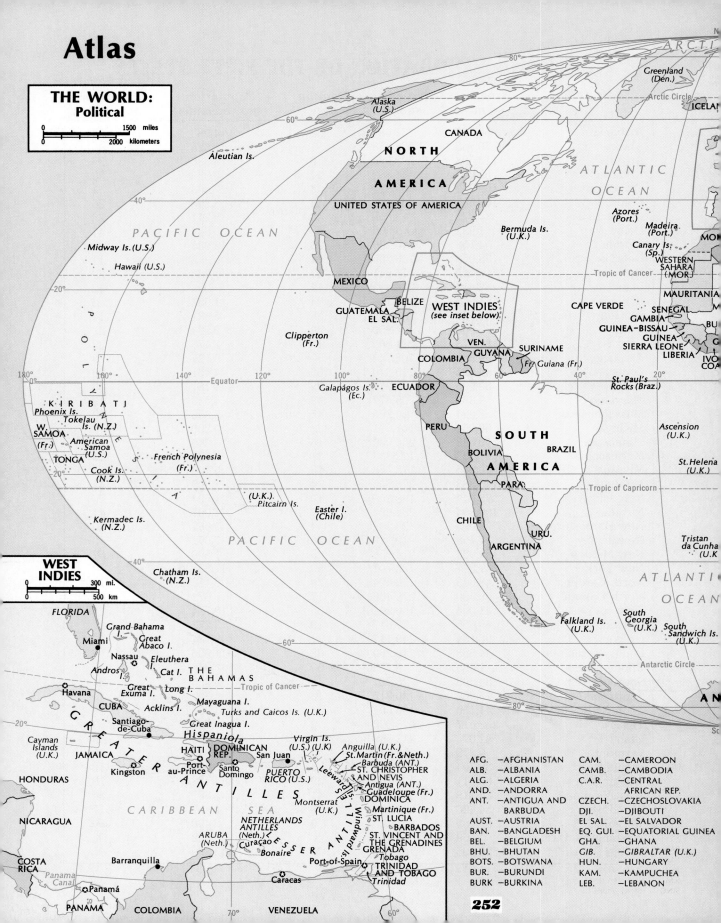

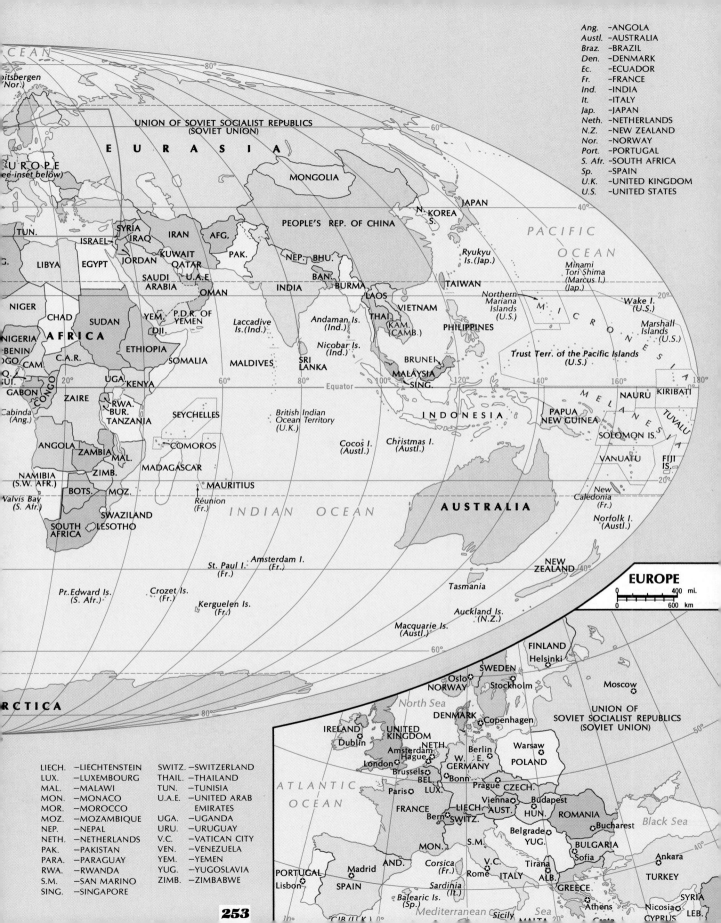

ASIA

ARCTIC OCEAN

Barrow

Beaufort Sea

Alaska (U.S.)

Fairbanks

Anchorage

Dawson

Juneau

Arctic Circle

Yukon R.

Bering Sea

Gulf of Alaska

PACIFIC OCEAN

Port Radium

Great Bear Lake

Great Slave Lake

CANADA

Thule

GREENLAND (Den.)

Pond Inlet

Baffin Bay

ICELAND

Godthaab

Labrador Sea

Churchill

Hudson Bay

Edmonton

Victoria
Vancouver
Seattle
Portland
Columbia

Calgary

Spokane

Regina

Lake Winnipeg

Winnipeg

Goose Bay

Seven Islands

Gander
St.John's

San Francisco

Salt Lake City

Great Salt L.

UNITED STATES OF AMERICA

Great

Denver

Colorado

Minneapolis
St.Paul
Milwaukee
Omaha
Chicago

Missouri R.

Lakes

Quebec

Montreal
Ottawa

Toronto

Detroit
Buffalo
Cleveland
Pittsburgh

Halifax

Boston

New York
Philadelphia

Los Angeles

San Diego

Phoenix

Kansas City

St. Louis

Cincinnati

Ohio R.

Washington
Baltimore

Norfolk

Guadalupe I. (Mex.)

Arkansas R.

Memphis

Tropic of Cancer

El Paso

Rio Grande

Dallas

Atlanta

Bermuda Is. (U.K.)

San Antonio

Houston

Mississippi R.

New Orleans

ATLANTIC OCEAN

Monterrey

G. of California

GULF OF MEXICO

Miami

Grand Bahama I.

Great Abaco I.

Nassau

Eleuthera I.

Den. —DENMARK
Fr. —FRANCE
Neth. —NETHERLANDS
Mex. —MEXICO
U.K. —UNITED KINGDOM
U.S. —UNITED STATES

MEXICO

Guadalajara

Mexico City

Orizaba

Havana

CUBA

Andros I.

Cat I.

Gr. Exuma I.

Long I.

THE BAHAMAS

Mayaguana I.

Acklins I.

Santiago-de-Cuba

Gr.Inagua I.

PUERTO RICO (U.S.)

Virgin Is. (U.S.&U.K.)

Cayman Islands (U.K.)

DOMINICAN REPUBLIC

Belmopan

BELIZE

JAMAICA

Kingston

HAITI
Port-au-Prince

Santo Domingo

ANTIGUA AND BARBUDA

ST. CHRISTOPHER-NEVIS

GUATEMALA

Guatemala

HONDURAS

Tegucigalpa

San Salvador

EL SALVADOR

NICARAGUA

CARIBBEAN SEA

Aruba (Neth.)

Neth. Antilles (Neth.)

Guadeloupe (Fr.)

DOMINICA

Martinique (Fr.)

ST. LUCIA

ST. VINCENT AND THE GRENADINES

GRENADA

Managua

San José

COSTA RICA

Panama Canal

PANAMA

Panamá

SOUTH AMERICA

TRINIDAD AND TOBAGO

NORTH AMERICA: Political

⚘ National capitals

• Other cities

0 ____ 500 miles

0 ____ 800 kilometers

256

West longitude

80° 70° 60° 50° 40°

Barranquilla
Cartagena
Maracaibo
10°
Valencia
Caracas
Barquisimeto
Port-of-Spain
TRINIDAD AND
TOBAGO
Cúcuta
San Cristóbal
Bucaramanga
Medellín
Bogotá
COLOMBIA
Cali
Malpelo I.
(Col.)

VENEZUELA
Orinoco R.

Georgetown
GUYANA
Paramaribo
SURINAM
Cayenne
Fr.
Guiana
(Fr.)

Col. —COLOMBIA
Fr. —FRANCE
U.K. —UNITED KINGDOM

Quito
ECUADOR
Guayaquil
Iquitos
Equator
0°
Amazon R.
Manaus
Belém
São Luís
Fortaleza

Trujillo
PERU
Callao
Lima
Cuzco
Arequipa
La Paz
Lake
Titicaca
BOLIVIA
Sucre

BRAZIL
Recife
Maceió
10°
Salvador
Brasília
(Federal
District)

PACIFIC
OCEAN

Chuquicamata
Antofagasta
20°
San Felix I.
(Chile)
San Ambrosio I.
(Chile)

PARAGUAY
Asunción
Tucumán
Belo
Horizonte
Rio de Janeiro
São Paulo
Niterói
Santos
Curitiba
Tropic of Capricorn

CHILE
Córdoba
Santa Fe
Paraná
Rosario
Buenos Aires
La Plata
ARGENTINA

Pôrto Alegre
URUGUAY
Montevideo
Rio de la Plata
30°

ATLANTIC
OCEAN

Valparaíso
Santiago
Juan Fernández Is.
(Chile)
Concepción
Mar del Plata
Bahía Blanca

40°

Punta Arenas
Strait of
Magellan
Falkland Is. (U.K.)
(Malvinas Is.)
257

SOUTH AMERICA:
Political

⊛ National capitals
● Other cities

0   500 miles
0   800 kilometers

90° 80° 70° 60° West longitude 50° 40° 30°

ATLANTIC
OCEAN

20°

Madeira Is.
(Port.)

Lisbon
PORTUGAL

SPAIN
Madrid

Valencia
Barcelona
Balearic
Is. (Sp.)

Bordeaux

FRANCE

Marseilles
Corsica

Sardinia

Palermo
Sicily

Naples

Rome

ITALY

Valletta

MALTA

Mediterranean
Sea

Crete
(Gr.)

Athens

GREECE

Tirana

Sofia

BUL.

ROM.

Bucharest

Belgrade

YUG.

Budapest

Vienna

Prague

Munich

POLAND

Wrocław

Warsaw

Berlin

GER.

Bonn
W.
GER.

Hamburg

Copenhagen

DEN.

Glasgow

UNITED
KINGDOM

IRE.
Dublin

London

Amsterdam
Hague
Brussels

Paris

Bern

Nice

Milan

Bordeaux

Bergen

Oslo

NORWAY

SWEDEN

Göteborg

Stockholm

Helsinki

FINLAND

Narvik

Murmansk

North
Sea

Barents Sea

Spitsbergen
(Nor.)

North
Land

Novaya
Zemlya

ARCTIC OCEAN

70° 80°

Tallinn

Riga

Kaliningrad

Leningrad

Archangel

Moscow

Kiev

Kharkov

Odessa

UKRAINE

Black Sea

Istanbul
(Constantinople)

İzmir

Ankara

TURKEY

Nicosia

CYPRUS

Beirut

Damascus

SYRIA

Jerusalem

ISRAEL

JOR.

Amman

Sinai
Pen.

IRAQ

Baghdad

Basra

Abadan

Kuwait

Manama

Riyadh

Doha

Abu Dhabi

UNITED ARAB
EMIRATES

SAUDI
ARABIA

Mecca

Red
Sea

AFRICA

YEMEN ARAB
REPUBLIC

San'a

Aden
Madinat
ash Sha'b

PEOPLE'S DEM.
REP. OF YEMEN

Empty Quarter

OMAN

Masqat

Socotra
(P.D.R. Yemen)

Arabian Sea

Saratov

Kazan

Volgograd

Krasnodar

Baku

Caspian
Sea

Aral
Sea

Volga R.

Kuibyshev

Orenburg

Ufa

Perm

Sverdlovsk

Chelyabinsk

Magnitogorsk

UNION OF SOVIET
(SOVIET UNION)

Omsk

Tomsk

Novosibirsk

Ob. R.

Yenisey R.

Tashkent

TURKESTAN

Tehran

IRAN
(PERSIA)

AFGHANISTAN

Kabul

Islamabad

PAKISTAN

Karachi

Hyderabad

Ahmadabad

Bombay

Hyderabad

INDIA

Madras

Laccadive Is.
(Ind.)

MALDIVES

Male

Colombo

SRI
LANKA

Jammu
and
Kashmir

Lahore

Delhi

New Delhi

TIBET

NEP.

Katmandu

Ganges R.

Indus R.

SINKIANG

Urumchi

Urumchi

INDIAN OCEAN

East longitude

BAN. — BANGLADESH
BHU. — BHUTAN
BUL. — BULGARIA
DEN. — DENMARK
GER. — GERMANY
IRE. — IRELAND
JOR. — JORDAN
KAM. — KAMPUCHEA
NEP. — NEPAL
ROM. — ROMANIA
YUG. — YUGOSLAVIA

1—ALBANIA
2—ANDORRA
3—AUSTRIA
4—BAHREIN
5—BELGIUM
6—BRUNEI
7—CZECHOSLOVAKIA
8—HUNGARY
9—KUWAIT
10—LEBANON
11—LIECHTENSTEIN
12—LUXEMBOURG
13—MONACO
14—NETHERLANDS
15—QATAR
16—SAN MARINO
17—SINGAPORE
18—SWITZERLAND

258

EURASIA: Political

Gr.	—GREECE
Ind.	—INDIA
Jap.	—JAPAN
Nor.	—NORWAY
Port.	—PORTUGAL
Sp.	—SPAIN
U.K.	—UNITED KINGDOM
U.S.	—UNITED STATES
U.S.S.R.	—SOVIET UNION

⊛ National capitals
● Other cities

0   800 mi.
0   1200 km

New Siberian Is.
Aleutian Is. (U.S.)
Bering Sea
Magadan
Kamchatka Pen.
S i b e r i a
Yakutsk
Lena R.
Sea of Okhotsk
UNION OF SOVIET SOCIALIST REPUBLICS
Kuril Islands (U.S.S.R.)
Krasnoyarsk
Sakhalin
Khabarovsk
Amur R.
Irkutsk
MANCHURIA
Harbin
Vladivostok
Sapporo
Sea of Japan
Ulan Bator
MONGOLIA
INNER MONGOLIA
Shenyang
Fushun
N. KOREA
Pyongyang
JAPAN
Tokyo
Yokohama
CHINA
Great Wall
Peking
Dairen
S. KOREA
Seoul
Kyoto
Nagoya
Kobe
Osaka
Tientsin
Pusan
Kitakyushu
Taiyuan
Tsingtao
Lanchow
Sian
Nanking
Shanghai
Hwang Ho
East China Sea
PEOPLE'S REPUBLIC OF CHINA
Wuhan
Chengtu
Chungking
Yangtze R.
Taipei
Ryukyu Is. (Jap.)
TAIWAN
Lhasa
Thimbu
BHU.
Kunming
Canton
Hong Kong (U.K.)
Brahmaputra
Macao (Port.)
BAN.
Dacca
Hanoi
PACIFIC OCEAN
Calcutta
Mandalay
BURMA
Bay of Bengal
Rangoon
Vientiane
LAOS
Hue
Da Nang
Manila
PHILIPPINES
Andaman Is. (Ind.)
THAILAND
Bangkok
VIETNAM
South China Sea
Davao
Mekong R.
KAM.
Phnom Penh
Ho Chi Minh City
Nicobar Is. (Ind.)
Bandar Seri Begawan
Djajapura
PAPUA NEW GUINEA
Lae
IRIAN JAYA
New Guinea
Port Moresby
Manado
MALAYSIA
Borneo
Sulawesi (Celebes)
Arafura Sea
Coral Sea
Medan
Kuala Lumpur
Pontianak
Samarinda
INDONESIA
Sumatra
Bandjermasin
Ujung Pandang
Timor
Palembang
Jakarta
Surabaja
Bandung
Java
AUSTRALIA

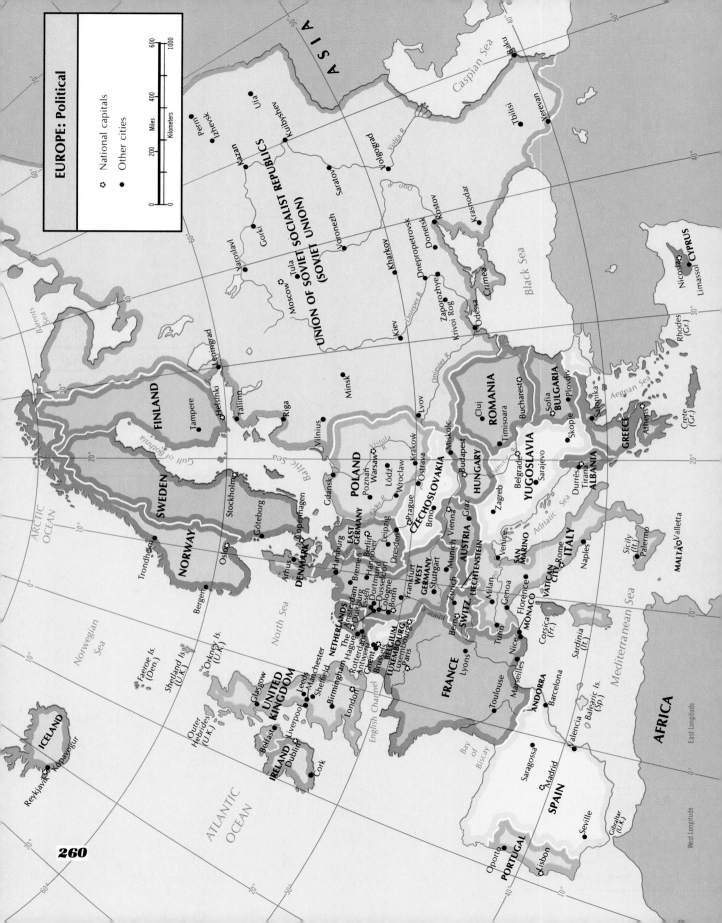

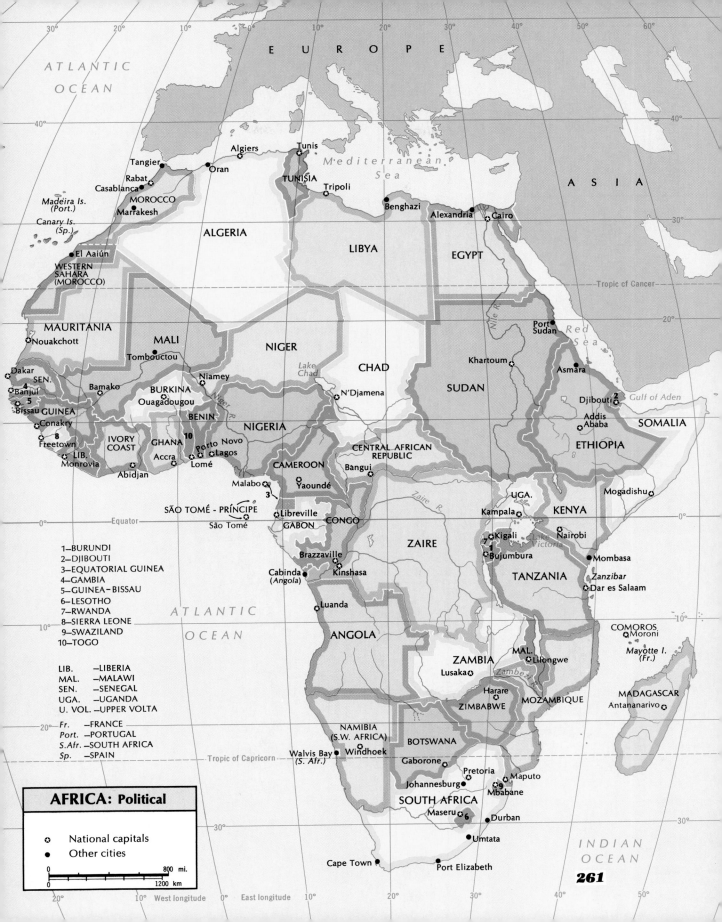

ATLANTIC
OCEAN

EUROPE

Mediterranean Sea

ASIA

ATLANTIC
OCEAN

Madeira Is.
(Port.)

Canary Is.
(Sp.)

Tangier
Rabat
Casablanca
MOROCCO
Marrakesh

Algiers
Oran
Tunis
TUNISIA
Tripoli

Benghazi
Alexandria
Cairo

El Aaiún
WESTERN
SAHARA
(MOROCCO)

ALGERIA

LIBYA

EGYPT

Tropic of Cancer

MAURITANIA
Nouakchott

MALI
Tombouctou

NIGER

CHAD

SUDAN

Port
Sudan

Red Sea

Dakar
SEN.
4 Banjul
5
Bissau GUINEA
Conakry
8
Freetown
LIB.
Monrovia

Bamako

Niamey
BURKINA
Ouagadougou
BENIN

Lake Chad

N'Djamena

Khartoum

Asmara

Djibouti 2
Gulf of Aden

Addis
Ababa

SOMALIA

ETHIOPIA

IVORY
COAST
GHANA
Accra
Abidjan

10
Porto Novo
Lomé
Lagos

NIGERIA

CENTRAL AFRICAN
REPUBLIC

Bangui

Mogadishu

Equator

SÃO TOMÉ - PRÍNCIPE
São Tomé

Malabo
3
Libreville
GABON

Yaoundé
CAMEROON

CONGO

Zaire R.

ZAIRE

UGA.
Kampala

KENYA

Nairobi

7 Kigali
1 Bujumbura

Lake Victoria

Mombasa

Equator

ATLANTIC
OCEAN

Brazzaville
Cabinda
(Angola)
Kinshasa

Luanda

TANZANIA

Zanzibar
Dar es Salaam

COMOROS
Moroni

Mayotte I.
(Fr.)

ANGOLA

ZAMBIA
Lusaka

MAL.
Lilongwe

MADAGASCAR
Antananarivo

Harare
ZIMBABWE

Zambezi

MOZAMBIQUE

Tropic of Capricorn

NAMIBIA
(S.W. AFRICA)

BOTSWANA

Walvis Bay
(S. Afr.)
Windhoek

Gaborone

Johannesburg

Pretoria
9
Mbabane

Maputo

SOUTH AFRICA

Maseru
6 Durban
Umtata

Cape Town

Port Elizabeth

INDIAN
OCEAN

1—BURUNDI
2—DJIBOUTI
3—EQUATORIAL GUINEA
4—GAMBIA
5—GUINEA-BISSAU
6—LESOTHO
7—RWANDA
8—SIERRA LEONE
9—SWAZILAND
10—TOGO

LIB. —LIBERIA
MAL. —MALAWI
SEN. —SENEGAL
UGA. —UGANDA
U. VOL. —UPPER VOLTA

Fr. —FRANCE
Port. —PORTUGAL
S.Afr. —SOUTH AFRICA
Sp. —SPAIN

AFRICA: Political

⊛ National capitals

• Other cities

0   800 mi.
0   1200 km

261

20°   10°   0°   10°
West longitude   East longitude

GAZETTEER

The Gazetteer is a geographical dictionary. It shows latitude and longitude for cities and certain other places. Latitude and longitude are shown in the form: 36°N/84°W. This means "36 degrees north latitude and 84 degrees west longitude." The page reference tells where each entry may be found on a map.

Key to Pronunciation

a	hat, cap	i	it, pin	ou	house, out	zh	measure, seizure
ā	age, face	ī	ice, five	sh	she, rush	ə	represents
ã	care, air	ng	long, bring	th	thin, both		a in about
ä	father, far	o	hot, rock	ᵀH	then, smooth		e in taken
ch	child, much	ō	open, go	u	cup, butter		i in pencil
e	let, best	ô	order, all	u̇	full, put		o in lemon
ē	equal, see	oi	oil, voice	ü	rule, move		u in circus
ėr	term, learn						

This Key to Pronunciation is from *Scott, Foresman Intermediate Dictionary*, by E.L. Thorndike and Clarence L. Barnhart. Copyright© 1983, by Scott, Foresman and Company. Reprinted by permission.

Africa (af′ ri kə). The earth's second largest continent. p. 18.

Amazon River (am′ ə zän   riv′ ər). Second longest river in the world. Tributaries rise in the Andes Mountains and Guiana Highlands. Flows into the Atlantic Ocean near Belém, Brazil. p. 257.

Antarctica (ant ärk′ ti kə). The earth's third smallest continent. p. 18.

Appalachian Mountains (ap ə lā′ chən moun′ tənz). A mountain range in eastern North America. Extends from Canada to Alabama. pp. 254–255.

Arctic Ocean (ärk′ tik ō′ shən). The large body of salt water north of the Arctic Circle. p. 18.

Asheville (ash′ vil). A city in the Blue Ridge Mountains in western North Carolina. (36°N/83°W) p. 56.

Asia (ā′ zhə). The earth's largest continent. p. 18.

Atlanta (ət lant′ ə). The capital of and most populated city in Georgia. (34°N/84°W) pp. 254–255.

Atlantic Ocean (ət lant′ ik ō′ shən). The large body of salt water separating North America and South America from Europe and Africa. p. 18.

Australia (ô strāl′ yə). The smallest continent on the earth. p. 18.

GAZETTEER

Baltimore (bôl′ tə mōr). The most populated city in Maryland. Located on Chesapeake Bay. (39°N/77°W) pp. 254–255.

Bartlesville (bärt′ əlz vil). A city in northeastern Oklahoma. Oil-producing area. (37°N/96°W) p. 159.

Bismarck (biz′ märk). The capital of North Dakota. Located on Missouri River. (47°N/101°W) p. 254.

Bonneville Dam (bän′ ə vil dām). Large dam on the Columbia River between Washington and Oregon. (46°N/122°W) pp. 254–255.

Boston (bôs′ tun). Capital of and most populated city in Massachusetts. Located on Massachusetts Bay. (42°N/71°W) pp. 254–255.

Cape Fear River (kāp fir riv′ ər). A river in North Carolina that flows southeast into the Atlantic Ocean. p. 56.

Chicago (shə käg′ ō). A city located in Illinois on the southern tip of Lake Michigan. One of eight cities in the United States with a population of more than 1,000,000. (42°N/88°W) pp. 254–255.

Columbia River (kə ləm bē ə riv′ er). A river that starts in the Rocky Mountains in Canada and flows into the Pacific Ocean along the Washington–Oregon boundary. p. 254.

Crowley (kraù′ lē). A community in southern Louisiana. Rice-farming area. (30°N/92°W) p. 145.

Dallas (dal′ əs). The second most populated city in northeastern Texas. Located on the Trinity River. (33°N/97°W). pp. 254–255.

Detroit (di troit′). The most populated city in Michigan. One of eight cities in the United States with a population of more than 1,000,000. (42°N/83°W) pp. 254–255.

Eastern Hemisphere (ēs′ tərn hem′ ə sfir). The half of the earth east of the Prime Meridian. p. 20.

Equator (i kwā′ tər). 0° line of latitude. A map line that circles the earth halfway between the two poles. p. 20.

Europe (yùr əp). The earth's second smallest continent. p. 18.

Fort Worth (fôrt wėrth). Fifth most populated city in Texas. Located on the Trinity River. (33°N/97°W) pp. 254–255.

Gary (gar′ ē). A city in northwestern Indiana. Located on Lake Michigan. Major steel-producing city. (42°N/87°W) pp. 254–255.

Greenwich (gren′ ich). A place in London, England. Located at 0° longitude. p. 25.

Gulf of Mexico (gulf′ ôv mek′ si kō). A body of salt water surrounded by the United States, Mexico, and Cuba. pp. 254–255.

Hannibal (han′ ə bəl). A community in Missouri located on the Mississippi River. The boyhood home of Mark Twain. (40°N/91°W) p. 106.

Hazard (haz′ ərd). A coal-mining city on the edge of the Appalachian Mountains in southeastern Kentucky. (37°N/83°W) p. 165.

Honolulu (hän əl ü′ lü). The capital and most populated city in Hawaii. (21°N/158°W) pp. 254–255.

Independence (in də pen′ dəns). City in western Missouri. Place where Santa Fe Trail began. (39°N/94°W) p. 89.

Indian Ocean (in′ dē ən ō′ shən). The large body of salt water between Africa and Australia. p. 18.

Indio (in dē ō′). A community in southeastern California. Date-farming area. (34°N/116°W) p. 14.

Juneau (jü′ nō). Capital of Alaska. Located on the Alaskan panhandle. (58°N/134°W) pp. 254–255.

Leningrad (len′ ən grad). The second most populated city in the Soviet Union. (60°N/30°E) p. 260.

London (lən′ dən). The capital and most populated city in the United Kingdom. Located along the Thames River. (52°N/0°longitude) p. 260.

Los Angeles (lô san′ jə ləs). One of eight cities in the United States with a population of more than 1,000,000. Located in southern California along the Pacific coast. (34°N/118°W) pp. 254–255.

Manaus (mə nous′). A city in Brazil. Located on a branch of the Amazon River. (3°S/60°W) p. 257.

Marana (mə rän′ ə). A community in Arizona. Cotton-farming area. (32°N/111°W) p. 140.

Mexico City (mek′ si kō sit′ ē). The capital of Mexico. One of the most populated cities in the world. (19°N/99°W) p. 256.

Minneapolis (min ē ap′ ə ləs). Largest city in Minnesota. Located on the Mississippi River at the Falls of St. Anthony. (45°N/93°W) pp. 254–255.

Mississippi River (mis ə sip′ ē riv′ ər). Second longest river in the United States. Rises in northern Minnesota and flows into the Gulf of Mexico near New Orleans, Louisiana. pp. 254–255.

Monhegan Island (män hē′ gən ī′ lənd). An island off the southern coast of Maine. (44°N/69°W) p. 169.

Montgomery (mənt gəm′ ə re). Capital of Alabama. Located on the Alabama River. (32°N/86°W) pp. 254–255.

Mount St. Helens (mount sānt hel′ ənz). An active volcano that is located in Washington. (46°N/123°W) pp. 254–255.

Nashville (nash′ vil). Capital of Tennessee. Located on the Cumberland River. (36°N/87°W) pp. 254–255.

New Hanover County (nü han′ ō vər koun′ tē). A county in southeastern North Carolina. p. 56.

New Orleans (nü ôr′ lē ənz). The most populated city in Louisiana. One of the busiest ports in the United States. Located near the mouth of the Mississippi River. (30°N/90°W) pp. 254–255.

New York City (nü yôrk′ sit′ ē). The most populated city in the United States. One of eight cities in the country with a popu-

GAZETTEER

GAZETTEER

GAZETTEER

lation of more than 1,000,000. Located in the state of New York at the mouth of the Hudson River. (41°N/74°W) pp. 254–255.

Northern Hemisphere (nôr′ ᴛнərn hem′ ə sfir). The half of the earth that is north of the Equator. p. 21

North Pole (nôrth pōl). The most northern place on the earth. p. 21

North Sea (nôrth sē). Part of the Atlantic Ocean between Great Britain and the European continent. p. 260.

Pacific Ocean (pə sif′ ik ō′ shən). The large body of salt water off the western coast of the United States. The earth's largest ocean. p. 15.

Philadelphia (fil ə del′ fē ə). The most populated city in Pennsylvania.One of eight cities in the United States with a population of more than 1,000,000. (40°N/75°W) pp. 254–255.

Pittsburgh (pits′ bərg). The second most populated city in Pennsylvania. The most important steel center in the United States. (40°N/80°W) pp. 254–255.

Portland (pôrt′ lənd). The most populated city in Oregon. Located on the Willamette River. (46°N/123°W) pp. 254–255.

Potomac River (pə tō′ mək riv′ ər). River on which Washington, D.C., is located. It also forms part of the boundary between Virginia and Maryland. p. 184.

Prime Meridian (prīm mə rid′ ē ən). 0° line of longitude that passes through Greenwich, England. It divides the earth into eastern and western hemispheres. p. 25.

Rockland (räk′ land). A city in southern Maine on the shore of Penobscot Bay. (44°N/69°W) p. 169.

Sacramento (sak rə ment′ ō). Capital of California. Located on the Sacramento River. (38°N/122°W) p. 14.

St. Augustine (sānt ô′ gə stēn). A city in Florida. It is the oldest city in the United States. (30°N/81°W) p. 24.

St. Joseph (sānt jō′ səf). A city in Missouri. Located on the Missouri River. (40°N/95°W) p. 106.

St. Louis (sānt lü′ əs). Most populated city in Missouri. Located on Mississippi River near the point where it is joined by the Missouri River. (39°N/90°W) p. 106.

Santa Fe (sant ə fā′). Spanish settlement started in 1609. Today the capital of New Mexico. (36°N/106°W) pp. 254–255.

Santa Fe Trail (sant ə fā′ trāl). Wagon trail over which supplies traveled from Independence, Missouri, to Santa Fe, New Mexico. p. 89.

Seattle (sē at′ əl). Largest city in Washington. Located on eastern shore of Puget Sound. (48°N/122°W) pp. 254–255.

South America (south ə mer′ ə kə). The earth's fourth largest continent. p. 18.

Southern Hemisphere (suᴛн′ ərn hem′ ə sfir). The half of the earth that is south of the Equator. p. 21.

South Pole (south pōl). The most southern place on the earth. p. 20.

Tenochtitlán (tä nôch tē tlän′). City in Mexico first built by Aztecs. The city no longer exists, but Mexico City has grown at the same location. (19°N/99°W) p. 82.

Tokyo (tō′ kē ō). Capital city of Japan. Located on island of Honshū on Tokyo Bay. (36°N/140°E) pp. 258–259.

Valley of Mexico (val′ ē ov mek′ si kō). Low area in Mexico surrounded by mountains. Mexico City is located in this valley. p. 82.

Washington, D.C. (wôsh′ ing tən DC). The capital of the United States. Located on the Potomac River. (39°N/77°W) p. 184.

Western Hemisphere (wes′tərn hem′ ə sfir). The half of the earth west of the Prime Meridian. The hemisphere in which all of South America and North America is located. p. 19.

Wilmington (wil′ ming tən). A city in North Carolina. Located on Cape Fear River. It is North Carolina's largest port. (34°N/78°W) p. 56.

Yuma (yü′ mə). A city in southwestern Arizona. Located where the Gila River joins the Colorado River. (33°N/115°W) pp. 254–255.

Capital Cities and State Flags of the Fifty States

STATE CHARTS

STATE CHARTS

STATE CHARTS

ALABAMA

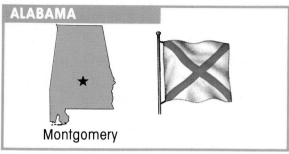

Montgomery

ALASKA

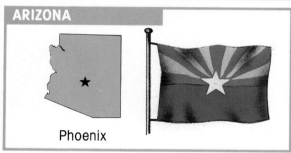

Juneau

ARIZONA

Phoenix

ARKANSAS

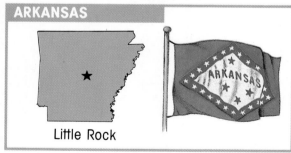

Little Rock

CALIFORNIA

Sacramento

COLORADO

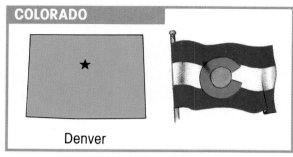

Denver

CONNECTICUT

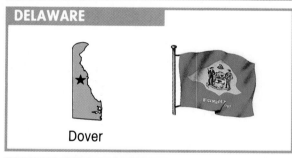

Hartford

DELAWARE

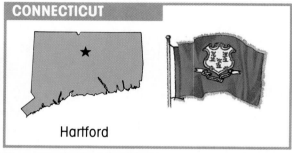

Dover

FLORIDA

Tallahassee

GEORGIA

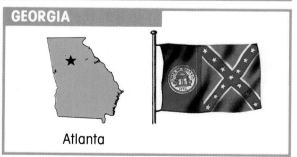

Atlanta

HAWAII

Honolulu

KANSAS

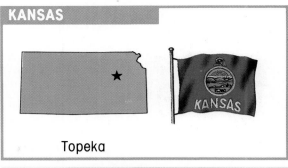

Topeka

IDAHO

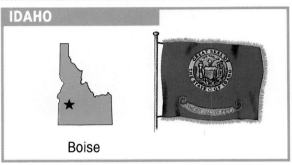

Boise

KENTUCKY

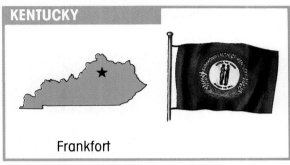

Frankfort

ILLINOIS

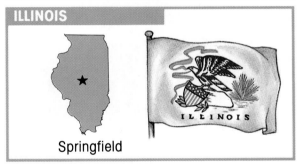

Springfield

LOUISIANA

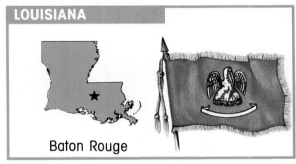

Baton Rouge

INDIANA

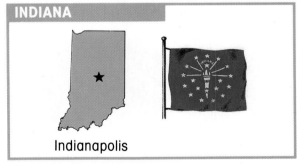

Indianapolis

MAINE

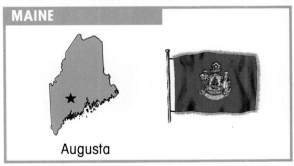

Augusta

IOWA

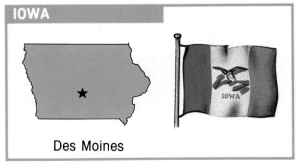

Des Moines

MARYLAND

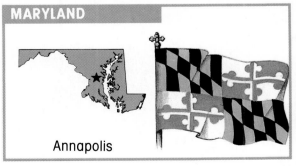

Annapolis

269

MASSACHUSETTS

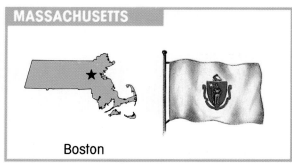

Boston

MONTANA

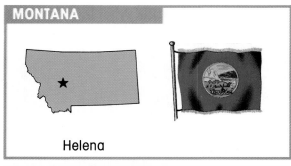

Helena

MICHIGAN

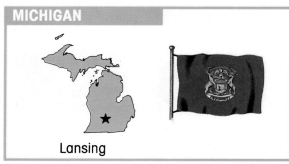

Lansing

NEBRASKA

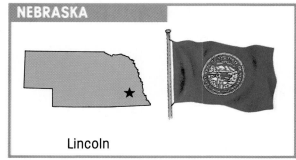

Lincoln

MINNESOTA

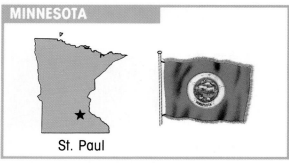

St. Paul

NEVADA

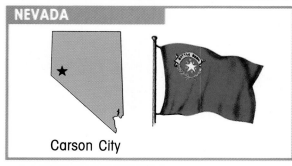

Carson City

MISSISSIPPI

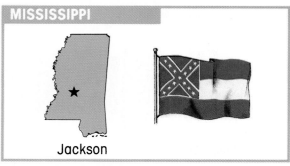

Jackson

NEW HAMPSHIRE

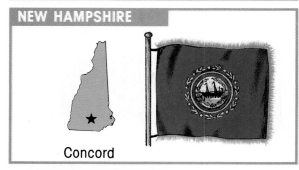

Concord

MISSOURI

Jefferson City

NEW JERSEY

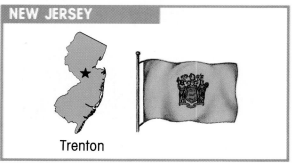

Trenton

NEW MEXICO

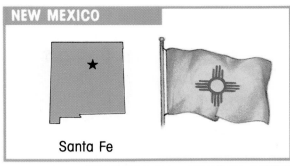

Santa Fe

OKLAHOMA

Oklahoma City

NEW YORK

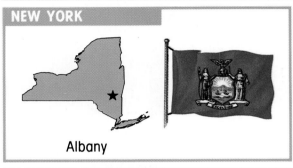

Albany

OREGON

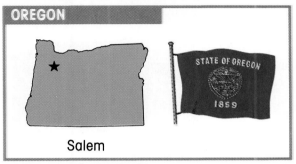

Salem

NORTH CAROLINA

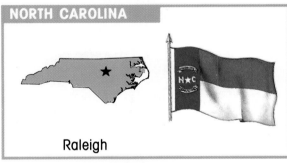

Raleigh

PENNSYLVANIA

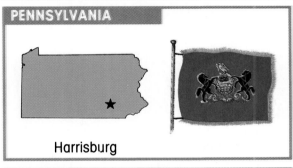

Harrisburg

NORTH DAKOTA

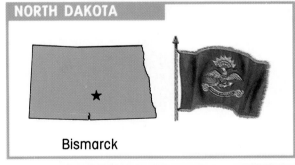

Bismarck

RHODE ISLAND

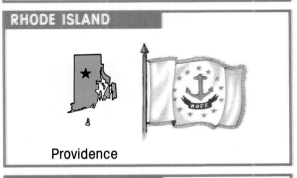

Providence

OHIO

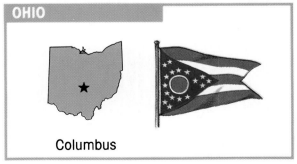

Columbus

SOUTH CAROLINA

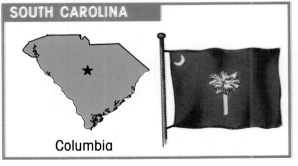

Columbia

STATE CHARTS

STATE CHARTS

STATE CHARTS

271

SOUTH DAKOTA

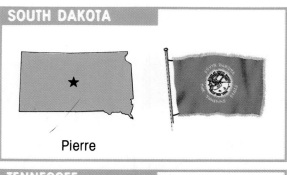

Pierre

VIRGINIA

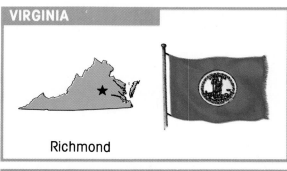

Richmond

TENNESSEE

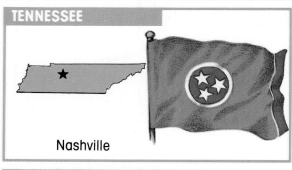

Nashville

WASHINGTON

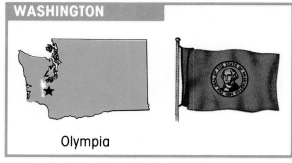

Olympia

TEXAS

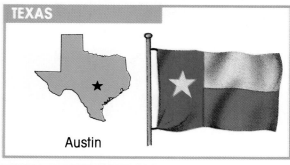

Austin

WEST VIRGINIA

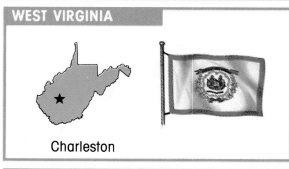

Charleston

UTAH

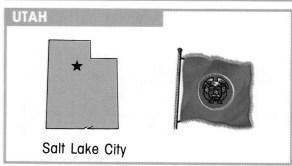

Salt Lake City

WISCONSIN

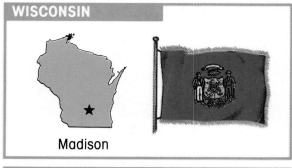

Madison

VERMONT

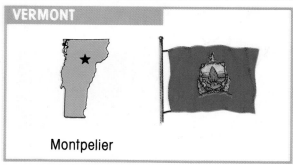

Montpelier

WYOMING

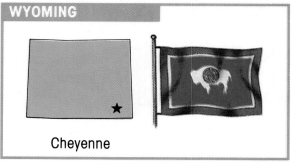

Cheyenne

THE EARTH: LAND AND WATER

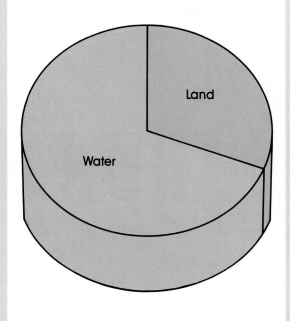

THE EARTH: LAND AREA BY CONTINENTS

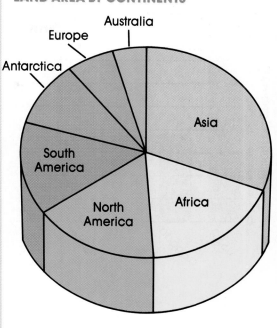

THE EARTH: LAND AREA BY COUNTRIES

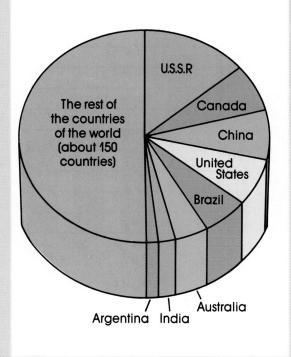

THE UNITED STATES: LAND AREA BY STATES

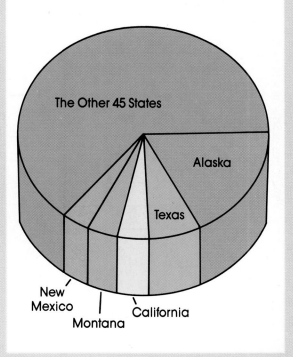

273

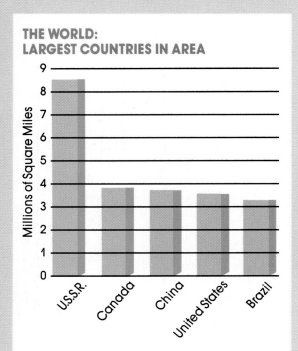

THE WORLD: LARGEST COUNTRIES IN AREA

Millions of Square Miles

U.S.S.R. · Canada · China · United States · Brazil

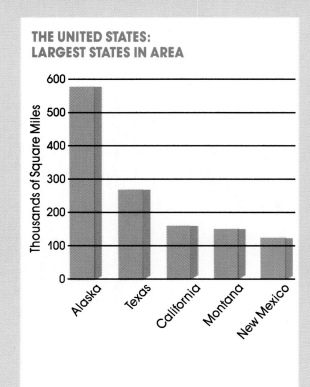

THE UNITED STATES: LARGEST STATES IN AREA

Thousands of Square Miles

Alaska · Texas · California · Montana · New Mexico

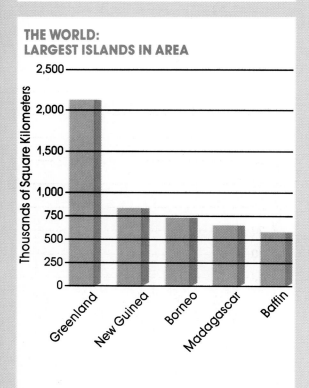

THE WORLD: LARGEST ISLANDS IN AREA

Thousands of Square Kilometers

Greenland · New Guinea · Borneo · Madagascar · Baffin

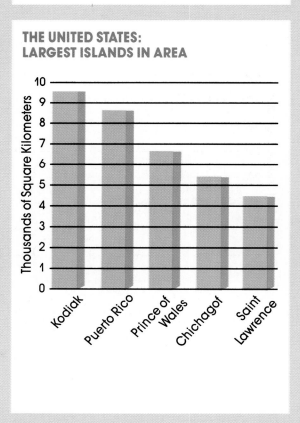

THE UNITED STATES: LARGEST ISLANDS IN AREA

Thousands of Square Kilometers

Kodiak · Puerto Rico · Prince of Wales · Chichagof · Saint Lawrence

THE WORLD: LONGEST RIVERS

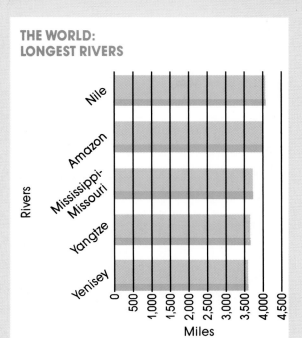

THE UNITED STATES: LONGEST RIVERS

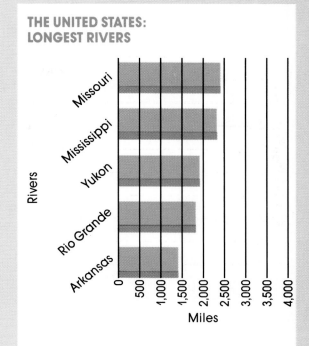

THE WORLD: LARGEST LAKES IN AREA

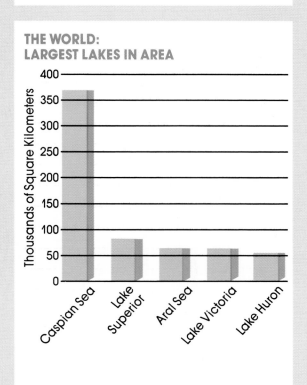

THE UNITED STATES: LARGEST LAKES IN AREA

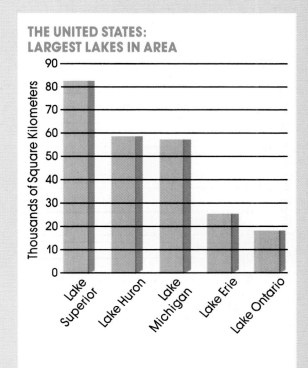

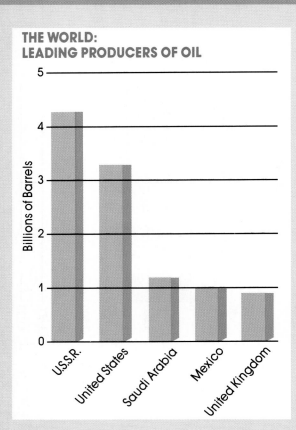

THE WORLD:
LEADING PRODUCERS OF OIL

Billions of Barrels

THE UNITED STATES:
LEADING PRODUCERS OF OIL

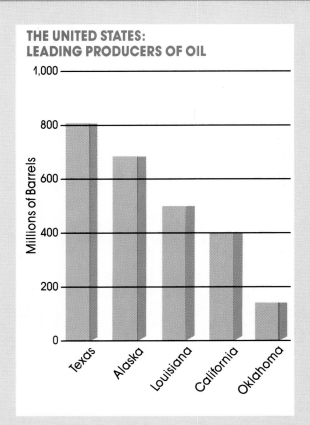

Millions of Barrels

THE WORLD:
LEADING PRODUCERS OF COAL

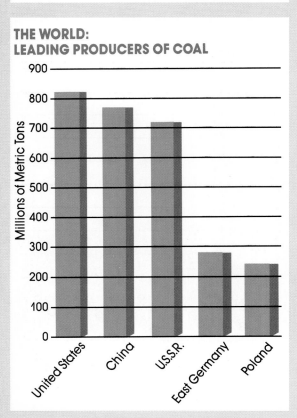

Millions of Metric Tons

THE UNITED STATES:
LEADING PRODUCERS OF COAL

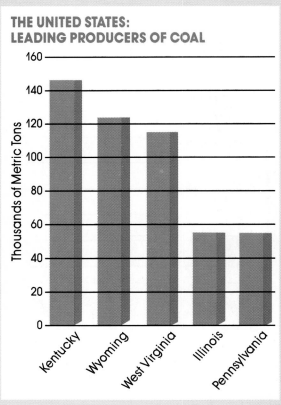

Thousands of Metric Tons

GRAPH APPENDIX   GRAPH APPENDIX   GRAPH APPENDIX

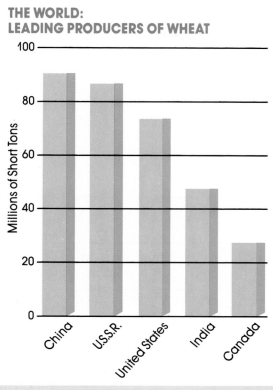

THE WORLD: LEADING PRODUCERS OF WHEAT

Millions of Short Tons

100 — 80 — 60 — 40 — 20 — 0

China · U.S.S.R. · United States · India · Canada

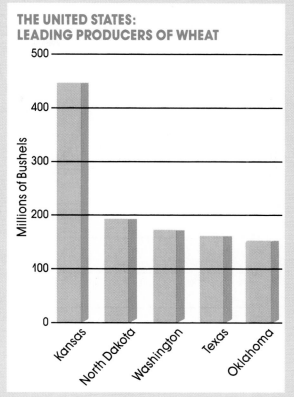

THE UNITED STATES: LEADING PRODUCERS OF WHEAT

Millions of Bushels

500 — 400 — 300 — 200 — 100 — 0

Kansas · North Dakota · Washington · Texas · Oklahoma

THE WORLD: LEADING PRODUCERS OF FISH

Millions of Metric Tons

12 — 10 — 8 — 6 — 4 — 2 — 0

Japan · U.S.S.R. · China · United States · Chile

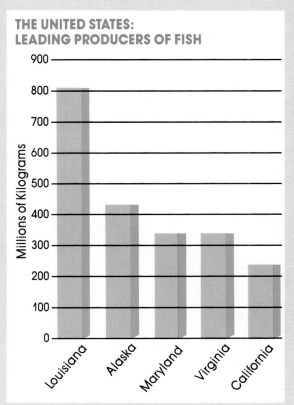

THE UNITED STATES: LEADING PRODUCERS OF FISH

Millions of Kilograms

900 — 800 — 700 — 600 — 500 — 400 — 300 — 200 — 100 — 0

Louisiana · Alaska · Maryland · Virginia · California

GRAPH APPENDIX   GRAPH APPENDIX   GRAPH APPENDIX

AVERAGE MONTHLY TEMPERATURES: ASHEVILLE, NORTH CAROLINA

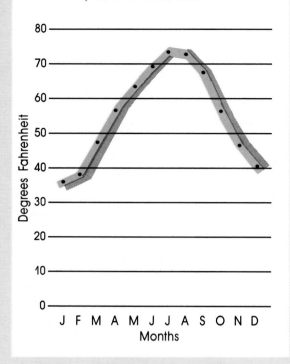

AVERAGE MONTHLY PRECIPITATION: ASHEVILLE, NORTH CAROLINA

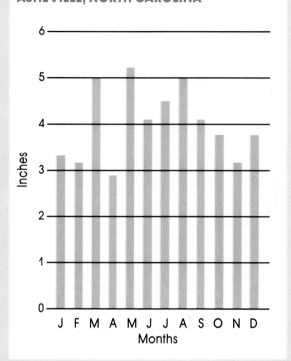

AVERAGE MONTHLY TEMPERATURES: BOSTON, MASSACHUSETTS

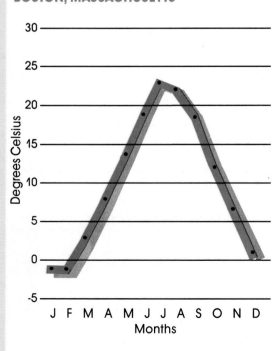

AVERAGE MONTHLY PRECIPITATION: BOSTON, MASSACHUSETTS

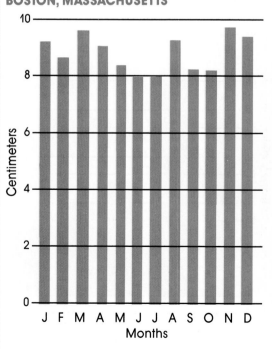

AVERAGE MONTHLY TEMPERATURES: SEATTLE, WASHINGTON

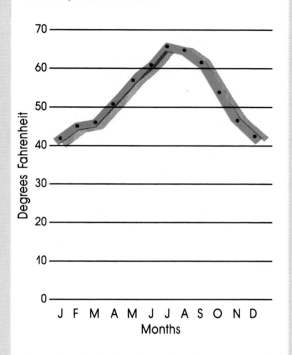

AVERAGE MONTHLY PRECIPITATION: SEATTLE, WASHINGTON

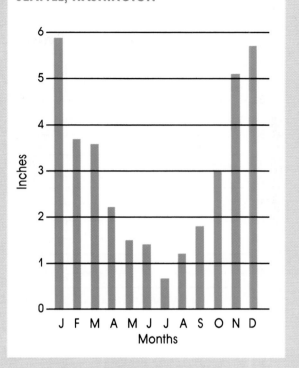

AVERAGE MONTHLY TEMPERATURES: NEW ORLEANS, LOUISIANA

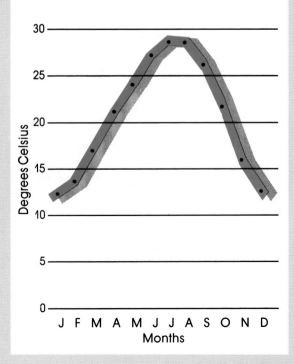

AVERAGE MONTHLY PRECIPITATION: NEW ORLEANS, LOUISIANA

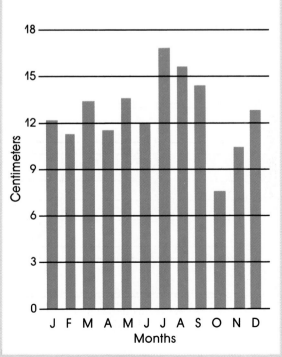

AVERAGE MONTHLY TEMPERATURES: WASHINGTON, D.C.

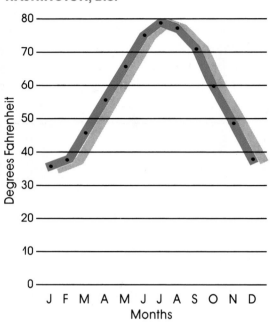

AVERAGE MONTHLY PRECIPITATION: WASHINGTON, D.C.

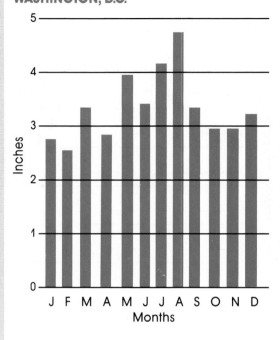

AVERAGE MONTHLY TEMPERATURES: LONDON, ENGLAND

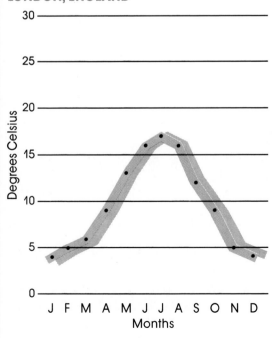

AVERAGE MONTHLY PRECIPITATION: LONDON, ENGLAND

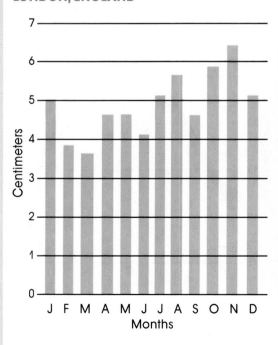

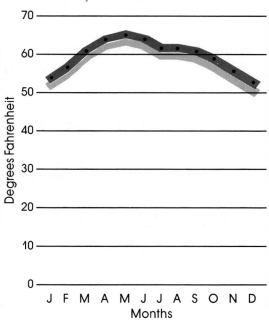

AVERAGE MONTHLY TEMPERATURES: MEXICO CITY, MEXICO

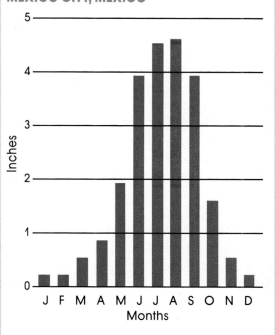

AVERAGE MONTHLY PRECIPITATION: MEXICO CITY, MEXICO

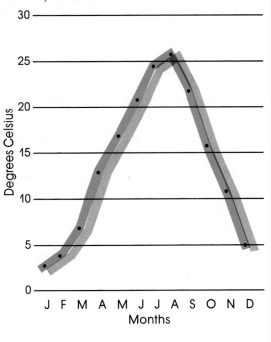

AVERAGE MONTHLY TEMPERATURES: TOKYO, JAPAN

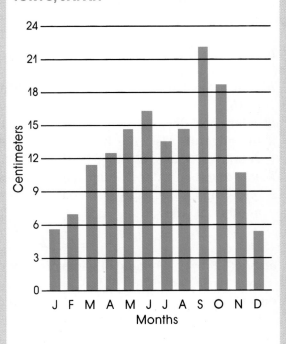

AVERAGE MONTHLY PRECIPITATION: TOKYO, JAPAN

GLOSSARY

The page references tell where each entry first appears in the text.

antenna (an ten′ ə). A wire or a metal rod that picks up radio waves or signals. An antenna is used in radio and television communications. p. 191.

apartment (ə pärt′ mənt). A single room or group of rooms in which a person or a family lives. p. 90.

architect (är′ kə tekt). A person who draws the plans for buildings and then guides the builders. p. 71.

archives (är′ kīvs). A place where important historical records, or papers, of a nation are kept. p. 226.

area (ãr′ ē ə). The land for several miles around a community. p. 64.

astronaut (as′ trə nôt). An American pilot or scientist who travels and works in space. p. 228.

auction (ôk′ shən). A public sale at which things are sold to the people who offer the most money for them. p. 152.

bar graph (bär graf). A kind of graph that shows information by using bars. p. 34.

bit (bit). A cutting tool at the end of a drill. p. 161.

border (bôr′ dər). To be next to or to touch the edge of. Also, the line between two countries, states, or other places. p. 17.

boundary (boun′ dər ē). A line that separates one community, state, or country from another. p. 105.

cable (kā′ bəl). A bundle of wires protected by a strong covering. p. 190.

canal (kə nal′). A waterway that people have dug out of the land. p. 185.

capital (kap′ ə təl). A city where laws and plans for a state or a nation are made. p. 13.

capitol (kap′ ə təl). A building where a state or national legislature meets to make laws for a state or a nation. p. 221.

card catalog (kärd kat′ ə lög). An alphabetical listing of all books in a library. The cards are filed in drawers. p. 58.

cargo (kär′ gō). Products, or goods, transported in a ship, train, or truck—for example, a cargo ship. p. 187.

causeway (kôz′ wā). A raised road usually built across shallow water. p. 82.

chamber of commerce (chām′ bər ov kom′ ərs). A group of business people who help their community. p. 64.

citizen (sit′ ə zən). A person who is a member of a community, a state, or a country. p. 76.

citizenship (sit′ ə zan ship). The way a person lives up to the responsibilities of being a citizen. p. 76.

civil rights (siv′ el rīts). The rights that all Americans are entitled to under the law, for example, the right to vote. p. 246.

Civil War (siv′əl wôr). The war between the North and the South begun in the United States in 1861 over the issues of independence for the South and slavery. p. 244.

climate (klī′ mit). The kind of weather a place has over a long period of time. p. 38.

colony (käl′ ə nē). A place that is located at a distance from the country that governs it. The United States was once a group of colonies ruled by England. p. 240.

communication (kə myü nə kā′ shən). The giving and receiving of information and ideas. p. 189.

community (kə myü′ nə tē). A place where people live, work, and play. A community has houses, stores, places of worship, and other buildings. p. 13.

compass rose (kum′ pəs rōz). A drawing that shows where north, south, east, and west are on a map. Sometimes a compass rose is called a direction finder. p. 8.

Congress (kong′ gris). The group of people who are elected to make laws for the United States. p. 173.

conservation (kon sər vā′ shən). The care of natural resources so that they will not be spoiled and wasted but will be used wisely. p. 170.

Constitution of the United States (kon stə tü′ shən). The set of laws by which the United States is governed. p. 226.

container (kən tā′ nər). A large metal box used to hold something for shipping. p. 67.

continent (kon′ tə nənt). A large body of land on the earth. The continents are North America, South America, Asia, Africa, Europe, Australia, and Antarctica. p. 18.

coordinates (kō ôr′ də nits). A set of numbers used to find a place on a map or globe. The numbers represent the place where the line of latitude and the line of longitude of a place on a map or globe meet. p. 26.

cotton boll (kät′ en bōl). The pod, or fruit, of the cotton plant, which contains the cotton fibers and seeds. p. 141.

cotton gin (kät′ en jin). A machine that removes the seeds from cotton and shapes the cotton into bales. p. 144.

council (koun′ səl). A group of men and women who are chosen by the people in a community to make laws and plans for the community. p. 215.

county (kount′ ē). A political division of a state. Most of our states are divided into counties. The center of government for a county is a community called a county seat. p. 56.

county fair (kount′ ē fār). A special occasion in a county when farmers and ranchers get together to enter their best animals and farm products in competitions, learn about new ways of raising crops and livestock, and exchange ideas. Many people also come to the fair to enjoy food, rides, and other events. p. 152.

creamery (krē′ mər ē). A place where butter and other dairy products are made. p. 136.

crop (krop). Plants that are grown in large amounts for food and other uses. p. 84.

crop duster (krop dus′ tər). A person who flies low in a special airplane that sprays insecticides on farm fields to protect the crops. p. 143.

cultivator (cul′ tə vāt ər). A farm machine, pulled by a tractor, that breaks up the soil and kills the weeds between rows of plants. p. 133.

custom (kus′ təm). The special way a group of people does something. p. 235.

dairy farm (dār′ ē färm). A farm on which the main work is raising cows for milk, butter, and cheese. p. 134.

date (dāt). A fruit that grows on date palm trees. p. 118.

Declaration of Independence (dek lə rā′ shən ov in də pen′ dəns). The paper that declared the American colonies to be free of British control and stated the reasons for their wish for such freedom. On July

GLOSSARY GLOSSARY GLOSSARY

4, 1776, this paper was signed by the leaders of the colonies. p. 226.

degree (di grē′). A unit for measuring latitude and longitude. Degree is also the unit for measuring temperature. The symbol for degree is °. p. 24.

delegate (del′ i gət). A person who represents a number of other people and speaks for them at a meeting or in a legislature. p. 240.

derrick (der′ ik). A steel tower that holds the drilling machinery over an oil well. p. 161.

desert (dez′ ərt). A region with very little rainfall and few plants. p. 116.

diagram (dī′ ə grăm). A drawing with labels, which can show what a thing is, how it works, and what the important parts are. p. 37.

dike (dīk). A bank of earth that is 1 or 2 feet (⅓ or ⅔ m) high and 4 or 5 feet (1 or 1½ m) wide. Dikes are used to hold water in flooded rice fields. p. 146.

division of labor (də vizh′ ən ov lā′ bər). To divide up a necessary job or work among several or many people in order to get the work done more quickly and efficiently. p. 82.

dock (dok). A kind of platform where ships load or unload their products in a port. p. 67.

east (ēst). The direction from which the sun seems to rise each morning. East is the opposite of west. When you face east, north is to your left and south is to your right. p. 7.

election (i lek′ shən). The choosing of a leader by voting. p. 215.

electricity (i lek tris′ ə tē). A form of energy that gives light and heat. p. 158.

encyclopedia (in sī kla pē′ dē ə). A set of books that gives detailed information on a great number of subjects. Subjects are listed alphabetically in the books. p. 59.

Equator (i kwā′ tər). A line drawn around the earth on maps and globes, halfway between the North Pole and the South Pole. The Equator divides the earth into the Northern Hemisphere and the Southern Hemisphere. p. 21.

export (ek′ spôrt). A product sold to another country. p. 67.

factory (fak′ tər ē). A building, or a group of buildings, in which machines and tools are used by workers to produce goods. p. 91.

fertilizer (fėr′ tə lī zər). Something put in soil to make crops grow better. p. 130.

fine (fīn). A certain amount of money paid as a punishment for not obeying a law. p. 218.

fish hatchery (fish hach′ ər ē). A place for hatching fish eggs. Wildlife conservation people raise fish in a hatchery and then put them in a body of water. p. 175.

fuel (fyü′ əl). Anything that is burned to make heat or to make power for running machines. p. 157.

globe (glōb). A model of the earth. A globe shows how the earth looks from far away. p. 5.

goods (gùdz). Things that are made, especially things that are made for sale. p. 93.

government (guv′ ərn mənt). The leaders of a group who make the laws and see that the laws are carried out. The group may be all the people of a nation, state, county, city, or town. p. 88.

GLOSSARY GLOSSARY GLOSSARY

governor (guv′ ər nər). The leader of a state's government who works with the state legislature to make laws for the state. A governor is elected by the people of the state. p. 222.

Governor's Mansion (guv′ ər nərz man′ shun). The home of a state governor. p. 222.

grain elevator (grān el′ ə va tər). A large building for storing grain. p. 109.

greenhouse (grēn′ hous). A building with a glass roof and glass sides that is kept warm for growing plants. p. 138.

Greenwich (gren′ ich). A place in England through which the Prime Meridian passes. Half of all longitude lines are west of Greenwich. The other half are east of Greenwich. p. 24.

grid system (grid sis′ təm). A set of horizontal and vertical lines that cross one another on a map. By using the grid system, you can find and describe the location of places on the map. p. 22.

gulf (gulf). A part of an ocean or sea that pushes into the land. p. 17.

harbor (här′ bər). A protected body of water that helps keep boats safe in stormy weather. p. 88.

harrow (har′ ō). A farming tool made with teeth or spikes used to break up and smooth the lumps of soil left by a plow. A harrow is pulled by a tractor. p. 131.

harvest (här′ vist). A gathering in of ripe crops from the land on which they grew. p. 131.

hay (hā). Grass that is cut and dried and used as food for livestock. p. 136.

hemisphere (hem′ ə sfir). A half of the earth. p. 20.

house raising (hous′ rā zing). A gathering of neighbors to help a person or family raise the frame of a house. p. 108.

import (im′ pôrt). A product brought from another country. p. 67.

income (in′ kum). The money that a person earns. p. 130.

Indies (in′ dēz). The name once given to eastern and southern Asia, later known as the East Indies. p. 236.

insecticide (in sek′ tə sīd). Insect-killing chemical often used by farmers to spray on crops. p. 143.

interview (in′ tər vyü). A face-to-face meeting of people to talk over a special subject. p. 73.

invent (in vent′). To make something no one else has ever made. p. 181.

irrigation (ir ə gā′ shən). Carrying water through pipes, ditches, or canals to lands that are dry. p. 118.

island (ī′ lənd). A body of land with water all around it. p. 16.

judge (juj). A person whose job is to hear and decide cases in a law court. Some judges are elected to the position. Other judges are named to the position. p. 218.

key (kē). A special part of a map that explains the symbols on a map. p. 8.

lake (lāk). A body of water that has land all around it. p. 17.

latitude (lat′ ə tüd). Distance, measured in degrees, north and south of the Equator. p. 24.

law (lô). A rule that people must obey. p. 13.

legislature (lej′ ə slā chər). A group of elected government leaders who make the laws of a state or nation. p. 221.

line graph (līn graf). A kind of graph that shows information by using lines. p. 35.

lint (lint). The long, strong white fibers of the cotton plant, which are used for making cloth and other products. p. 141.

livestock (līv′ stok). Farm animals such as cows, horses, sheep, and pigs. p. 149.

lobster (lob′ stər). A sea animal about 12 inches (31 cm) long with two big claws and eight legs. Lobsters are used for food. p. 167.

longhouse (long′ hous). A house built by Native Americans, which was added to as a family grew larger. p. 97.

longitude (lon′ jə tüd). Distance, measured in degrees, east and west of the Prime Meridian. p. 24.

magazine (mag ə zēn′). A collection of stories and articles by different writers, usually printed every week or every month. p. 193.

map (map). A flat drawing that shows what the earth, or part of the earth, looks like. p. 8.

mayor (mā′ ər). A community leader whose job is to help make the laws and to see that the laws are carried out. p. 215.

militia (mə lish′ ə). A citizen army partly trained for war. Also groups of soldiers trained to protect the American colonies against outside attacks. p. 242.

mill (mil). To remove the hard outer shell of rice by machine. Also the building where machines grind grain into flour. p. 148.

mineral (min′ ər əl). A substance found in the earth, such as coal, oil, iron, and gold.

A mineral is taken from the earth by mining. p. 156.

mine shaft (mīn shaft). A kind of tunnel that has been dug downward from the surface of the earth to where coal or some other minerals are found. p. 165.

model (mod′ əl). A small copy of a real thing, for example, a model car. The globe is a model of the earth. p. 4.

monument (mon′ yə mənt). Something set up to keep a person or an event from being forgotten. A monument may be a building, statue, arch, column, or tomb. p. 225.

mountain (moun′ tən). Land that rises high above the land around it. p. 16.

national forest (nash′ ə nəl fôr′ ist). A forest that belongs to all the people of a country, or nation. National forests are cared for by the government of a nation. p. 173.

natural resource (nach′ ər əl ri sôrz′). Something useful to people and supplied by nature, such as land, water, forests, and minerals. p. 38.

newspaper (nüz′ pā pər). Sheets of paper printed every day or week, telling the news and having ads and other useful information. p. 193.

north (nôrth). The direction toward the North Pole. North is the opposite of south. When you face the sun in the morning, north is to your left. p. 7.

North Pole (nôrth pōl). The most northern place on the earth. p. 7.

ocean (ō′ shən). A very large body of salt water on the earth. The names of the oceans are the Atlantic Ocean, the Pacific

Ocean, the Indian Ocean, and the Arctic Ocean. Another word for ocean is *sea*. p. 16.

offshore oil platform (ôf′ shôr′ oil plat′ fôrm). A large structure of either steel or concrete that is located in an ocean or gulf. The platform has equipment for drilling wells as well as living space for workers and a helicopter landing deck. p. 161.

pasture (pas′ chər). A field in which animals eat grass and other plants. p. 134.

penalty (pen′əl tē). A punishment, such as paying a fine or going to jail, for not obeying a law. p. 218.

peninsula (pə nin′ səl ə). A piece of land that sticks out into the water. A peninsula has water almost all the way around it. Most of Florida is a peninsula. p. 16.

pesticide (pes′ tə sīd). A chemical used to control or destroy insects and other pests harmful to farm crops. p. 109.

petroleum (pə trōl′ lē əm). An oily dark liquid that is found in the earth. p. 157.

physical feature (fiz′ ə kəl fē′ chər). A part of the earth. Rivers, lakes, seas, and mountains are examples of physical features. p. 16.

pictograph (pik′ tə graf). A kind of graph that uses symbols instead of numbers. p. 33.

pie graph (pī graf). A kind of graph drawn in the shape of a circle. Sometimes a pie graph is called a circle graph. p. 36.

Pilgrim (pil′ grəm). One of a group of people who came from England to America on a ship called the *Mayflower*, looking for a place where they could freely practice their own religion. They landed in Massachusetts in 1620. p. 238.

pipeline (pīp′ līn). A system of pipes that carries certain substances, such as water or petroleum, over long distances. p. 162.

plain (plān). A large area of flat grasslands. Nebraska is a plain state. p. 16.

plantation (plān tā′ shən). A very large farm or estate. p. 132.

planter (plān′ tər). A farm machine, pulled by a tractor, that makes small holes, drops seeds into them, and covers the seeds with soil. p. 131.

plow (plou). A tool farmers use to prepare soil for planting by turning it over and shaping it into rows. p. 131.

pollute (pə lüt′). To spoil by adding something. For example, rivers, lakes, and oceans are polluted by dumping trash in them. p. 170.

population (pop yə lā′ shən). The number of people in a place. p. 34.

port (pôrt). A place where ships and boats load and unload products. A port offers protection from waves and wind. p. 54.

precipitation (pri sip ə tā′ shən). All the forms of water that fall to the earth. Rain, snow, and sleet are forms of precipitation. p. 41.

Prime Meridian (prīm mə rid′ ē ən). The line of longitude from which other lines of longitude are measured. The Prime Meridian is numbered 0°. p. 24.

print (print). Words stamped in ink on paper. Print is an important means of communication. p. 193.

product (prod′ əkt). Something that people make or grow. p. 66.

profit (prof′ it). The difference between the amount of money a product costs a person and the amount of money that person sells the product for. p. 104.

property (prop′ ər tē). Land, houses, or other buildings owned by people in a community.

Property also may mean anything that a person owns. p. 212.

property tax (prop′ ər tē taks). A certain amount of money paid by people who own land, houses, or other buildings in a community. The amount of the tax depends on how much the property is worth. p. 212.

ranch (ranch). A large farm for raising cattle, sheep, or horses. p. 149.

ranger (rān′ jər). A person whose job is to take care of national forests or national parks. p. 173.

raw materials (rô mə tir′ ē əlz). Substances found in nature that can be made into finished products. For example, iron ore is a raw material that can be made into steel. p. 180.

recreation (rek rē ā′ shən). Play, games, and sports. p. 73.

refinery (ri fī′ nər ē). A factory with machines that change a natural resource to make it pure or to make different products from it. An oil refinery turns crude oil into gasoline, diesel oil, lubricating oil, and other useful products. p. 162.

religious freedom (ri lij′ əs frēd′ əm). The freedom to practice any religion. p. 85.

reporter (ri pôr′ tər). A person who gathers the news for a newspaper. p. 194.

river (riv′ ər). A long, narrow body of water that flows through the land toward a lake, sea, or ocean. p. 17.

rodeo (rō′ dē ō). A series of contests that show the skills of cowhands. p. 153.

satellite (sat′ ə līt). An artificial object that circles the planet Earth carrying communications equipment. p. 191.

scale (skāl). The size of a model drawing, or map, compared with what it stands for. On a map, scale shows distance. A scale of miles on a map tells how many miles on the earth one inch stands for. The scale used for a model or a drawing tells how big something is. p. 10.

service (sėr′ vis). Work that helps other people, rather than work in which a product is made. p. 94.

sightseeing (sīt′ se ing). Seeing places of interest. p. 111.

slavery (slāv′ə rē). A system under which some people are permitted to buy, sell, and own other people, usually for their labor. One of the reasons the American Civil War was fought. p. 244.

south (south). The direction toward the South Pole. South is the opposite of north. When you face the sun in the morning, south is to your right. p. 7.

South Pole (south pōl). The most southern place on the earth. The South Pole is in Antarctica. p. 7.

specialize (spesh′ ə līz). To concentrate on doing one job or one part of a particular process, so that one becomes very good and very quick at that job. Specializing allows division of labor. p. 82.

spring (spring). Water that bubbles up from under the ground, sometimes forming a pond or a stream. p. 104.

state (stāt). A part of a country. There are 50 states in the United States. p. 13.

suburb (sub′ ərb). A community near a large city. p. 183.

subway (sub′ wā). An electric train that travels underground. p. 183.

survey (sər vā′). To measure the land and make maps to show its physical features and to set up its boundaries. p. 105.

surveyor (sər vā′ ər). Someone who measures land and makes maps. p. 242.

symbol (sim′ bəl). A drawing that stands for a real thing or place. On a map, a dot is a symbol for a city. p. 8.

table (tā′ bəl). A list of facts and information. p. 31.

tax (taks). A certain amount of money that people pay to a community, state, or national government. Tax money is used to pay for the many needed services in the community, state, or nation. p. 212.

taxicab (tak′ sē kab). A special car. People pay the owner or driver of the car to drive them from place to place. p. 182.

temperature (tem′ pər ə chər). Amount of heat or cold. p. 38.

thermometer (thər mäm′ ə tər). A tool that is used to measure the temperature of the air. Liquid in the glass tube of a thermometer rises when the air becomes warmer and falls when the air becomes colder. A thermometer measures the temperature in units called degrees. p. 38.

time line (tīm līn). A scale drawing, standing for a period of time, on which dates are shown. A time line tells when things happened and the order in which they happened. p. 43.

tractor (trak′ tər). An important farm machine with a powerful motor used to pull tools and other machines on a farm. p. 131.

trade (trād). The buying, selling, or exchanging of goods. p. 82.

transportation (trans pər tā′ shən). The carrying of people and products from place to place. p. 83.

tribe (trīb). A group of families who share the same way of life. p. 235.

valley (val′ ē). A lowland between hills or mountains. p. 82.

veterinarian (vet ər ə när′ ē ən). A doctor who treats animals that are sick or hurt. p. 151.

vote (vōt). A way of choosing a leader, particularly in government. p. 215.

weather (weTH′ ər). The way the air is at a certain time: sunny or cloudy, hot or cool, windy or calm, dry or wet. p. 38.

well (wel). A hole dug in the earth to get water, oil, gas, or steam. p. 116.

west (west). The direction in which the sun seems to set at night. West is the opposite of east. When you face west, north is to your right. South is to your left. p. 7.

White House (hwīt hous). The building in Washington, D.C., where the President of the United States lives and works. p. 225.

windmill (wind′ mil). A machine that uses the power of the wind to pump water from under the ground to the surface. p. 150.

ZIP code (zip kōd). A group of numbers used in mailing addresses to speed up mail delivery. p. 197.

INDEX

INDEX

INDEX

INDEX

INDEX

INDEX

INDEX

INDEX   INDEX   INDEX

CREDITS

Cover: Silver Burdett & Ginn

Graphs, charts, and time lines: Laura Shallop

Maps: R.R. Donnelley Cartographic Services; General Drafting Co., Inc.

Contributing artists: Rick Del Rossi, Don Dyen, Michelle Epstein, John Holder, Peter Krempasky, Trudy McDonald

Unit One 2: *l.* Peter Byron for Silver Burdett & Ginn; *r.* Joe Viesti for Silver Burdett & Ginn. 3: IMAGERY for Silver Burdett & Ginn.
Chapter 1 4: *l.* Courtesy Chevrolet Motor Division; *r.* Silver Burdett & Ginn. 5: *l.* NASA; *r.* Silver Burdett & Ginn. 6: NASA. 8: Dan De Wilde for Silver Burdett & Ginn. 9: Silver Burdett & Ginn. 10: Dan De Wilde for Silver Burdett & Ginn. 13: Alec Duncan/Taurus Photos.
Cameron Davidson/Bruce Coleman; *m.* Eve Arnold/Magnum; *b.* Tim McCabe/Taurus Photos. 17: Jeff Foott/Bruce Coleman. 20–21: © 1988 Loren McIntyre/Woodfin Camp & Associates. 25: J. Oetzel/Tom Stack & Associates.
Chapter 2 30–31: Silver Burdett & Ginn. 32: Eric Carle/Shostal Associates. 38: Dan De Wilde for Silver Burdett & Ginn. 40: Culver Pictures. 43: Tom Stack/Tom Stack & Associates. 44: NASA.

Unit Two 48: G. Cloyd/Taurus Photos. 49: *t.* Francene Keem/Leo DeWys, Inc.; *b.* © Jim Cartier/Photo Researchers, Inc. 50: Leon Dishman/Shostal Associates. 50–51: *l.* Paul Conklin; *r.* Eric Carle/Shostal Associates.
Chapter 3 all photos by Michal Heron for Silver Burdett & Ginn except as otherwise noted. 52–53: Ken Taylor for Silver Burdett & Ginn. 62: *t.* Courtesy, New Hanover County Museum. 70, 72: Courtesy, DEG Film Studios, Inc. 77: Nelson-Bohart/Tom Stack & Associates.
Chapter 4 80–81: © M. MeDici. 81: Dave Millert/Tom Stack & Associates. 83: *l.* Robert Frerck/Odyssey Productions; *r.* J. Messerschmidt/Bruce Coleman. 84: *t.* The Granger Collection; *b.* J. Messerschmidt/Bruce Coleman. 85: *t.* The Granger Collection; *b.* James Blank/Bruce Coleman. 86: Kamiam Samoul. 87: The Granger Collection. 88: © Joyce Photographics/Photo Researchers, Inc. 89: The Granger Collection. 90: Paul Conklin. 91: *l.* Robert Frerck/Odyssey Productions; *r.* Bob Daemmrich. 92: General Dynamics. 93: MacDonald Photography for Silver Burdett & Ginn. 94: *l.* Robert Frerck/Odyssey Productions; *r.* Don Arns/Tom Stack & Associates. 97: Courtesy Tillicum Village. 98: Shostal Associates. 99: J. Messerschmidt/Bruce Coleman.
Chapter 5 102–103: Bob Greenlee for Silver Burdett & Ginn. 104: *l.* The Picture Gallery of Canadian History, Vol. 1, by C.W. Jefferys. Reprinted by permission of McGraw-Hill Ryerson Ltd. Photo courtesy of Minnesota Historical Society; *r.* Minnesota Historical Society. 105: Crow Wing County Historical Society; Photo by Sothers Studio. 107: Missouri Historical Society. 108: Bob Greenlee. 109: © 1988 Nathan Benn/Woodfin Camp & Associates. 110: C.C. Lockwood/Bruce Coleman. 111: Tom Campbell/Click, Chicago. 112: *l.* Bob Greenlee; *r.* Mark Twain Museum. 113: *l.* Raymond Baymes, Click, Chicago; *r.* Bob Greenlee. 114: Culver Pictures. 115: *t.l.* Photographic Resources; *b.l.r.* © 1988 Nathan Benn/Woodfin Camp & Associates. 116: Dennis Doran/West Stock, Inc. 117: The Coachella Valley Historical Society. 118,119: Bill Mollet. 120: *l.* National Date Festival; *r.* Dennis Doran/West Stock, Inc.

Unit Three 124: Craig Aurness/West Light. 125: *t.* © 1988 Robert Frerck/Woodfin Camp & Associates; *b.* Photri. 126: *l.* Karl Kummels/Shostal Associates; *inset* Grant Haller/Leo DeWys; *r.* David Falconer. 127: *t.* C.B. Jones/Taurus Photos; *b.* David Falconer.
Chapter 6 128–129: Rod Planck/Tom Stack & Associates. 128: *inset* McNee/Tom Stack & Associates. 129: *inset* Darryl Baird. 130: Silver Burdett & Ginn. 131: Paul Conklin. 132: The Granger Collection. 133: *t.* Tim McCabe/Taurus Photos; *b.* Kennedy/Texas Stock. 135: E.R. Degginger. 136: *t. m.* Robert Frerck/Odyssey Productions; *b.* L.L.T. Rhodes/Taurus Photos. 137: *l.* Robert Lee, II; *r.* E.R. Degginger. 138: *l.* Kenneth W. Fink/Bruce Coleman; *r.*

E.R. Degginger. 139: Jamie Tanaka/Bruce Coleman. 142: John Hoffman/Bruce Coleman. 143: Darryl Baird. 144: Dan de Wilde for Silver Burdett & Ginn. 146: © Eastcott-Momatiuk/Photo Researchers, Inc. 148: Dan De Wilde for Silver Burdett & Ginn. 149: Ken Cole/The Stockhouse, Inc. 150: D.K. Langford. 151: Skeeter/Texas Stock. 152: Len Berger/Berg & Associates. 153: Chris Minerva/Manhattan Views.
Chapter 7 156-157: Cass Germany. 160: Bartlesville Area History Museum and Archives, Bartlesville Public Library. 161: Walter Frerck/Odyssey Productions. 162: *t.* k© 1988 Martin Rogers/Woodfin Camp & Associates; *b.* Jim McNee/Tom Stack & Associates; *inset* Walter Frerck/Odyssey Productions. 163: *l.* Caron Pepper/Tom Stack & Associates; *r.* © 1988 Bill Strode/Woodfin Camp & Associates. 165: Erich Hartmann/Magnum. 167: Steve Solum/Bruce Coleman. 168, 169: Robert Frerck/Odyssey Productions. 170: Brian Parker/Tom Stack & Associates. 171: Erich Hartmann/Magnum. 172: *l.* Augustus Upitis/Shostal Associates; *r.* Culver Pictures. 174: Helen Rhode/AlaskaPhoto.
Chapter 8 178–179: Bob Daemmrich. 179: Rick Browne/Stock, Boston. 180: The Granger Collection. 182: Frank Cezus-Click, Chicago. 185: William Wright/Taurus Photos. 186: Photoworld/FPG. 187: © Jerry Wachter/Photo Researchers, Inc. 189: Dan De Wilde for Silver Burdett & Ginn. 190: Courtesy Bell Labs. 192: © 1988 Michal Heron/Woodfin Camp & Associates. 193, 195: Dan De Wilde for Silver Burdett & Ginn. 194: Silver Burdett & Ginn. 196: *l.* Silver Burdett & Ginn; *r.* Cecile Brunswick/Peter Arnold Inc. 197: *k l.* Bob Daemmrich; *r.* © Mindy Klacman/Photo Researchers, Inc. 198: J. Zehrt/FPG.

Unit Four 202: Bob Daemmrich for Silver Burdett & Ginn. 203: *t.* Silver Burdett & Ginn; *b.* Judy White/Berg & Associates. 204: Charles Anderson/Monkmeyer Press. 205: *t.* Steve Strickland/West Light; *b.* © 1988 Jim Anderson/Woodfin Camp & Associates.
Chapter 9 206–207: M. Getz/FPG. 208: Bob Daemmrich. 209: M. Wootton/H. Armstrong Roberts. 210: © David Weintraub/Photo Researchers, Inc. 211: Cary Wolinsky/Stock, Boston. 212: Bob Daemmrich. 213: *l.* Silver Burdett & Ginn; *r.* Bob Daemmrich. 214: Steve Leonard/Click, Chicago. 215: Michal Heron. 216: © 1988 Lester Sloan/Woodfin Camp & Associates. 217: Suzi Barnes/Tom Stack & Associates. 218: Eldred Wade/Shostal Associates. 219: Silver Burdett & Ginn. 220: *t.l.* Keith Gunnar/Bruce Coleman; *l.m.* Ken Taylor/Wildlife Images for Silver Burdett & Ginn; *l.b.* Steve Solum/Bruce Coleman; *t.r.* Robert Weinreb/Bruce Coleman; *m.r.* Rick Myers/Tom Stack & Associates; *b.r.* Jerry Hout/Bruce Coleman. 221: *l.* Joel Brown/Shostal Associates; *r.* Nancy Simmerman/Bruce Coleman. 222: Karl Kummels/Shostal Associates. 225: *l.* Owen Franken/Stock, Boston; *r.* Craig Aurness/West Light. 226: *l.* Stacy Pick/Stock, Boston; *r.* Andrew Harman/Folio, Inc. 227: Courtesy of the Harvard University Portrait Collection. 228: Larry Smith/H. Armstrong Roberts. 229: Jim Whitmer.
Chapter 10 232-233: E.R. Degginger/Bruce Coleman. 234: Steven Alexander/Shostal Associates. 235: North Dakota Travel Department. 236: The Granger Collection. 237: Silver Burdett & Ginn. 238: *The Thanksgiving Feast* N.C. Wyeth, courtesy of the Metropolitan Life Insurance Company—photo by M. Varon, 1985. 239: © 1988 Marion Hubbell/Woodfin Camp & Associates. 240: The Granger Collection. 241: Howard Foote/Shostal Associates; *inset* © George Jones, III/Photo Researchers, Inc. 242: The Granger Collection. 243: Nina Tisaro. 244: The Granger Collection. 245: Hank Morgan/Rainbow. 246: Matt Herron/Black Star. 247: Silver Burdett & Ginn; *inset* Rhoda Sidney for Silver Burdett & Ginn.

A B C D E F G H I J—RRD—97 96 95 94 93 92 91 90 89